Edward Arber, Thomas Cooper

An Admonition of the People of England. 1589

Edited by Edward Arber

Edward Arber, Thomas Cooper

An Admonition of the People of England. 1589
Edited by Edward Arber

ISBN/EAN: 9783337009069

Printed in Europe, USA, Canada, Australia, Japan

Cover: Foto ©ninafisch / pixelio.de

More available books at **www.hansebooks.com**

The English Scholar's Library.

No. 15.

An Admonition to the People of England.
1589.

The English Scholar's Library.

T[HOMAS]. C[OOPER].

[Bishop of WINCHESTER.]

An Admonition to the People

of England.

1589.

Edited by EDWARD ARBER,
HON. FELLOW OF KING'S COLLEGE, LONDON; F.S.A.,
PROFESSOR OF ENGLISH LANGUAGE AND LITERATURE
SIR JOSIAH MASON'S COLLEGE, BIRMINGHAM.

1, MONTAGUE ROAD, BIRMINGHAM.
15, August, 1882.
No. 15.
(*All rights reserved.*)

CONTENTS.

	PAGE
Bibliography	vi
INTRODUCTION	vii–xii

An Admonition to the People of England	1
To the Reader	3–6
The Contents of this Treatise	7–8
An Admonition to the Church and people of England to take heede of the contempt of those Bishops and Preachers, which God hath sent to them as messengers to bring vnto them the doctrine of their Saluation	9–29
Against the slaunderous Libels of late published vnder a famed and fond name of MARTIN MARPRELATE	29–60
Answers to generall quarrels made against the Bishops	61–119
Answeres to the Aduersaries of Bishops Liuings ...	120–179

BIBLIOGRAPHY.

ISSUES IN THE AUTHOR'S LIFETIME.

1 & 2. [January] 1589. London 4to. See title page at *p.* 1.
Two editions [of this year]; one containing 252 *pp.*, the other 245 *pp.*
Lowndes Bibl. Manual.
The present reprint is from a copy containing 245 *pp.*

ISSUES SINCE HIS DEATH.

3. 1847. 94, High Holborn, London. 8vo. [*Puritan Discipline Tracts.*] An Admonition to the People of England against MARTIN MAR-PRELATE. [Edited by JOHN PETHERAM.]

4. 15 August, 1881. Birmingham. The present impression.

∴ *All as separate publications.*

Mr. PETHERAM in his *Introduction* to No. 3, thus discriminates between 1 and 2 :—

First Edition, 1589 [? 252 *pp.*].	Second Edition, 1589 [? 245 *pp.*].
Does not contain these words	I will now come to answere briefly some particular slanders vttered against some Bishops and others by name, *p.* 24 [*p.* 28].

The following variations were pointed out in *Hay any work for Cooper?* 1589 (to be reprinted in the present Series) between these two impressions.

The Libeller doth but dreame, let him and his doe what they *dare*, *p.* 40.	The Libeller doth but dreame, let him and his doe what they *can*, *p.* 40 [*p.* 33].
I will not deny it, *p.* 135.	That is not yet proved, *p.* 135 [*p.* 105].

INTRODUCTION.

NOT only in justice to the Prelates attacked in the *MARTIN MARPRELATE Controversy*, but also in order to understand aright the later works of that Ecclesiastical Dispute, it is necessary to reprint this *Admonition*: although, at the first sight, it may not appear so inviting as many of the other works in this Series.

Only some few pages (29–60 of the present edition) are a specific reply to the *Epistle* which appeared in the previous November. But the writer took the occasion to gather together all the Puritan arguments of his time; to state them in the fullest possible manner, indeed, almost to exaggerate them; and then coming to close quarters with his antagonists, to confute all their assertions, with facts and arguments that apparently carried conviction to his own mind.

So that this *Admonition* is, for us, a complete and official exposition of the Protestant view of Ecclesiastical Government, some four months after the defeat of the Spanish Armada; in contradistinction to the Puritan view of the same, as expressed in UDALL's *Demonstration of Discipline*, already printed in this Series.

Thus the reader can now view exactly the two poles of thought in that Conflict of Opinion: out of which, that Uprising against Compulsion in Religion, that Assertion of the innate right of the Individual Judgement to decide for itself in such matters, that Challenge that the Christian Church is but a voluntary association for good purposes, slowly came into existence, and crystallized themselves into organizations and schools of thought—known successively, as Separatism, Puritanism, Nonconformity, and Dissent. This gradual untrammeling of English thought was the fostering of the spirit of liberty, and has been one of the greatest blessings that has come to our nation: so that, with a clear view, we now can readily distinguish between things secular and spiritual, between what is naturally due to our Humanity, and what is a part of the Divine message of the Divine Will concerning it.

II.

IT WAS a clever ruse of the Bishop of WINCHESTER to call this treatise an *Admonition*; and to publish it with his initials only, T. C.: which were also the famous initials of THOMAS CARTWRIGHT, the celebrated Puritan Divine of Cambridge, who had written the *Second Admonition to the Parliament* in 1572; and whose hunted life, with its many imprisonments and judicial examinations, was one long Struggle against the System, of which the present text is an earnest and eloquent Apology. We must discard rank, title, and power in our estimate of Men: and the long suffering CARTWRIGHT is, in all respects, the greater being than his sometime associate among the Fellows of Trinity College, Cambridge, physical-force JOHN WHITGIFT, afterwards Archbishop of CANTERBURY. So that the Champions of both sides of this great struggle, at one time, sat side by side in that beautiful College.

CARTWRIGHT led the Puritan thought *within* the Church, and wrote *against* the Brownists. One must study his life, and see how many things he suffered at the hands of the Bishops, to realise their active secular power of imprisonment, fines, &c.: and then, the studied moderation, the thin veil of mildness of this *Admonition* will be seen at once, to be what Lord BACON would call "a Place of Persuasion."

III.

How could Protestants and Puritans agree? They represented opposite casts of mind, different standards of judgement, contrary ways of thinking, and conflicting currents of argumentation.

Their starting points were far asunder. The Protestants looked back to the Past. To them, the Fathers were still a living authority; the power of whose dead hand controlled much of their thoughts. They rested on the Law of the land, unreformed as yet, for want of time; so that the Protestant Bishops were shorn of but little of the earthly splendour and pomp of their Roman Catholic predecessors. They looked to the Prince as GOD's Vicegerent, as the only Source of all authority in the nation; by whose personal favour Bishops rose or fell, and the Church prospered or was persecuted.

So that much of Bishop COOPER's *retrospect* in this *Admonition* is undoubtedly true in fact, and just in statement.

But the life of nations is not in the Past, but in the Present. So the Puritans were the better exponents of the life of England at this time, of the gathering forces which were (through many a struggle) to shape out its after history. They would readily acknowledge TERTULLIAN, AUGUSTINE, JEROME, BASIL, AMBROSE, and the rest, as being very good people in their way; and would regard their life and opinions with deep interest, as so many experiments in the social life of their several times: but felt that they were of little or no authority for them, and that each Age, in its own Present, had the indefeasible Right, as well as the clear Duty of solving its own problems, in the best way it could. Their appeal was to Reason, as against Authority; and especially to the immense powers of the patient Human Mind, under the teaching of the Scriptures. Lastly, they worked for, and rested on the People; as contrasted, either with the Prince, or the privileged classes.

Both sides had drawbacks. With the Bishops, there was, in many who held Spiritual Office, much corruption of life. The Puritans, on the other hand, seemed to have felt the need of a spur of an Infallible System, "of One Only Form of Church Government," as a kind of ecclesiastical battering ram that was to knock down everything before it: but, as we know, the sense of its infallibility died out within the next two or three generations. So that Bishop COOPER's challenge, at *p.* 62,

> Onely this I desire, *That they will lay downe out of the worde of God some iust proofes, and a direct commaundement, that there should bee in all ages and states of the Church of Christ, one onely forme of outwarde gouernement.* Secondly, *that they will note and name some certaine particular Churches, either in the Apostles time, or afterward, wherein the whole Gouernement of the Church was practised, onely by Doctours, Pastours, Elders, and Deacons, and none other, and that in an equalitie, without superioritie in one aboue an other,*

was really never answered, and never could be affirmatively, from history. Their real strength lay in a full appreciation of the Wants of the Time, and of the duty of preparing for the generations that were to come after.

So the Protestants contentedly looked backward; the Puritans earnestly looked forward. It was the differing outlook of Age and Youth again.

IV.

IT WAS evidently the Bishop's purpose herein to gather into his arms all possible arguments that the Puritans could allege against Episcopacy; and to wrestle with them for a fall. It would certainly seem (unless the Bishop has much overstated his opponents' case), that there was a great amount of free speech in England on this matter, at that time. People were evidently in the habit of expressing their mind very freely upon the subject; much more than our general history would lead us to realize.

V.

OME of the side arguments in this *Admonition* are very interesting, and constitute it a kind of Landmark in the story of the Growth of our Political Ideas. Take, for instance, the old theory of a Subject's duty, as stated by the Bishop, at *p.* 156.

Wee owe to the Prince, honour, feare, and obedience: obedience (I say) in al those things that are not against the worde of God and his commandementes. Those things that God commaundeth, a Christian Prince cannot forbid: Those things that God forbiddeth, no Prince hath authority to command. But such things as be external, and by Gods word left indifferent, the Prince by his authoritie may so by lawe dispose, either in commanding, or forbidding, as in wisedome and discretion he shall thinke to make most to the glory of God, and to the good and safe state of his people. Among these things external, I think lands, goods, and possessions to bee, and therefore that the same ought to be subiect to taxe and tribute in such sort, as the lavves and state of the country requireth : yea, and if there shall happen in any country a magistrate, which by violence and extortion shall vvrest more vnto him of the lands and substance of the people, then lavv and right requireth : I see no cause vvarranted by Gods vvorde, that the inferiour subiects can rebell, or resist the prince therein, but that they shal euidently shew themselues to resist the ordinance of God. For they haue not the sworde of correction committed into their hande, and often times God by euil princes correcteth the sinnes of the people. Wherefore, if subiects resist the hard dealings euen of euil Magistrates, they do in that respect striue against God himselfe, who will not suffer it vnpunished.

This is said by an Ecclesiastic, who, by virtue of his profession, was supposed to know more of the Divine Will in relation to Politics and the Constitution of Human Society, than any layman could arrive at.

What a Progression in Thought was there, therefore, made within the next two generations. Just sixty years (to a month, if not to a week) after this was written, this conception of Kingship was beheaded in the person of CHARLES I.; and the Hierarchy itself (as it was a class and a force in the national society when this was written) had passed away for ever. This prodigious change of opinion, this liberation of thought, this difficult and trying movement from a mere subserviency to Authority, to the fullest exercise of human intelligence, brought about by some of the greatest thinkers England ever possessed, is one of the most interesting studies in the whole of our English History.

VI.

EGARDED as an argument, this *Admonition* is a Masterpiece of inconclusive reasonings. The principles advocated by the Puritans are, for the most part, entirely accepted; the conclusions following from those principles are also theoretically admitted, fully : so far, then, the Bishop agrees with his opponents; and the state of public opinion at the time rendered this the most advisable course. But then, the facts which led the Puritans into the thinking out of these arguments, are either denied, or else by some logical illusion, are spirited away. There is a careful avoidance of specific facts; everything is dealt with in a general way.

It is an interesting study to note the Bishop's logical shifts, to see him flying, now to the text of Scripture; and when that will not serve, to the gloss of the Fathers, as interpreting it; both these failing, to the simple will of the Prince, being a Christian ; or if not, to the statute Law of the realm : or, all these not serving, to that Fear of Change and Dread of the Unknown, which is often really nothing else but moral cowardice.

So that to this tangled mass of reasonings, much of it but pure sophistry, may be put the appeal of Lord BACON, already printed by us.

Again, to my Lords the Bishops, I say, That it is hard for them to avoid blame—in the opinion of an indifferent person—in standing so precisely upon altering nothing. *Leges, novis legibus non recreatæ, acescunt,* " Laws not refreshed with new laws, wax sour." *Qui mala non permutat, in bonis non perseverat,* " Without change of ill, a man cannot continue the good." To take away many abuses supplanteth not good orders, but establisheth them. *Morosa moris retentio res turbulenta est, æque ac novitas:* " A contentious retaining of custom is a turbulent thing, as well as innovation." A good husband-[man] is ever proining in his vineyard or his field: not unseasonably, indeed; not unskilfully; but lightly he findeth ever somewhat to do.

We have heard of no offers of the Bishops of Bills in Parliament, which, no doubt, proceeding from them, to whom it properly belongeth, would have everywhere received acceptation. Their own *Constitutions* and *Orders* have reformed them little.

Is nothing amiss? Can any man defend the use of Excommunication as a base process to lackay up and down for duties and fees? it being a precursory Judgement of the Latter Day.

Is there no mean to train and nurse up ministers?—for the yield of the Universities will not serve, though they were never so well governed—to train them, I say, not to preach (for that every man confidently adventureth to do) but to preach soundly, and to handle the Scriptures with wisdom and judgement.

I know " prophesying " was subject to great abuse; and would be more abused now, because [the] heat of contentions is increased: but I say the only reason of the abuse was because there was admitted to it a popular auditory, and it was not contained within a private Conference of Ministers.

Other things might be spoken of.

Introductory Sketch, &c., No. 8. pp. 160-1. 1879.

VII.

BUT our more immediate concern with this *Admonition* is its relation to the *MARTIN MARPRELATE Controversy,* which we are reprinting, and out of which it sprang. The denials or palliations to the specific charges against individual Prelates, we will consider in *Hay any work for Cooper?* which is the Martinist reply to this *Admonition.* For convenience of the student we have inserted between [ ], the references to the edition of the *Epistle* already included in this Series.

We have only space here to indicate one or two places where the Bishop, in retaliation, tries his hand at the Martinist style, and attempts some shrewd hits at the Puritans.

One is at *pp.* 71-72, where the Right Reverend Father endeavours to give a black and white portrait of *MARTIN MARPRELATE*, of which we shall hear again in *Hay any work for Cooper?*

But the conclusion of the *Admonition* contains the Bishop's Parthian dart; wherein he winds up a magnificent series of special pleadings for the lordly possessions of the English Hierarchy, by thus likening the Puritans to *JUDAS ISCARIOT*, who grumbled "*because he was a thief.*"

The affection of them, which at this day speake so much against the Landes and liuings of bishops, and other Cleargie men, is much like the dealing of those persons, that murmured against *Marie* of *Bethania*, which in the house of *Simon* the leper, in testimonie of her thankfulnesse, for the great mercies that shee had receiued of Christ, powred vpon his head the precious oyntment of Spikenard. For euen in like manner our gracious Queene, when God had deliuered her out of the iawes of the greedie lyons, and cruell wolues that sought her blood, and by his mightie hand had set her in the throne of this her Fathers kingdome: to testifie her thankefull minde, and to shevve her liberall and bountifull heart towarde the Church of God, shee povvred vpon it this plentifull gift, towarde the maintenance of the Ministers and Preachers of his vvorde, that shee might declare to the worlde, that in imbracing the Gospell, and restoring the same to this Realme, shee had not that minde and affection, vvhich some other haue shewed, that is, vnder colour thereof, to make the increase of her owne benefite, and the commoditie of her Crowne. But as then *Iudas* and some other Disciples murmured at *Marie*, and vnder pretence of holinesse and charitie toward the poore, founde great fault with that superfluous excesse (as they thought it) euen so nowe, many Disciples among vs, with like colour of religion and holinesse, and of zeale towarde the perfection of the Church (forsooth) murmure at the liberal benefit of our prince, which she hath bestowed vpon the Church, and think the same a great superfluitie, that might bee better imployed sundry wayes, to the benefite of the common weale. VVhatsoeuer is pretented, I pray God the cause of the griefe bee not the same that Iohn 12. *Iohn* mentioneth to haue beene that, which first began the murmuring at that time. *pp.* 178-9.

AN ADMONITION
TO THE PEOPLE OF ENGLAND:

VVHEREIN ARE ANSVVERED, NOT ONELY THE slaunderous vntruethes, reprochfully *vttered by* Martin *the Libeller, but also* many other Crimes by some of his broode, *obiected generally against all Bishops, and the* chiefe of the Cleargie, purposely to *deface and discredite the present* state of the Church.

*Detractor et libens auditor, vterque
Diabolum portat in lingua.*

Seene and allowed by authoritie.

Jmprinted at London by the Deputies of Christopher Barker, Printer to the Queenes most excellent Maiestie.

1 5 8 9.

TO THE READER.

I Am not ignorant (Gentle Reader) what daunger *I drawe vpon my selfe, by this attempt to answere the quarrels and slaunders of late time published in certaine Libelles, against the Bishops and other chiefe of the Clergie of the Church of England. We see the eagernesse and boldnesse of their spirit that be the authors of them: we taste alreadie the bitternes of their tongues and pennes. The raging furie of their reuenge vpon all which they mislike, themselues dissemble not, but lay it downe in words of great threatnings. I must needs therfore looke for any hurt, that venemous, scoffing, and vnbridled tongues can worke toward me. And how shoulde I hope to escape that, when the Saints of God in Heauen doe feele it? In the course of their whole Libell, when they speake of* Peter, Paul, *or the* Blessed Virgin Marie, &c: *whome other iustlie call Saintes, their phrase in derision is,* Sir Peter, Sir Paule, Sir Marie. *Surely it had becommed right well the same vnmodest Spirite, to haue said also* Sir Christ, *and so throughly to haue bewrayed himself. Seeing they haue sharpned their tongues and heart's against heauen, wee poore creatures on earth must be content in our weaknesse to beare them. The dartes, I confesse, of deceitfull and slaunderous tongues, are verye sharpe, and the burning of the woundes made by them, will as hardly in the hearts of many bee quenched, as the coales of Iuniper. But I thanke God I feare them not, though they bring mee greater harme, eyther in credite, liuing or life, then I trust that God that seeth, knoweth, and defendeth the trueth will suffer them.* Ambrose *beeing in case somewhat like, sayeth thus,* Non tanti est vnius vita, quanti est dignitas omnium Sacerdotum. *If I therefore shoulde hazarde the one for the defence of the other: I trust the godlye woulde iudge that I did that duetie which I owe to the Church of God, and to my brethren of the same function and calling.*

What is the cause why wee bee with such spight and malice discredited? Surely, because as the duty of faythfull Subiectes dooth binde vs, liuing in the state of a Church refourmed, we doo indeuour to preserue those Lawes, which her Maiesties authoritie and the whole state of the Realme hath allowed and established, and doe not admitte a newe platforme of gouernment, deuised, I knowe not by whome.

The reasons that moue vs so to doe, are these two. First, wee see no proofe brought out of the word of God, that of necessitie such forme of Gouernement ought to be: Secondly, that by the placing of the same, it woulde bring so many alterations and inconueniences, as in our opinion would bee dangerous to the Prince and to the Realme. Some of those inconueniences I haue in this treatise laid downe, and leaue them to the consideration of them, whom God hath set in place of gouernment.

It may be some will iudge that I am worldly affected, because I shewe my selfe so much grieued with losse of our credite, and hinderance of good name among the people. In trueth, although

[Bp. T. Cooper.
Jan. 1589.]

*a godly Minister shoulde haue no worldly thing so deere vnto him,
as his credite: yet if the hurt went no further then to our selues,
wee should make lesse account of it.   But, seeing by our reproche
and infamie, the doctrine which wee teache is greatly hindered, we
ought by all lawfull meanes to defend it.   Christ himselfe, in this
respect, answered such reproches, as the enemies obiected against
him.   As,* that hee vvas a friende vnto Publicanes and
sinners: That hee vvrought his miracles by the   Matth. 9.
power of Beelsebub: That hee broke the Sabbaoth   Matth. 12. Iohn 8.
day: That hee was a Samaritane: That hee had
a deuil &c.   Saint Paul *also to the* Corinthians *against his
Aduersaries sheweth, that hee was not a* vaine Promiser: *That
hee was not* light *and* vnconstant, *and* a wauering Teacher:
That hee did not teache craftily, *or* corruptly dispensing the
worde of God: *That hee did not* teach ambitiously, as seeking
his owne glorie &c.   *The like did a nomber of learned Fathers
of the Primitiue Church, at large answering those vile*   Tertul
and reprochefull Slaunders raysed against the Christians   Iustin. Melito, &c.
in those dayes. Augustine *in a whole woorke answered Assertions
falsly fathered vpon him: and so did many other.   Wee seeke not
therein our own prayse and commendation.   If I doe insert
particular prayses and commendations, I must say vnto the*
Libellers, *as* S. Paul *sayde to the* Corinthians, Si insipiens fui
in laudando, vos me coegistis.   *If I haue bene foolish in
ouermuch praising, your immodest reproches, vntrueths, and
slaunders do driue me to it.   In this mine answere, I seeke not to
satisfie all kinde of men, but onely the moderate and godly.   For
the malicious Back-biter and Rayler will neuer be satisfied: but
the more he is answered, the worse he will be.   If my defence may
take moderate place with the better sort, I shall be glad: if not, I
may not be excessiuely grieued with sorowe, but I must say with*
Paul, Gloria nostra hæc est, testimonium conscientiæ nostræ.

And with Iob, Ecce in cælis testis meus. *This witnesse in heauen, and the witnesse of our owne heart and conscience, is sufficient to comfort vs. And for our further helpe, we must pray with* Dauid, *who was lamentably beaten and bitten with viperous tongues,* Leade vs, O Lorde, in thy righteousnesse, because of our enemies: make thy way plaine before vs. *This God I trust, will deliuer vs from the daunger of euill tongues, and open their eyes and hearts, that they may see and vnderstande what hinderance they bring to the Gospel of Christ, which they will seeme to professe so earnestly. Amen.*

(∴)

The Contents of this Treatise.

AN Admonition to beware of the contempt of the Bishops and other Preachers. ... ... Page 1. [*p.* 9]
The end which the enemy of the Church of God respecteth in woorking their discredite. ... ... pag. 23. [*p.* 22]

Answeres to the vntrueths and slaunders vttered in Martins late Libell. ... ... pag. 33. [*p.* 29]
    Against my Lord of Canterburie. ... pag. 37. [*p.* 32]
    Against my Lord of London. ... ... pag. 51. [*p.* 41]
    Against the Bishop[s] of Rochester, Lincolne, and Winchester. ... ... pag. 62, 63 &c. [*pp.* 49, 50 &c.]

The causes why the Bishops desire to maintaine the present state of the gouernment of the Church, and what inconueniences they fear vpon the alteration thereof will come to the state of the Realme. ... ... pag. 79 &c. [*p.* 61]

Answeres to certaine generall Crimes objected to all the Bishops without exception · as first,
    The Crime of Simonie and Couetousnesse. pag. 96. [*p.* 73]
    The dispensing with Banes for money. ... pag. 100. [*p.* 76]
    The Sale of Christian libertie in Marriages. pag. 103. [*p.* 78]
    That they make lewde and vnlearned Ministers for money. ... ... pag. 108. [*p.* 82]
    That they maintain an vnlearned Ministery, and therby be occasion of Reuoltings, and many other mischiefs to the Prince and the Common weale · But it is declared that there is no such vnlearned Ministery as they pretend, and therefore can not bee an occasion of Reuolting, or any other like mischiefes, but that there bee other true and right causes to redresse, of which it behoueth them that God hath set in place, in time to haue speciall regarde, for feare lest those mischiefes that be pretended, doe increase. ... ... pag. 109 &c. [*p.* 83]

The Crime of mainteyning Pilling and powling Courts.	pag. 135. [*p.* 101]
The Crime of abusing Ecclesiastical discipline.	pag. 141. [*p.* 105]
The Crime of ambition and griedie seeking after Liuings and promotion.	pag. 144. [*p.* 107]
That Bishops are carnally disposed: which they shewe by hoarding vp great summes of money, by purchasing Landes for their wiues and children, by furnishing their tables with plate and guilded Cups, by filling their purses with vnreasonable Fines and Incomes.	pag. 148. [*p.* 110]

That the Prince ought to take away their great Lands and Liuings, and set them to meane Pensions, that in pouertie they may be answerable to the Apostles. ... ... pag. 157. [*p.* 116]

Which they take vpon them to proue by the whole course of the Scriptures. ... ... pag. 162. [*p.* 120]

  The Lawe. ... ... pag. 166. [*p.* 124]
  The Prophets. ... ... pag. 177. [*p.* 131]
  The example of Christ. ... ... pag. 190. [*p.* 140]
  and the doctrine of his Apostles. ... pag. 221. [*p.* 162]

Answere to the prescription of the old Lawe, vvith the true meaning thereof. ... ... pag. 166. [*p.* 124]

Ansvvere to the Allegations out of the Prophets, noting hovve absurdly and affectionately they be abused. ... ... pag. 177 &c. [*p.* 131]

Answere to the example of Christ, and the true doctrine that is to be taken of the same. pag. 191 &c. [*p.* 141]

Answere to the doctrine of the Apostles, declaring hovv the same is rightly to be vnderstanded. pag. 221. [*p.* 162]

A Declaration, how Ministers haue bene maintained from the beginning; wherein is shevved, that they haue had both Lands, Houses, Rents, and Reuenues. ... ... pag. 231 &c. [*p.* 169]

A Declaration, that the wealthie state of the Church was not the chiefe cause of setting vp Antichrist in his Throne, as it is pretended: but that the Histories of that time do declare other causes of more importance, which also beginne to growe among vs, and therefore good heede to be taken in time. ... ... pag. 238 &c. [*p.* 174]

¶ AN ADMONITION
to the Church and people of England,

to take heede of the contempt of those Bishops and Preachers, which God hath sent to them as messengers to bring vnto them the doctrine of their Saluation.

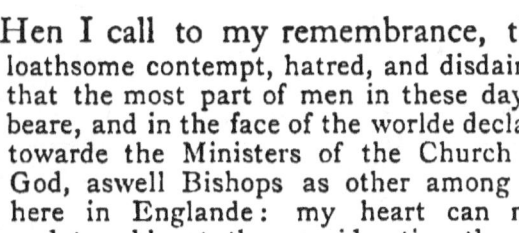Hen I call to my remembrance, the loathsome contempt, hatred, and disdaine, that the most part of men in these dayes beare, and in the face of the worlde declare towarde the Ministers of the Church of God, aswell Bishops as other among vs here in Englande: my heart can not but greatly feare and tremble at the consideration thereof It hath pleased God now a long time most plentifully to powre downe vpon vs his manifold and great benefites of wealth, riches, peace and quietnesse, euen in the middest of the flames of discord, dissention and miserie rounde about vs, yea, and that more is, by the space of these thirtie yeeres, by the continuall preaching of the Gospell hath called vs vnto him (as before time he called his chosen people of the Iewes by his Prophets) and yet do we not onely not shew any sound token, either of our returning to him that called vs, or of our thankefull receiuing his worde which he hath sent vs, or of conforming our liues thereunto, as hee willeth vs: but also euidently to the eyes and eares of all men, shew our hatred and misliking of those reuerend persons, whome it hath pleased God to vse as his messengers to call vs vnto him, and as his instruments to bring vnto vs the glad tidings of the Gospel, which before with sworde and fire was taken from vs. For who seeth not in these dayes, that hee who can most bitterly inueigh against Bishops and Preachers, that can most boldely blaze their discredites, that can most vncharitably slaunder their liues and doings, thinketh of himselfe, and is esteemed of other, as the most zealous and earnest furtherer of the Gospel? Yea, they thinke it almost

the best way, and most ready, to bring themselues in credite and estimation with many. A lamentable state of time it is, wherein such vntemperate boldnesse is permitted without any bridle at all. What man therefore that feareth God, that loueth his Church, that hath care of his Prince and countrey, can remember this thing, and not dread in his heart the sequele thereof? When the *Israelites* derided and contemned the Prophets which God had sent among them, his wrath was so kindled, that hee brought the *Assyrians* vpon them to their confusion. When the tribe of *Iuda* did the like to *Ieremie* and other messengers of God, they were cast into the captiuitie of *Babylon*. When the Iewes reprochefully vsed Christ, and with vvicked slaunder persecuted his Apostles that brought to them the light of saluation, their Citie and Temple vvas burned, their people slaine, and (as Christ threatned) their countrey made desolate, and giuen ouer to the spoyle. And shall wee thinke that God vvill not remaine the same God tovvards vs? Is his minde changed? is his iustice slaked? is his hand shortned, that either he wil not, or cannot reuenge, as he hath bin wont to doe? No (good Christians) let vs neuer deceiue our selues with such vaine and godlesse cogitations. God remaineth alwayes one, and is not mutable. His benefits to the Israelites and Iewes were neuer greater, then they novv these many yeeres haue bene toward vs: they were neuer more earnestly, eyther by Gods blessings allured, or by preaching called to repentance then vve haue bene. And yet our vnthankefulnesse, in some respectes is greater then theirs, and our vncourteous vsing of his messengers not much inferiour: yea, if the willes of many were not brideled by Gods singular grace, in our Prince and gouernours, it is to bee feared, it woulde shewe it selfe as outragious as theirs did. We haue iust cause therefore to feare the like plague, which they in like case sustained: And surely, it cannot bee, but that it hasteneth fast upon vs.

marginal references: 4. Reg. 17. & 18. — 4. Reg. 24. — Matth. 23. Luke 13.

Obiection.

But some will say (I knowe) That I doe great iniurie to the Prophets, the Apostles, and other messengers of God, to compare them vvith such vvicked men, such blinde guides, such couetous hypocrites, such antichristian Prelates, such symonicall Preachers, as our cleargie men novv are.

Answere.

I doe not compare them (good Reader) in worthines of grace and vertue, but in likenesse of office and ministerie. These haue brought vnto this realme, the same light of the gospell, the same trueth of doctrine, the same way of saluation, that the Apostles brought to the people of God in their time. They are the mouth of God whereby hee speaketh to vs and calleth vs to his knowledge, as hee did his chosen by other in the Primitiue church. And howsoeuer by the libertie of this time, it pleaseth men in the heate of their spirite to boyle out with reprochfull choler against them: yet I am sure, they are not able to vse more bitter and vncourteous speech, then the like affection vttered against the Prophets, against Christ himselfe, and his Apostles, as after more euidently shall appeare. I knowe, they being but fraile and sinfull men in comparison of those blessed Saints of God beforetime, may giue more iust cause of reproche, and minister more matter to euill tongues, then they did: And yet I doubt not, but the tenth part of that euill that vnthankefull mindes vtter against them, shall neuer be found to be true. They that haue the feare of God, will not rashly iudge of other, and christian charitie will hide the blemishes and faultes of their brethren, and specially of the preachers of the gospell sincerely teaching Gods trueth. Charitie woulde consider, that the times are dangerous, and that we are lighted into these corrupt and perillous last dayes, whereof Christ prophecied in the Euangelists, and therfore may thinke our selues thrise happy, if wee haue tollerable Ministers, though they bee farre from that rule that Christian perfection requireth.

These dayes bee like the times *Nazianzen* writeth of. *VVhen they heare any thing spoken of a Minister or Priest,* <small>Apolog.</small> *they by and by conceiue that of all, which is reported of one. And wee are become a Theater, not to Angels and men, (as that Champion Saint* Paul *sayth,) But wee are become a Stage to the most vile and abiect men at all times, and in all places, in the Streetes, in Shoppes, at Tables, at Feasts, at Councels, euen to the very playing scaffolds, which I speake with teares, and are scoffed at, euen of the vile and contemptible players. &c.*

The time was (sayth *Caluine*) *when no man durst open his mouth against the Ministers or Preachers of the worde: But nowe* there is no speech more plausible. None of these base persons would speake a word, if they did not see themselues backed by men of great authoritie, and receiue reward for so dealing. Such vntrueths woulde soone vanish and bee forgotten, vnlesse they were nourished by them for whose pleasure they were deuised. It may be hardly thought, that the true zeale of God, and loue of his Gospell is in that heart, that can easily breake out to the discrediting of the ministers and teachers thereof. They woulde rather sigh in their hearts and groane in their consciences, and pray vnto God in the spirit of mildenes, to take away such blemishes from the face of his Church, and to amende the faults thereof, if not all at once, yet by little and little, as to his gratious prouidence might seem best. For surely where hatred and contempt of the ministers is, there all goodnes must needes growe to confusion. And that maketh mee to feare, that to our great euil, the ruine of the gospell is at hand among vs. For where God is loued and feared, there his word is imbraced, and his ministers reuerenced.

This is the cause of all euil (sayth Chrysostome) *that the authoritie of spirituall gouernours is decayed, no reuerence, no honor, no feare is vsed toward them.* Obey your gouernours (saith *Paul*) *and be subiect to them.* But now al things are ouerthrowen and cleane confounded: Neither speake I this for the gouernours sake, but for your owne. And a little after, *He that honoureth the Priest honoureth God, and hee that despiseth the Priest, by little and little falleth to this also, that he will vse reproch against God himself.* He that receiueth you (sayth Christ) receiueth me. And in another place, sayth the Scripture, *Haue his Priestes in honour.* Hence commeth it (sayth Cyprian) *that the bonde of the Lordes peace is broken: Hence is it that brotherly loue is violated: Of this cause is it, that trueth is corrupted, vnitie is broken, that men leane to Schismes: because Priests are slaundered, Bishops are enuied, and euery man, either complaineth that hee is not ordeined rather then another, or else disdaineth to haue another aboue him.* &c.

<small>In 2. epist. ad Tim. 2. 1.</small>

<small>Matt. 10.</small>

The Iewes were esteemed to despise God, because they made so small account of his seruant *Moses*. And to *Samuel* (saith the Lord) *They haue not despised thee, but me.* Yea, if it be an euill Minister, (sayth Chrysostome) yet God marketh, that for his sake thou doest reuerence and obey him, that is not worthie honour of himselfe, and therefore will he pay thee

<small>Nom. 16.</small>

thy rewarde. *If he that receiueth a Prophet in the name of a Prophet, receiue the rewarde of a Prophet, it cannot be that he that reuerenceth and obeyeth his ordinarie Minister, shall want his reward.* Christians should remember that Bishops and Preachers are *the Angels of God*, the *Ambassadours of* Mal. 2. *Christ*, the *Ministers of our saluation*, and therefore 2. Cor. 5. Ephes. 2. that they can not be slaundered or abused, but the reproche must touche God himselfe. *Esay* sheweth, when Esay. 57. the vnthankeful and disobedient Iewes did mocke the Prophets, did put out their lips, and lell out their tongues in disdaine of them, that God was dishonoured with the reproch thereof. Happily it will be doubted, whether our Bishops and Preachers bee the Ministers and messengers of God, or no. Yea, some dare affirme boldly, that in deede they be not. But (good Christians) beware of such cogitations, as displeasant and misliking affections may raise in you. If they be not the ministers and messengers of God, if they bee not sent of him, then it is not the message of God that they haue brought vs: it is not his worde that they haue taught vs: they bee not Gods Sacraments that they deliuered vnto vs, and so doe a great nomber of vs remain as no Christians. Though they were such vnworthie persons, as the vnthankfull mindes of many doe imagine them, or as the vncharitable tongues and pennes of some of late time haue blazed them: yet bringing nothing vnto you, but Gods will out of his holy Scriptures, (for in deede they haue not done otherwise, howsoeuer their doctrine be defaced) you should assuredly be perswaded, that they are the instruments of Gods blessing vnto you. *Although they that bee superiours*, saith Chrysostome, *and Gouernours*, Chrysost. in *were euill, and spotted with manye faultes: yet shoulde* 2. ad. Corin. *not the Disciples withdrawe them from their instruction.* For if Christ speaking of the Doctours of the Iewes, that because they sate in *Moyses Chayre, they were worthie to bee heard of their Disciples, although their workes were not commendable: what fauour are they worthie of, which contemne and trample vnder foote (as it were) the Prelates of the Church, which by Gods goodnesse liue moderately? If it bee a foule matter for one to iudge an other, howe much more is it vnlawfull to iudge their Maisters and instructers?* Baalam was a couetous prophet, and yet by him GOD blessed his people. Nowe surely, if you haue receiued at their handes the blessing of Gods trueth, and the light of

his holie word, as in deede you haue: the cogitation of this
benefite shoulde moue your mindes more fauourably to thinke
of them, and more charitably to iudge of their doinges. Or
if you doe not, looke that you leaue not great occasion to
men to thinke of you, that you make light accompt of that
doctrine of the Gospell, which aswell their predecessours as
they, haue, and doe daily preach vnto you: and so that you
bee not those men that you would pretende to be. For men
will thinke this: If these people did fauour the Gospell, they
woulde rather seeke meanes to hide the blemishes and
imperfections of their Prelates and Preachers, then thus
odiously to amplifie and paint foorth their discredite to
their vtter shame and reproche in the worlde. For, as
much as in them lyeth, through their sides (in the heartes
and mindes of manie) they giue a mortal wound to the
doctrine, which by them hath now these manie yeeres beene
taught in this Realme. For will men iudge (trowe you) that
after so great darknesse and ignoraunce of Gods woorde, as
the Churche of Christ is reported by vs to haue beene wrapped
in, that God woulde restore and sende vnto the same the
light of his trueth, by so wicked and naughtie instruments,
as these men be imagined to be? (For they condemne not
onelie those Bishops and ministers that be now in place, but
their predecessors also, whose place these men occupie, and
whose doctrine they confirme.) Men will thinke surely,
either that that doctrine which we call darknesse and errour,
was the true light, or that these Preachers can not be so euill
persons, as malice doth make them. Christ would not suffer
that the deuill shoulde vtter any thing to the glorie of God,
and will he suffer deuillish and Antichristian persons to bee the
chiefe Preachers and restorers of his Gospell? GOD
alwaies hath appointed godlie men to be the teachers and
reuiuers of his trueth, as *Abraham* with the other Patriarches,
Moses, Aaron, Dauid, the *Prophets,* the *Apostles.* And in our
dayes *Luther, Zuinglius, Oecolampadius, Cranmer, Ridley,
Iewell, &c.* For God is neuer destitute of his godly captaines
to gouerne his Church, and to set foorth his word.

Obiection.

Oh, but our Bishops and preachers bee couetous: they giue not to the
poore: they imbesill the goodes of the Church: they bee woorkers and
clokers of Simonie: they hinder reformation of the Church, &c.

Answere.

But how know you that? It were safe for your consciences first to trie and knowe the trueth, before you rashly, to condemnation, iudge your brother. Common speeches, and coniecturall collections doe oftentimes prooue false. Doe you think that al is true which is spoken of your selues? I appeale to your owne consciences. Surely hee must bee a very happie man in these dayes, of whome some euill is not spoken, which, in his owne conscience, hee knoweth not to bee true. Nowe if this may, and doeth happen to most priuate persons, howe is it not likely that it happeneth also to Bishops and ecclesiasticall Ministers? Yea, of all other it is most like, that they shoulde feele the bitternesse of false and backbiting speeches: The Ministers of God haue beene alwayes subiect to that crosse. And in these dayes, they haue to doe with so manie and diuers kindes of enemies, as it is not possible for them to escape the daunger thereof. On the one side is the *Papist*, whose errours they confute, whose obstinacie they punish: On the other side are the *phantasticall spirites of Anabaptists, Of the families of the loue*, and sundry others of the like sort, whose wickednesse and corrupting of the church, is by our ecclesiastical gouernors drawen into the light, reproued, and repressed. Yea, and beside these, there are an infinit number of *Epicures*, and *Atheistes*, which hate the Bishops and speake euil of them, and wish them to be taken away: partly because they are as bridles to their loose and wicked life: partlie because they staye from them, that spoyle and praye, which nowe for a fewe yeeres with great hope they haue gaped after, and with much adoe is holden out of their iavves. Moreouer, who knoweth not that they which haue the office of iudging, correcting, and reproouing other, bee their doinges neuer so sincere, shall often light into the displeasure and misliking of manie, and thereby gette misreport? Therefore seeing Bishoppes, and other chiefe of the Clergie, are besette with so manie difficulties, and lie in danger of so manie aduersaries: no maruaile though their blemishes bee amplified, and (as the prouerbe is) of euerie moul-hill made a great mountayne. Yea, no maruaile, though their best doinges and sincerest meaninges, by mislikers are depraued, and with harde and vncharitable interpretations wrested to their reproofe.

Chrys. in 2. ad. Timoth.

Wherfore al Christians that haue the feare of God, and loue his trueth, but principally the chiefe gouernours, that haue authoritie to deale with the Clergie, ought to take great heed, that by such deprauing reports they bee not carried to mislike or discredite them, which neuer iustly deserued so great reproofe. Let them diligently consider what may fall vnto themselues also, beeyng in place subiect to like obliquie. What meant Saint *Paul*, when he saide, *Against an elder, receiue no accusation vnder two or three witnesses?* Surely hee did see that the office of teachers and reproouers, iudges and gouernors, lieth in great daunger of euill speech and false accusations, and therefore would not haue them rashly condemned, either in priuate or publike iudgement, much lesse to bee defaced and contemned, to be disobeyed and resisted, yea, though they were more grieuous offenders, then standeth with the worthinesse of their offices. *Aaron* had grieuously offended, and greatly distained his calling, when hee was the Minister to make the golden Calfe, and to further the peoples horrible and shamefull idolatrie. I trust all the enemies that the Bishops and Clergie men of *England* haue, shall neuer be able to prooue, that in this time of the Gospell, any one of them did euer commit an offence either so horrible, and displeasant in the sight of God, or so hurtfull and offensiue to the Church. And yet after that, when *Corah, Dathan* and other did call him proude Prelate, and sayde that hee, and his brother vsed tyrannie ouer the people of God, howe grieuously God did take it, and howe dreadfull punishment came vpon them for misusing the Ministers of G O D, the historie doeth sufficiently declare: yea, though many of the offenders were of the highest state, birth, and linage, among the people.

1 Tim. 5.

Nom. 16.

Obiection.

But it is a common Obiection, and many thinke they sufficiently excuse their contempt, when they say, That our Bishops and Preachers speake well, and teach other to doe well, but they followe not the same themselues, and therefore men doe not beleeue them, nor be any thing mooued with their preaching.

Answere.

But I say vnto you, if you followe any doctrine in respect

of the person that speaketh it, you doe not like good Christians: yea, if Paul speake any thing of himselfe, you doe not well, if in that respect you beleeue him : but you shoulde embrace his doctrine and followe his teaching, because he is the Apostle and messenger of God sent to deliuer his holy will out of the scriptures, and as it were from the mouth of God himselfe. 1. Thes. 1.

Obiection.

It will be sayd that Bishops should be The light of the world, the salt of the earth, patternes and examples to the flocke of Christ. Matth. 5. 1. Pet. 2.

Answere.

I graunt they should be so, and if they be not, the daunger is theirs : but Christ is the iudge, whose office thou mayest not presume without danger, to take vpon thee, in iudging his Minister. If they be not such as they shoulde be, wilt thou headlong therefore runne to thine owne perdition, and cast thy selfe into the danger of Gods wrath and displeasure, aswell by reiecting the trueth of his doctrine, as also by rashly iudging and condemning his Minister? Doest thou not remember that Christ sayeth, *That men shall make an accompt of euery idle worde that they speake?* And shall they not make a streight account, thinke you, for their vncurteous and vusauorie speeches, for their vncharitable and bitter raylings against them, by whose meanes they haue receiued the doctrine of saluation? Who can bee worse then a Publicane? And yet the Pharisey is greatly reproued, for that he spake so contemptuously of the Publicane, and so arrogantly preferred himselfe before him. The Chrys. in epist *Pharisey* (sayth *Chrisostome*) *by his euill speech did* ad Rom. *hurt the Publican nothing, but rather did him good, yea, though the thinges were true that hee spake of him. Wee also drawe vnto our selues extreame euill, by our euill speeches, euen as the Pharisey (as it were) did thrust a sworde into himselfe, and receiuing a sore wounde, departed. Let vs therefore rule our vntamed tongues, least wee also haue a like rewarde: for if hee that spake euill of a Publican, escaped not punishment, what defence shall we haue, that are wont to raile against our fathers? If Marie which once blasphemed her brother, was so sore punished, what hope of health* Rom. 14. Matth. 12.

shall we haue, which dayly ouerwhelme our superiors with railing speeches and taunts?

They that haue the right feare of God, looke first into their owne bosomes: they bee inquisitiue of their owne liues: they sit as iudges and examiners of their owne consciences: but nowe a dayes (the more it is to bee lamented) men forget them-selues: they looke not into their owne doings: they cast that end of the wallet behinde them, wherein their owne faultes are wrapped and be alwayes curiously prying into the liues and doings of other, and specially of Gouernours, Bishops, and Ecclesiasticall Ministers. In them, if they see neuer so light a blemish, if in their face they can finde neuer so small a warte, or espie in their eye neuer so little a moate, they are esteemed by and by misshapen Bishops, blinde guides, Monsters of Antichrist, not meete for any roome in Christes Church, not to bee suffered in any Christian commonweale. Yea, they loath their doctrine, Counsell and instruction, be it neuer so true and good: they will not take any aduise at their hands: yea, they say their teaching can doe no man good. Thus doe they make those men stumbling stockes for themselues to perdition, whome GOD of his singular grace and prouidence hath sent with his worde among them, as Ministers of their saluation.

Thinke of Bishops and Preachers, how basely and vncharitably soeuer it shall please you, they are not onely the Surgeons of your soules, but your spirituall fathers also. A naturall childe, though he suffer griefe and iniuries at his fathers hande, will not be in a rage against him, but will take the hurts patiently and mildely, so long as any way they may be borne. Although hee see faultes in his father, (as that he is euill of sight, or doateth for age, or that he be weake and staggereth as hee goeth, yea, and sometime falleth to the grounde) he will not therefore vndutifully chide his father, but by such meanes as hee can wil helpe, and with his best indeuour, wipe away the filth, that he gathereth by his oft falling: hee wil bee mindeful of that good lesson, *Noli*
Eccle. 3. *gloriari in ignominia Patris tui, neque enim tibi tam gloria quàm probrum est.* So surely, those good and kindly children that loue God their great father, wil vse themselues toward their spiritual fathers in his Church. If *Noah* happen in his sleepe to lye somewhat vncomely, and leaue open his nakednesse, they will not follow the example of cursed *Cham*,

and with derision fetch not their brethren onely, but their fathers enemies also to beholde it, that hee may bee for euer shamed, and the aduersaries mouthes opened against him: They will rather with blessed and obedient *Sem* and *Iaphet*, take the garment of christian charitie, and going backwarde hide their fathers nakednesse, yea, and happily with the rusling of their feet, or by casting on of the garment, purposely wake him out of his sleepe, that he may vnderstand howe vncomely hee doth lie, in the derision, not onely of their vnkind brother, but of other also that seeke his reproche, and by that meanes be taught to take heed that he doe not fal on sleepe againe in such vncomely maner.

Chrysostome complaineth at this vnkindnesse: *What coulde be more happie then they? what more miserable then wee? for they gaue their blood, and their life for their Maisters, but wee will not vouchsafe to vtter so much as a few wordes for our common fathers, when wee heare them reproched, backbited, slaundered, both of their owne and of others: for wee neither reproue or represse such cursed speakers: yea, I woulde to God we our selues were not the first accusers. Surely wee heare not such opprobrious rebukes at the mouthes of Infidels, as wee see powred out against our superiours, by them that are of the same religion.* Thus much haue I spoken, and the longer stoode vppon this matter (the Lord knoweth) not so much to helpe the credite of them that bee blamed, as, if it may be possible, to turne away from vs Englishmen the great daunger of our vnkindenesse in abusing them, by whome God hath deliuered vnto us so great and inestimable benefites.

Chrys. in Epist. ad Rom.

Obiection.

Some perchance will aske me, whether I entend by this meanes to cloake and hide the corrupt and naughtie life of the chiefe ministers of the Church, whereby they slaunder the Gospel, deface their calling, and be an open offence to a great number of godly.

Answere.

I answere, God forbid that I should haue any such meaning. Their great offences I greatly reproue, and thinke them woorthy, vpon triall of trueth, not only of blame, but also of more sharpe punishment, then any other, for that the offence giuen by them is greater. And we haue a Prince and

Magistrate, who by Gods lawe, if there be so iust cause, both may, and ought to deale with them, neither can their authoritie bee refused, they claime not exemption.

But as for their smaller faultes, Christian charitie forceth me to winke at them, because I know greater matter in my selfe. And I see they are men, and no Angels, and they liue in a perillous time, and haue many occasions to offend, so that it is harder for them to stande vpright, then for some other that are in priuate state. Hee is an Angell that neuer falleth, hee is no man. Men are fraile, and in daunger to sinne, though they haue otherwise great graces. If any of them haue fallen with Aaron, to anie great and horrible offence, I trust they are with him also risen by repentaunce, and with teares, in the mercie of God, washed away their wickednesse: Or, if they haue not, I must needes say with Christ, *Better it were that a Milstone were hanged about their neckes, and they cast into the sea*, then that by their continuance in euil, they shoulde bee occasion that anie shoulde fall from God, or reiect his Gospell. As their vertues are more profitable and beneficial to the Church of God, then the vertues of other priuate persons: so are their vices and faults more hurtfull and daungerous. They stande on an high place where all mens eyes are fastened vppon them: their least faultes cannot be hidde, and the greatest are of all men abhorred. A wart in the face, and a blemish in a Bishoppe, is no small disfiguring of either of them. If other mens faults be seene, the offence is not accounted great: but if a bishops be espied, it is esteemed, not according to the greatnes of the thing, but according to the dignitie of the person. *Hee that knoweth the will of his Master and doth it not, shalbe beaten with many stripes.*

Sacerdos (saith *Chrysostome*) *si pariter cum Subditis peccat, non eadem sed acerbiora patietur.* If a Priest shall offend as the inferiour doeth, hee shall suffer not the same punishment, but farre greater.

In Matt. 9. homil. 27.

It behooueth them therefore in the feare of God, to looke more diligently about them then any other, and specially in these miserable dayes, wherein all mens eyes are so curiously set vpon them, that they almost cleane forget to looke any thing vpon themselues, or to finde fault with any other, then with Ecclesiasticall persons and officers.

Obiection.

Heere some perchaunce will take mee in mine owne turne, and conclude against all that hitherto I haue spoken, yea and against the whole purpose of my writing: That if Bishoppes offences be so grieuous and hurtfull, more then other mens are, and that our Bishops and Ecclesiastical Ministers, are seene to commit so foule and heynous faultes: that they are worthie of all that euill that is spoken against them, and that I cannot iustly blame these persons, that with great zeale doe reproue these their doings, so hurtful to the Church of Christ, and so dangerous to the people of God.

Answere.

Surely, if all bee true that is written and spoken against them, (as I trust, and in part I knowe, it is not) I must needes confesse, and were wicked if I woulde denie, that they had iustly deserued whatsoeuer euill coulde bee vttered of them. For sure I am, if, as I say, all were true that is spoken, that they should be as detestable as anie heretikes that euer were in the Church, yea, as the Pope and Antichrist himselfe, whose pillars and vpholders, they are called and accounted with many. And yet can I not excuse them, which in such manner doe persecute them with the bitternesse of their tongue and penne, no more then I can excuse *Nabuchodonosor*, or any other tyrant that plagued the people of God, offending against his lawe. For whatsoeuer God in his prouidence respected, they looked only to the satisfying of their couetous, ambitious, cruell and bloody affection: And so, whatsoeuer God regardeth in chastening his negligent Ministers, or in waking them out of sleepe with the spurre of infamy and reproch: yet by their virulent and vnseasoned speeches that are vsed, by the scornfull and disdainefull reproches, by the rash and vncharitable vntruethes, I feare it may bee too truely gathered, that they which bee the instruments thereof, seeke to fulfill their enuious, proude and disdainefull appetites, or the working of some other purpose, which they looke to bring to passe, by the discrediting of the Bishops, and other chiefe of the Clergie, which be as great blockes and stops in their way. *Qui habet aures ad audiendum, audiat.* But let such persons in time take heede, when God as a mercifull father, hath chastised his children sufficiently, and stirred them to remember their dueties, that he cast not the rod into the fire, as before time he hath vsed to doe, and bring the rewarde of their vnchristian dealing vpon their owne heads. If right zeale, with conscience and detestation of euil, were the roote of these inuectiues, which so boyle in loathsome choller and bitter gall against the Bishops and other of the Clergie: surely, the same spirit would mooue them to breake out into like vehement lamentations against the euils and vices, which shew themselues in a great number of this Realme: I meane, the deepe ignorance and contempt of God in the midst of the light of the Gospell, the heathenish securitie in sinne and wickednesse, the monstrous pride in apparell, the voluptuous riot and sensualitie, the excessiue buildings and needelesse nestes of mens treasures, which bee as cankers consuming the riches of this Realme.

What shall I say of the loosenesse of whoredome and adulterie? the wrongfull wrestling by extortion, bribery, and vsury? the crafty cosening for priuate commoditie? the libertie in false swearing and periurie? with the heape almost of all other vices wherewith mans life may be distained? so that if some stay were not by moderat gouernment, and some meane number restrained in conscience, by the doctrine of the Gospell: it were greatly to be feared, that our wickednesse would growe in haste to such perfection, as it woulde presently pull out of heauen Gods wrath against vs. But all these thinges are wrapt vp in deepe silence among most of these men, vnlesse it bee to vpbraid Bishops as causes thereof, and the corrupt gouernment, as it is thought, of this Church, with the rich and wealthy states of Bishops, pretended to bee the onely cause of Gods indignation toward vs. But this is the wicked working of the deuill, to turne mens eyes from their owne sinnes, that they may not acknowledge them, and by repentance turne away the displeasure of God and his iustice hanging ouer vs, and, if it be possible, also to destroy the course of the Gospell, that hath bene so long with so small fruit among vs.

But here I haue to aduertise the godly, and chiefely the Prince and Magistrates, that they be not abused and ledde by the cunning that Sathan hath alwayes vsed, to deface the glory of God, and disturbe his Church. When Sathan seeth the doctrine of Trueth to spring vp amongst men, and somewhat to prosper: when hee seeth wickednesse and vice by diligent preaching to bee repressed, and thereby his kingdome of errour and wickednesse to decay, and the glorie of God to increase: then hee bestirreth him by all meanes hee can. And if by Gods good prouidence the Princes and Magistrates bee such, as by sword and fire he cannot either ouerthrowe it, or worke some mischiefe against it: then seeketh hee by lying and slander to discredit and deface the messengers that GOD sendeth with his worde, and instruments that he vseth to aduance and sette foorth his trueth, by this meanes to worke hinderance to the trueth it selfe. When *Ieremie* preached the will of God earnestly and truely vnto the Iewes, were there not false Prophets, and other very neere the Prince, which perswaded him and other rulers, that hee was a naughtie man, not worthie to liue? that hee was an enemie to his Countrey? that hee conspired with the *Babylonians*, and was with money or otherwise corrupted by them, to perswade the people of *Iuda*, not to refuse their subiection? When God by the Iewes in captiuitie, Hest 3. and 4. and by the fauour of the Queene *Hester*, began to spread his knowledge among the Gentiles, so that their heathenish idolatrie was somewhat blemished, the deuil raised vp a fit instrument by such meanes as before is mentioned, to worke their confusion. For *Haman* came to king *Assuerus*, and said, *There is a people dispersed throughout all the prouinces of thine Empire, not agreeing among themselues, vsing newe lawes, and contemning thy ordinances, and thou knowest it is not expedient for thy kingdome, that they should be suffered to waxe so insolent. And if it shall please thee to appoynt, that they may be all put to death, I will bring in tenne thousand talents into the kings treasure.* It was a shrewd tale to perswade a Prince. For he tempered his hateful and slaunderous lying with the sweete sawce of gaine and commoditie. The subtile Sathan did see, that sometime they which otherwise are good Princes, when hope of great benefite is offered, will be more easily perswaded to some kinde of hard dealing, which otherwise they themselues would not like. When *Iohn Baptist* was sent to prepare the way for the comming of Christ, though hee were a man of very austere liuing, did not the Pharisees perswade the people and chiefe rulers, that hee was but an hypocrite? that hee was possessed with a deuill, and therfore that his Matth. 11. doctrine should not be beleeued? When Christ himselfe came, a perfect patterne of all temperance and godly vertue, ^{Iohn 8.} did they not say, that he was a glutton, and a wine bibber? a Samaritane? a friend of Publicanes and sinners? a worker with deuils? a seducer of the people? &c. and by this means in the hearts of many wrought the discredite both of his doctrine, and of his myracles? In like manner dealt Sathan with his instruments against the Apostles and godlie professors of Christian religion in the Primitiue Church, as it appeareth in the Ecclesiasticall Histories and aunciet ^{Tertull. Apolog. in Epist. Mar. Collec. apud Euseb.} Fathers. For malitious tongues and pennes did spreade abroade of them, that they murdered their children, and did eate them: that vsually at their assemblies they committed incest: that they woorshipped the sunne: that they worshipped an asse head: that they were traitours to the Empire: that they were generall enemies of all mankinde: with an infinite number of other like false and slaunderous crimes, and by this meanes the wicked enemies of Christ raised those grieuous and terrible persecutions, wherewith the Church was vexed the space of three hundred yeeres vnder the Emperours. Yea, and this craft of the deuill ceased not vnder the Christian Emperours. For then stirred hee vp schismes and factions, errours and heresies, almost in number infinite, and still by backebiters and slaunderous instrumentes, defaced and brought out of credite the godly and learned bishops, which were as the pillars of Christian trueth, against the enemies of God and his Church.

Constantine that woorthy and godlie prince, at the beginning fauoured and furthered all those reuerend and learned Bishops that did mainteine the doctrine of *Nicene* Councell against the *Arians:* but after that *Eusebius* of *Nicomedia*, the great patrone of that heresie, had procured friendes in the court, and therby crept in some credite with the Emperour, he, and the residue of his sort, deuised shamefull slaunders against *Athanasius* and other, that, in the ende, with great displeasure of the Emperour, he was banished into *Fraunce*, and there ^{Theod. lib. c. 26. Athan. Apol. 2. Socrat. lib. 1. cap. 30. Theodor.} continued all the reigne of the saide *Constantine*. His enemies with great impudencie, had charged him with shamefull vntruths, as that he cruelly and vniustly had excommunicated diuers persons: that as a couetous extortioner, he had oppressed the countrey of

Egypt with exactions: that he had committed adultery with a strumpet, who was brought before his face to auouch it to be true: that he had murthered *Arsenius*, and vsed his arme to worke sorcery: that he sent money to one that went about treason against the Emperour: that he had affirmed in threatning wordes, that he would cause the citie of *Alexandria* to send no more tribute-corne to *Constantinople* for the Emperors prouision, as before time it had vsed to doe. As they dealt with *Athanasius*, so did they in like manner with *Eustathius, Macarius*, and al other godly Fathers which defended the true faith of Christ, and set themselues against the indeuours of heretikes, and other seditious and factious spirites. And in like maner were other vsed after that time, as *Ambrose, Cyrill*, and *Chrysostome*. It were a matter almost infinite to recite the examples thereof, and to shewe how like they are to the attempts of some in these dayes. [Socrat. lib. 1. cap. 35.]

And although it pleased GOD by strange meanes at that time to reproue sundrie of those shamefull vntrueths deuised against manie: yet by stoute affirmation and colourable proofe, thorow friendship, many of them tooke suche effect, that sundrie woorthie and good men were put out of their bishoprikes, driuen into banishment, and put to death, to the great trouble of the Church, and exceeding hinderaunce of christian faith for the space of many yeeres. We reade in histories, that *Philip* king of *Macedony*, a subtile and politique prince, who is thought to haue conquered more by craft and cunning, then by force of warre and dint of sworde, minding to bring the *Græcians* vnder his subiection, in concluding an agreement with them, conditioned that they shoulde deliuer vnto him their Orators as the very firebrands of discord among them, and the onely occasioners of that displeasure and misliking, that was betweene him and them. At which time *Demosthenes* one of the Orators, speaking for himselfe, admonished the *Athenians* to call to their remembraunce, the parable betweene the shepheardes and the wolues. The wolues pretending desire of agreement between them and the shepheards, perswaded them, that all the cause of their displeasure, was the vnseàsonable barking of the dogges: and promised great amitie, so that they woulde put away their ill-fauoured curres and mastiues. But when the dogs were remooued, the wolues tooke their pleasure in spoyling the flocke more cruelly then euer they did before. So (saieth *Demosthenes*) this King *Philip*, vnder pretence of friendship, seeking his owne benefite, would haue you deliuer vp your Orators, which from time to time call vppon you, and giue you vvarning of his subtile and craftie deuises, to the ende, that when you haue so done, ere you bee ware, he may bring you and your citie vnder his tyrannie. And this saying of *Demosthenes* proued after verie true indeede. Euen so (good Christians) the subtile serpent Sathan, prince of darknesse, seeking to bring the Church of *England* vnder his kingdome againe, from which by the mightie hand of God it hath beene deliuered, indeuoureth cunningly to perswade the shepheardes, that is, the chiefe Gouernours of this realme to put away their barking dogges, that is, to put down the state of Bishops, and other chiefe of the Cleargie, to take away their lands and liuings, and set them to their pensions, the sooner by that meanes to worke his purpose. And heerein he turneth himselfe into an Angel of light, and pretendeth great holines, and the authoritie of Gods worde, and the holy Scriptures. For such a subtile *Protheus* he is, that he can turne himselfe into all maner of shapes, to bring forward his deuise.

The craftie enemie of the Church of GOD, doeth well knowe the frailetie and corruption of mennes nature, that they will not of themselues easily bende to that is good, vnlesse they bee allured vnto it, by the hope of benefite. He vnderstandeth that *Honos alit artes*, and if he shall by any cunning bee able to pull away the reward of learning, hee right well seeth that hee shall haue farre fewer dogges to barke at him, and almost none that shall haue teeth to bite those hell houndes, that hee will sende to deuoure and destroy the flocke of Christ. Happily there may bee some young Spanielles that will quest lauishly ynough, but hee will not feare them, because hee knoweth they will haue no teeth to bite. If the state of the Cleargie shall bee made contemptible, and the best reward of learning a meane pension: hee foreseeth that neither yong flourishing wittes will easily incline themselues to godly learning, neither wil their parents and friendes suffer them to make that the ende of their trauaile. To bring this to pass, hee worketh his deuises by sundry kindes of men: first, by such as be Papists in heart, and yet can clap their handes, and set forwarde this purpose, because they see it the next way, either to ouerthrowe the course of the Gospell, or by great and needlesse alteration, to hazard and indanger the state of the common weale. The second sort are certaine worldly and godlesse Epicures, which can pretend religion, and yet passe not which end thereof goe forwarde, so they may bee partakers of that spoyle, which in this alteration is hoped for. The thirde sorte, in some respect the best, but of all other most dangerous, because they giue the opportunity and countenance to the residue, and make their indeuours seeme zealous and godly.

These bee such which in doctrine agree with the present state, and shewe themselues to haue a desire of a perfection in all things, and in some respect, in deede, haue no euill meaning, but through inordinate zeale are so caried, that they see not howe great dangers by such deuises they drawe into the Church and state of this Realme. Howe great perils, euen small mutations haue brought to Common-weales, the knowledge of Histories, and the obseruation of times, will easily teach vs.

Obiection.

But in this place mee thinketh I heare some crie out with earnest affection against me, and say, that I shewe my selfe to bee a carnall man, and in this matter of the Church vse carnall and fleshly reasons out of humaine policie, and do not stay my conscience vpon Gods word and the holy Scriptures, whereunto only in the gouernment of the Church wee shoulde cleaue, though all reason, and policie seeme contrary.

Answere.

If I doe staye my selfe, and grounde my conscience vpon humane policie, in any matter of faith and religion, I must needes confesse myselfe to be worthie great blame: But if in some things perteining to the externall fourme of gouernement, or the outwarde state of the Church, I haue respect to Christian policie, not contrary to Gods word, I see no iust cause, why I shoulde be misliked, if, in consideration of the corrupt affection of mans nature, I wish the state of a Christian Church and common weale to bee such, that yong and towardly wittes, not yet mortified by God's spirit, may bee allured with the hope of benefite, to the studie of learning, and principally of the holy Scriptures, leauing the secret direction of their minde to God. I trust no man can with good reason reprooue this my desire, and in the course of my writing, no man shall iustly say, that either I doe staye mine owne conscience, or will other men to grounde theirs, vpon reason and policie only, without the word of God. For neither will the feare of God suffer mee so to deale, in matter of such weight, neither doe I see, that by such meanes I can further the cause that I write of.

Many Pamphlets haue bene of late yeres partly written, and partly printed, against the whole gouernment of the Church by Bishops, and those in sundrie sortes, according to the nature and disposition of the Authors, but in all, great protestation of euident and strong proofe out of the Scriptures, and other writers : But especially there is one which I haue seene, the writer whereof maketh this solemne protestation following.

That as he looketh to be acceptable to the Lord, at the iudgement of the immaculate lambe, in his accusation that he maketh against the Clergie of this Realme, he will not cleaue to his owne iudgement, nor will followe his owne braine, nor wil of himself inuent ought, nor vntruly blame ought, but will faithfully and truely, sincerely and incorruptly, rehearse the holy Scriptures, and the sentences, actes, and deedes of other learned men, which determine and agree vpon those things, that hee layeth downe against them.

You may well vnderstand therefore, that such an accusation will not bee answered and shifted away with humane reason onely. The matter must haue more pith and substance in it. But howsoeuer that accusation will bee answered, I woulde the authour had perfourmed his protestation as faithfully, as, to carry some credite and fauour, he layde it out solemnely. Then shoulde not his writing containe so many vncharitabe, and contemptuous speeches, so many slaunderous vntruethes, so many wrested Scriptures, so many false conclusions, so many impertinent allegations, as he doth vse.

The purpose to perswade so great and daungerous a mutation in a common weale, shoulde haue carried with it, not onely more trueth, and comelinesse of speech, but also more weight of matter, and sounde substance of proofe. But such is the libertie of this time, and such is the maner of them, that to slaunder and deface other, passe not what they speake or write.

I will nowe come to answere briefly some particular slanders vttered against some Bishops and other by name.

Against the slaunderous Libels of late published vnder a fained and fonde name of MARTIN MARPRELATE.

OH my good Brethren and louing Countrey men, what a lamentable thing is this, that euen nowe, when the viewe of the mightie Nauie of the *Spaniards* is scant passed out of our sight: when the terrible sound of their shot ringeth, as it were, yet in our eares: when the certaine purpose of most cruel and bloody conquest of this Realme is confessed by themselues, and blazed before our eyes: when our sighes and grones with our fasting and prayers, in shewe of our repentance, are fresh in memorie, and the teares not washed from the eyes of many good men: when the mightie workes of God, and his marueilous mercies in deliuering vs, and in scattering and confounding our enemies, is bruted ouer all the world, and with humble thanks renowmed by all them that loue the Gospell: when our Christian duetie requireth for ioy and thankesgiuing, that we should be seene yet still lifting vp our hands and hearts to heauen, and with thankefull mindes setting foorth the glorie of God, and with *Moses* and the Israelites singing prayses vnto his Name, and saying, *The Lord hath triumphed gloriously, the horse and the Rider, the Ships and the Saylers, the souldiers and their Captaines hee hath ouerthrowen in the Sea: the Lorde is our strength, the Lorde is become our saluation, &c.* That euen nowe (I say) at this present time, wee shoulde see in mens handes and bosomes, commonly slaunderous Pamphlets fresh from the Presse, against the best of the Church of Englande, and that wee shoulde heare at euery table, and in Sermons and Lectures, at priuate Conuenticles, the voyces of many not giuing prayse to God, but scoffing, mocking, rayling, and deprauing the liues and doings of Bishoppes, and other of the Ministerie, and contemptuously defacing the state of Gouernment of this Church, begunne in the time of that godly and blessed Prince, King *Edward* the sixt, and confirmed and established by our most gracious Soueraigne. What an vnthankfulneses is this? what a forgetting of our duetie towarde God, and towarde our brethren? what a reproche to our profession of the Gospell? what an euident testimonie to the Aduersarie, of our hypocrisie, and deepe malice layde vp in the bottome of our breastes, euen in the middest of our troubles, when these Pamphlets were in penning? The common report goeth, and intelligence is sundry wayes giuen, that the Enemies of this lande haue rather their malice increased towarde vs, then sustained a full ouerthrowe: and therefore by confederacie, are in making prouision for a newe inuasion, more terrible in threatning, then the other. Which may seeme more easie to them, because they now know their owne wants, and our imperfections: For which vndoubtedly, they will prepare most carefully. *For the children of this worlde, are wiser in their generation, then the children of God.* What then meaneth this vntemperate, vncharitable and vnchristian dealings among our selues, at such an vnseasonable time? but as it were, to ioyne handes with the Seminaries, Iesuites, and Massing priests, and other Messengers of Antichrist, in furthering their deuises, by distracting the mindes of the Subiects, and drawing them into partes and factions, in increasing the nomber of Mal-contents, and mislikers of the state: which make no account of religion, but to make their commoditie, though it bee with spoyle of their owne countrey, if opportunitie serue? In pulling away the good and faithfull hearts of many subiects from her Maiestie, because she mainteineth that state of Church-gouernment, which they mislike, and which is protested to them, to bee prophane and Antichristian.

There are of late time, euen within these fewe weekes, three or foure odious Libels against the Bishops, and other of the Clergie, printed and spread abroad almost into all Countreyes of this Realme, so fraught with vntruthes, slaunders, reproches, raylings, reuilings, scoffings, and other vntemperate speeches: as I thinke the like was neuer committed to Presse or paper, no not against the vilest sort of men, that haue liued upon the earth. Such a preiudice this is to the honour of this State and Gouerment, as neuer was offered in any age.

For these things bee done with such impudencie and desperate boldnesse, as if they thought there were neither

Prince, nor Lawe, nor Magistrate, nor Ruler, that durst controll them, or seeke to represse them.

The Author of them calleth himselfe by a fained name, *Martin Marprelate*: a very fit name vndoubtedly. But if this outragious spirit of boldenesse be not stopped speedily, I feare he wil proue himselfe to bee, not onely *Mar-prelate*, but *Mar-prince*, *Mar-state*, *Mar-lawe*, *Mar-magistrate*, and all together, vntil he bring it to an Anabaptisticall equalitie and communitie.

When there is seene in any Common wealth such a loose boldenesse of speech, against a setled lawe or State, it is a certaine proofe of a loose boldenesse of minde. For, *Sermo est index animi*, that is, Such as the speeche is, such is the minde. *Ex abundantia cordis os loquitur.* It hath also in all Histories bene obserued, that loose boldenesse of minde toward the Superiours, is ioyned alwayes with contempt: and contemptuous boldenesse is the very roote and spring of discord, dissention, vprores, ciuill warres, and all desperate attemptes, that may breede trouble and danger in the State. Yea, and if they be hardened with some continuance of time, and hope of impunitie, and some multitude of assistance gathering vnto them: what may followe, I leaue to the wisedome and discretion of them, that God hath set in place of Gouernment.

These Libellers are not contented to lay downe great crimes generally, as some other haue done, but with very vndecent tearmes, charge some particular Bishops with particular faultes, with what trueth you shall now vnderstand.

They first beginne with *the most Reuerend, the Archbishop* of *Canterburie*: which crimes and reproches, because they are many, and of no weight or likelihoode of trueth, I take onely the chiefe, and note the pages wherein they are, setting the answere after, answering them very briefly.

But in those that touch my Lord of *London*, because they are by lewd tongues drawen into more common talke, and his person most slaunderously inueighed against and discredited: I thought it necessarie the thinges should bee more fully and amplie declared, that the trueth of them might be better conceiued.

For as much as I haue not bene curious in all my life to examine the doings of other, hauing ynough to do with mine owne, I haue in these matters vsed the instruction of them, whom no honest man may in Christian duetie suspect of vntrueth: and therefore in conscience I thinke the things to be true as I haue layde them downe.

An answere to such thinges as the most Reuerend *the Archbishop of Canterburie is particularly charged withall in the Libel.*

Libel. pag. 2.[*p*. 5.]His Grace I warrant you, will carie to his graue, the blowes &c.

Answere. God be thanked, he neuer felt blowe giuen by him or any other in that cause, except the blovves of their despitefull and malitious tongues, vvhich notvvithstanding hee contemneth, remembring how true it is that *Hierome* saith, *Istæ machinæ hereticorum sunt, vt conuicti de perfidia ad maledicta se conferant.* When heretikes are conuinced of falsehood and vntrueths, their shift is to flee to railing and slandering. And againe, *Detractio vilium satis hominum est, et suam laudem quærentium.* To backebite is the shift of base men, and such as seeke their owne praise.

He did indeede peruse *Doctor Bridges* booke before it went to the Presse, and hee knovveth that the sufficiencie thereof causeth these men thus to storme, as not being able otherwise to answere it: which maketh them so bitterly to inueigh against his person, and therefore, *Si insectari personam deploratæ causæ signum est* (as it is in deede) *illorum causa est deploratissima.*

Libell Pa. 3.[*p*. 5.]It is shame for your Grace *Iohn of Cant.* that Cartwrights bookes are not ansvvered.

Answere. Hee neuer thought them so necessarie to be answered, as the factious authors of the Libel pretend. And of that opinion are not a fevve wise and learned men, that beare good will vnto the party, and with all their hearts wishe, that God woulde direct him to vse his good giftes to the peace and quietnesse of the Church. There is sufficient written already to satisfie an indifferent reader. Hee that with indifferent minde shall read the answere of the one, and the replie of the other, shall see great difference in learning betweene them.

The desire of disputation is but a vaine brag: they haue

bene disputed and conferred with oftner then either the worthines of their persons or cause did require. Wherin their inability to defend such a cause hath manifestlie appeared, as it is vvell knowen to very many, wel able to iudge. But what brags are here by the Libeller vttered, which doe not agree with the old *Heretikes and Schismatikes*?

His Grace threatned to send Mistres *Lawson* to Bridewel, because &c. Libel. pag. 10. [*p.* 11.]

This is a notorious vntrueth. For neither did hee, nor D. *Perne* euer heare (but of this Libeller) that shee spake anie such wordes of him. But in trueth, asvvell for the immodestie of her tongue, vvherein she excelleth beyond the seemelinesse of an honest woman, as also for her vnwomanlie and skittish gadding vp, and downe to Lambehith, and from thence in company vnfit for her, without her owne husband, he threatned to send her to Bridevvell, if she reformed not the same : which he meaneth to peforme, if she continue her lightnesse. And yet *Dame Lawson* so notorious, for the vilenesse of her tongue, and other vnwomanly behauiour, is one of *Martins* cononized Saints: *Quia quod volumus sanctum est*, as *Augustine* said of their predecessors the *Donatists*. It is likewise an vntruth, vvhich is reported in that page of her words spoken by M. *Shaller*. For surely if she had vttered them, hee would haue sent her thither without faile. But *Dame Lawson* glorieth in her owne shame, and so do her teachers. Answere.

That which he calleth a Protection, *Chard* had from the Lords of her Maiesties priuie Counsell, vpon charitable and good causes moouing their Lordships.

He seemeth to charge the Archbishop with infidelitie &c. Libel. pag. 15

This needeth no answere, it sheweth of what spirit they are. Answere.

Touching the *Premunire &c.* Libel pag. 21

The Libeller doth but dreame, let him and his doe what they can. Answere.

The same may bee answered to their threatning of fists &c.

That which hee speaketh of buying a Pardon &c. as it is most vntrue, so is it slaunderous to the *State*. If there were any such matter, it may soone appeare by search: but the impudencie of these men is great, and villanous slaunder will neuer long be without iust reward.

Libel. pag. 22.[*p.* 21.] He saith we fauour Recusants rather then Puritans &c.

Answere. Herein he doeth notoriously abuse vs: though the Recusant for the most part, behaueth himself more ciuilly before the Magistrate then doth the *Puritane:* who is commonly most insolent, and thereby deserueth more sharpe wordes and reproofes then the other.

That which he speaketh of the *Recusants* threats against *Puritane* Preachers, hath no sense. For how can the *Recusant* so threaten the *Puritane*, when he neuer commeth to heare his Sermons? But these wicked *Martinists* account her Maiesties louing subiectes, liking and allowing the orders of the Church, and procuring the contrary to be reformed by authoritie, as Papists and Recusants. By which sinister practise and iudgement many are discomforted, and obedience greatly impeached.

Libel. pa. 23 [*p.* 22.] Doth your Grace remember, what the Iesuite at Newgate &c.

Answere. No truely, for he neuer heard of any such matter, but by this lewde Libeller: neyther doeth he thinke that there was euer such thing spoken. Schismatikes are impudent lyars, the worlde knoweth what he hath euer bene, and vvhat hee is: he doth disdaine to answere such senselesse calumniations.

That which hee speaketh of *Thackwell* the Printer &c. is a matter nothing pertaining to him. M. *Richard Yong*, was the dealer therein without his priuitie, who is able to iustify his doings in that matter, and to conuince the libeller of a malicious slaunder. The man is knowen and liuing : the Libeller may talke with him, and knowe his owne wickednesse. *The mouth that lyeth killeth the soule. The Lord will destroy lying lippes, and the tongue that speaketh proude things.*

Waldegraue receiued iustly according to his deserts, hauing founde before that time, greater fauour than he deserued, being a notorious disobedient and godlesse person, an vnthriftie spender, and consumer of the fruits of his owne labours, one that hath violated his faith to his best and dearest friends, and wittingly brought them into danger, to their vndoing. His wife and children haue cause to curse all wicked and vngodly Libellers.

The Calumniation touching the Presse and Letters Pag. 24.[*p.* 23.] in the Charterhouse (which presse *Waldgraue* himselfe soulde to one of the *Earle of Arundels* men, as it is since confessed) must receiue the same answere with the other of *Thackwell:* sauing that to M. *Yong* must bee added also, some other of greater authority, who can tel *Martin*, that his spirite is not the spirit of God, which is the spirit of trueth, but the spirite of Sathan, the author of lyes. Charge them, O shamelesse man, with this matter, who are able to answere thee, and not the Archbishop, whome it toucheth not, though it becommeth not euery common and base person, to demaund an account of the doings of men in authoritie.

The decree there mentioned, being first perused by the Queenes learned counsell, and allowed by the Lords of her Maiesties most honorable priuie Counsell, had his furtherance in deede, and should haue, if it were to doe againe. It is but for the maintenance of good orders among the printers, approued and allowed by the most, the best, and the wisest of that company, and for the suppression of inordinate persons, such as *Waldegraue* is.

Hee erected no newe Printer, contrary to that decree: but vsed meanes by vvay of persvvasion for that party, Pag. 25. commended to him by his neighbors, to be a very honest and poore man, hauing maried also the vvidowe of a Printer: and hee did vvery vvell like and allovve of his placing by such, as haue interest therein. Neither did hee euer heare, (but by this Libeller vvho hath no conscience in lying) that hee euer printed any such bookes. This I knowe of a certaintie, that *Thomas Orwin* himselfe hath vpon his booke oath denied, that he euer printed, either *Iesus Psalter*, or *Our Lady Psalter*, or that he euer was any vvorker about them, or about any the like bookes. *But the poisoned serpent careth not whome hee stingeth.*

Whether *Waldgraue* haue printed any thing against the state, or no, let the bookes by him printed, be iudges.

I doe not thinke, that eyther hee, or any *Martinist* euer heard any Papist say, that there vvas no great iarre betvveene the Papistes and the Archbishop in matters of Religion. It is but the Libellers Calumniation. If they did, vvhat is that to him? I thinke *Martin* him selfe doubteth not of the Archbishops soundnesse in such matters of Religion, as are in controuersie betwixt the Papists and vs. If hee doe, the matter is not great.

The *Vniuersitie* of *Cambridge*, where hee liued aboue thirtie yeeres, and publiquely red the Diuinitie Lecture aboue seuen yeeres, and other places where he hath since remained, vvill testify for him therein, and condemne the Libeller for a meere *Sycophant*, and me also of follie, for ansvvering so godlesse and lewde a person.

It is no disparagement to receiue testimonie of a mans aduersarie: and therefore if Master *Reinolds* haue giuen that commendation to his booke in comparison of others, it is no impeachment to the trueth therof. I haue not seene *Reinolds* his booke: the Libel is so full of lies, that an honest man can not beleeue any thing conteined in it.

My Lorde of *Canterburie* would be sorie from the bottome of his heart, if his perswasion, and the grounds thereof were not Catholike: hee detesteth and abhorreth schismaticall grounds and perswasions: and thereunto hee professeth himselfe an open enemie, which he woulde haue all *Martinists* to knowe.

That of the Spaniards stealing him away, &c. [*p.* 24] is foolish and ridiculous. I would the best *Martinist* in *England* durst say it to his face before witnesse.

Hee firmely beleeueth that Christ in soule descended into hell. All the *Martinists* in Christendome are not able to proue the contrary: and they that indeuour it, doe abuse the scriptures, and fall into many absurdities.

Hee is likewise perswaded that there ought to be by the worde of God a superioritie among the Ministers of the Church, which is sufficiently prooued in his booke against *T. C.* and D. *Bridges* booke likewise, and he is all times ready to iustifie it, by the holy Scriptures, and by the testimony of all antiquitie. *Epiphanius* and *August*[*ine*]: account them heretikes, that holde the contrary. The Arguments to the contrary, are vaine, their answeres absurd, the authorities they vse, shamefully abused, and the Scriptures wrested.

He hath shewed sufficient reason in his booke against *T.C.* why Ministers of the Gospell, may be called Priests. The ancient fathers so cal them. The church of *England* imbraceth that name, and that by the authoritie of the highest court in *England*. And why may not *Presbyter* be called Priest?

In these three points (whereof the last is of the least

[Bp. T. Cooper. Jan. 1589.]

moment) he doth agree with the holy Scriptures, vvith the vniuersall Church of God, vvith all antiquitie, and in some sort with the Church of *Rome*. But hee doth disagree from the Church of Rome that now is in the dregges, vvhich it hath added : as, that Christ should harrow hell : that the Pope should be head of the vniuersall Church : that hee, or any other Priest, should haue authoritie ouer Kinges and Princes to depose them, to deliuer their subiects from the othe of their obedience. These thinges haue neither the vvord of God, nor the decrees of ancient Councels, nor the authoritie of antiquitie to approoue them, but directly the contrarie. As for the name of Priest, as they take it, hee doth likevvise condemne in our Ministers, neyther doe themselues ascribe it to them. And therefore the Libeller in these poyntes vvriteth like himselfe.

Touching Wigginton, &c.   Libel. pag. 26. 27.

That vvhich he speaketh of *Wigginton*, is like the rest, sauing for his saucie and malapert behauiour   Answere. tovvarde the Archbishoppe : vvherein in trueth, hee did beare vvith him too much. *Wigginton* is a man vvell knovven vnto him, and if hee knevve himselfe, hee vvould confesse that hee had great cause to thanke the Archbishoppe. As hee vvas a foolish, proude, and vaine boy, a laughing stocke for his follie to all the societie with whom hee liued : so doeth hee retaine the same qualities being a man, sauing that his follie, pride, and vanitie is much increased : so that nowe hee is become ridiculous euen to his owne faction.

The honestest, the most, and the best of his parish did exhibite to the high Commissioners, articles of very great moment against him : the like whereof haue seldome bene seene in that Court. The most and woorst of them are prooued by diuers sufficient witnesses, and some of them confessed by himselfe, as it appeareth in record. For which enormities, and for that hee refused to make condigne satisfaction for the same, and to conforme himselfe to the orders of the Church, by lawe established : he was by due order of lawe deposed from his Ministerie, aud depriued of his benefice, and so remayneth, being vnfit and vnworthie of either.

The tale of *Atkinson* is a lowde, notorious, and knowen lie. For neither did he euer say so to the Archbishop, neither would hee haue taken it at his hands, neither was that any cause of *VViggintons* depriuation : but vanitie and hypocrisie causeth this man to haue so small conscience in lying, according to that saying, *Omnis hypocrisis mendacio plena est.*

That heathenish vntruth vttered diuers times in this booke, that the Archbishoppe should accompt preaching of the word of God to be heresie, and mortally abhorre and persecute it, is rather to bee pitied then answered. If man punish not such sycophants, God will do it, to whose iust iudgement the reuenge of this iniurie is referred. He doth bridle factious and vnlearned Preachers, such as the more part of that sect are, who notwithstanding crie out for a learned Ministerie, themselues being vnlearned, and so would be accounted of all men, if it were not *propter studium partium.* I say with S. *Hierome, Nunc loquentibus et pronunciantibus plenus est orbis: loquuntur quæ nesciunt, docent quæ non didicerunt, magistri sunt cum discipuli antè non fuerint.* The world is full of them that can speake and talke: but they speake the thinges they knowe not: they teach the thinges they haue not learned: they take vpon them to teach before they were schollers to learne. Indeede our Church is too full of such talkers, rather then sober teachers, whome hee professeth himselfe greatly to mislike. Otherwise hee defieth all *Martinistes* in *Englande*, and doeth appeale vnto the whole State of the learned and obedient Clergie for his innocencie therein.

Libel. pag.31[*p.* 28.]Touching master Euans, &c.

Answere. That of *Euans* concerning the Vicarage of *Warwike*, is maliciously reported. He reiected him for lacke of conformitie to the orders of the Church. If hee haue done him any wrong thereby, the lawe is open, hee might haue had his remedie. That honourable person mentioned by the Libeller, I am sure, accepted of his answer. And I knowe, that according to his honourable disposition, hee thinketh himselfe greatly abused by the libeller in this point. But what careth such a corner-creeper what he saith of any man, be hee neuer so honourable? The rest of that tale is vntrue, not worth answering. And if the relator thereof durst appeare and shewe himselfe, *Martin* could not be long vnknowen. If any of his men at any time reported, that hee shoulde say, hee woulde not be beholding to neuer a noble man in this land, &c. hee sheweth himselfe to be of the Libellers conditions, that is, a common lyar. For hee neuer spake the wordes to any man, neither doeth he vse that familiaritie with his men.

But the Libeller careth not what hee speaketh, either of him, or of his men, so that he may fill vp his libel with vntrue slaunders.

That which followeth of the Archbishops words to the knight, that he was the second person of the land, &c. is of the same kinde. The knight I am sure is liuing, let him be examined of that matter. True it is, that there was a good knight with him, an olde friend of his about such a sute: but that he euer spake any such wordes vnto him, as the Libeller woulde make the worlde beleeue, is most false: the Knight liueth and can testifie the same. But the Libeller thinketh all men to be as proude and malapert as himselfe and other of his faction are, whose pride the world seeth, and it is vntolerable.

He was neuer *D. Perns* boy, nor vnder him at any time, but as felow of the house where he was master. Pag. 32[*p.* 29.] Neither did he euer cary his, or any other mans cloake bagge: Although if he had so done, it had bin no disgrace to him. Better mens sonnes then the Libeller is, haue caried cloake-bags. But the lewde man is not ashamed to lye in those things, that are open to euery mans eyes: such is his malice and impudencie.

How *Dauisons* Catechisme was allowed, or how long in perusing, I know not: some paultrie pamphlet Pag. 34. belike it is, like to that busie and vnlearned *Scot*, now termed to be the author thereof. *D. Wood* is better able to judge of such matters, then either *Dauison*, or any *Martinist*, that dare be knowen.

  Touching the Apocrypha, &c.   Libel. pag. 37. [*p.* 34.]

He gaue commandement in deede, and meaneth to see it obserued. For who euer separated this *Apocrypha* from the rest of the *Bible*, from the beginning of Christianity to this day? Or what Church in the world, refourmed or other, doth yet at this present? And shal we suffer this singularitie in the church of England, to the aduauntage of the aduersary, offence of the godly, and contrary to al the world besides? I knowe there is great difference betweene the one and the other: yet all learned men haue from the beginning, giuen to the *Apocrypha* authoritie, next to the Canonicall Scriptures. And therfore such giddie heads, as seeke to deface them, are to be bridled. A foule shame it is, and not to be suffered, that such speeches should be vttered against those bookes, as by some hath bene: enough to cause ignorant people to discredite the whole Bible.

Libel. pag.44[p. 40.] Touching Dr. Sparke, &c.

Answere. Their Honors that were then present, can and wil, I am sure, answere for the bishops to this vntrueth. They made report to diuers in publike place, and some to the highest, of that conference, after an other sort, and to another end, then the Libeller doth. That seely *Obiection* God knoweth, was soone answered in few words, viz. That the translation read in our Churches, vvas in that point according to the *Septuagint*, and correspondent to the Analogie of faith. For if the word be vnderstood of the Israelites, then is it true to say, that *they were not obedient to his commandement*: but if of the signes and vvonders, that *Moses* and *Aaron* did before *Pharao*, or of *Moses* and *Aaron* themselues, then is it on the other side true, that *they were obedient to his commandement*. This might haue satisfied any learned and peaceable Diuine, and pacified their immoderate contention against the booke of common praier. This was then, and is now, the answere t·that friuolous obiection, and this is the *Nonplus* that the Libeller vaunteth of. More modestie might haue become *D. Sparke*, and the reporter, euen *conscientia suæ imbecillitatis*, in that conference.

Libel. pa. 50. [p. 50.] Touching Patrike, &c.

Answere. He neuer made *Patrike* Minister, neither intended to make him, neither was hee of his acquaintance at all in *Worcester*. It is vvel knovven that the Archbishoe hath not ordeined moe, then onelie two Ministers, since his comming to this Archbishoprike. And therefore this *Calumniation* must be placed vvith the former.

Thus is this godlesse Libeller answered in fevv vvords, touching such matters wherwith he chargeth the most reuerend father the Archbishop of *Cant.* whereby the world may perceiue, with what spirit he is possessed. The wise *Prouer. 24.* man saith, *that destruction shall suddenly come vpon the backbiter and calumniator.* The *Psalmist* saith, *The Lord* *Psalm. 55.* *wil destroy lying lips, and the tongue which speaketh proud things*: and *that death shal suddenly come vpon them, and hell shall receiue them.* S. *Ambrose* saith, *that Detractors are scarcely to be accounted Christians.* And *Cyprian* saith, *Non qui audit, sed qui facit conuitium, miser est.* Not he that is railed at, but he that raileth, is the wretched man. The wicked Iewes, when they could not otherwise answere Christ, called him Samaritan, and saide he had a deuill, and shortly after tooke up stones, and cast at him. So the Anabaptists, within our memory, after slaunderous and opprobrious calumniations against the godly preachers and magistrates then liuing, fell to blowes and open violence. The Libeller in this booke hath performed the one, and threatned the other.

> This haue I laid downe word by worde, as I receiued the same from my Lorde of London: who desireth to haue the matter heard by indifferent Iudges, and will shew the Suggestions to be very vntrue.

And as to *Martins* lewd exclamation against the B. of *London* concerning the cloth thought to be stollen from the Dyars, this is the truth of the case: that vpon notice giuen to the said B. that such like cloth was wayued within his Manor of *Fulham*, and left in a ditch there, and no owner knowen, hee presently hoping to take them that brought it thither, or at the least to saue the same from purloyning or miscarying, appoynted the same to be watched diuers nights: and in the end hearing neyther of the owners, nor of them that so waiued it, willed the same to bee brought to his house in Fulham, and there to be kept for him or them which by law ought to haue it, were it in respect of the first property, or of the alteration thereof by means of the liberties. Whereupon, a good space after, the Dyars indeed came to the Bishop, and claimed the cloth, and sought by earnest means to haue it again, without making any proofe, that the cloth was theirs, or that the same cloth was it, for which the theeues were executed, or that fresh sute was made after the saide theeues for the same. But vpon conference had with learned Lawyers therein, it was resolued, that the propertie of this cloth was altered and transferred to the lyberties: and so it seemeth the Dyars themselues haue found, els would they by lawe haue sought remedy therefore yer [*ere*] nowe, it beeing well nie towards three yeares since. Yet neuerthelesse, so far hath the said bishop beene from exacting the extremity, that offer hath bene made to the Dyars of a good part of the cloth, where in rigour of the law, they haue lost all: And further to restore all, or to make sufficient recompence therefore, if by law it ought to be so, vpon the examination of the trueth of the case. And as for *Martins* erronious iudgement, that this is theft, beeing taken and claymed by right and lawe, as aforesayd, because the true owners are defeated (as hee saith) surely, hee might knowe if it were matter for his humor, that the Lavve vvorketh this in other cases, as in strayes proclaymed and kept a yeere and a daye, according to the law, the propertie is altered, and transferred to the Lord from the true ovvner: so is it for stolen cattell, brought *bona fide* to the ouert market: The first ovvners propertie is gone, and the buyer hath it: And so is it for waiued goods, as was this cloth. And to shewe that the sayde Bishop had not so great a desire to detaine the cloth as the Libeller hath presumed, hee often times asked an officer of his, howe it happened that the Dyars came not for it: for hee was euer ready, and yet is, to deliuer it to them, or the value thereof, if it prooue to be theirs. And thus much is to be answered to that matter.

The Libeller obiecteth against the Bishop as a great heinous fault, that of his Porter he made a Minister: which, al things considered, he thinketh that doing to be iustifiable and lawfully done, and not to lacke example of many such that haue bene after that sort admitted, both since her Maiesties comming to the Crown, by many good Bishops, and by sound histories Ecclesiasticall, that vvhere the Church by reason of persecution or multitude of Hamlets, and free Chappels, which haue commonly very small stipends for the Minister, honest godly men, vppon the discretion of the Gouernors of the Church, haue and might be brought in to serue in the want of learned men, in prayer, administration of Sacraments, good example of life, and in some sort of exhortation. And this man therefore, when the Bishop founde him by good and long experience to be one that feared God, to be conuersant in the scriptures, and of very honest life and conuersation: he allowed of him, to serue in a small congregation at *Padington*, where commonly for the meannesse of the stipend, no Preacher coulde be had, as in many places it commeth to passe where the Parsonage is impropriat, and the prouision for the Vicar or Curat is very smal. And how this poore man behaued himselfe there, time and tryall proued him: for he continued in that place with good liking of the people 8. or 9. yeres, till he grew dull of sight for age, and thereby vnable for to serue any longer. It is to be founde among the Greeke Canons, that in *Spaine* and *Africa* when the Goathes and Vandalles had by extreme persecution made hauocke of the Church men, those fewe that were left there aliue, made their moane to the Churches of *Rome* and *Italy*, that their Churches stoode emptie, because they could get none to serue, no not such as were vnlearned. Whereby it appeareth, that in the time of necessitie, and such great want, the Church did allowe of very meane Clarkes, and so did they in the beginning of hir Maiesties raigne. But *Martin* and his complices, hauing a desire to throwe out of the Church, the booke of common prayer, would rather haue the Churches serued by none, then by such as by praier and administration of Sacraments should keepe the people together in godly assemblies. But this Libeller being as a botch in the body, wherunto all bad humors commonly resort, and fewe good, was content to take this report of this poore man, and not at all to make mention, as he might haue done, of that precise and straight order which the Bishoppe obserueth in making Ministers. For most true it is, that the said B. admitteth none to orders, but such as he himself doth examine in his owne person in poynts of Diuinitie, and that in the latin tongue, in the hearing of many: whereby it commeth to passe, that none lightly come at him, but such as be Graduats, and of the vniuersities. But *Martin* neither himselfe nor his cole cariers seeke for any thing that is commendable, but like the spider that gathereth all that may turne to poyson.

Further, for lacke of true matter, *M. Maddockes* must be brought in by the Libeller to furnish his railing comedy. It were ynough to say of that thus much, that the most reuerent Father the Archbishop of *Canterburie* examining that matter betweene the Bishop and *Maddockes*, with some other Bishops assisting him, founde the matter to make so sore against the Bishop, that *Maddockes* himselfe was content before them to aske him forgiuenes, and to promise that he would euer after haue a reuerent regard of his duetie towards the saide Bishop, as his Ordinarie. For if he should so vntruely haue played with the name of *Aelmer*, by turning it into the name of Mar-elme, hee shoulde haue spoken against his conscience, as he himselfe knoweth, and all the Court, and her Maiestie her selfe can testifie, that it was a most shamefull vntrueth blased abroade by one *Lichfield* a Musicion, which is nowe departed.

Here might bee noted, howe *Doctor Perne*, beeing at no meane mans table, and hearing of such slanderous rayling of felling of the Elmes at *Fulham*, he asked one of the company being an ancient Lawyer, howe long the Elmes of *Fulham* had bene felled. Said the Lawyer, some halfe yere past. Nowe truly saide *D. Perne*, they are marueilouslie growen in that time, for I assure you I vvas there vvithin these foure daies, and they seeme to be tvvo hundred yeeres old. And maister *Vicechamberlaine* at her Maiesties being at *Fulham*, tolde the Bishop that her Maiestie misliked nothing, but that her Highnesse lodging was kept from all good prsopects by the thicknesse of the trees. Lo, you may see hereby, that the Libeller to set out his *Pasquill*, raketh all things by all reportes from all the Sycophants in the world, and maketh no choice of man or matter, so that it may serue his turne.

And for any Letter written by the maister of Requests so iestinglie, as the Libeller reporteth, Maddockes hath deceiued him: for there vvas no such matter, nor the man for whome the Bishop wrote, was none of his seruant, nor is.

Nowe commeth in Dame *Lawson* to frumpe the bishoppe vvith impudent and vnvvomanlie speech, and vnfit for that sexe, whome *Paul* vtterly forbiddeth to speake in the congregation. But considering the circumstaunces of time, place, and persons, it is to bee thought that Dame *Lawson* came at no time to the bishoppe in that brauerie: for if she had, the bishop is not so soft, but shee shoulde haue felt of Discipline, and of the Queenes authoritie. Surelie the bishop and such other of the Reuerend fathers that are so bitten by this Libeller, may comfort themselues by the example of *Athanasius* and others as I before haue said, which were most shamefully accused by the heretikes, of murder, robbery, enchantment, whoredome, and other most detestable crimes, to deface them to the worlde, to the ende that their heresies might be the better liked of. But *Martin* remember that saying, *Væ homini per quem scandalum venit,* and that *Iude* saith, *that* Michael *when he disputed with the Deuill about the body of* Moses, *the Angell gaue no railing sentence against him, but said, the Lord rebuke thee, Satan.* And if it pleased you to remember that booke that is fathered vpon *Ignatius* in *Greeke* which attributeth so much to the bishops, you would be good master to bishops, against whom so vnreuerently you cast out your stomacke.

And for your iesting at the Bishop for bowling vpon the Sabboth, you must vnderstand that the best expositor of the Sabboth, which is Christ, hath saide, that the Sabboth was made for man, and not man for the Sabboth : and man may haue his meate dressed for his health vpon the Sabboth, and why may he not then haue some conuenient exercise of the body, for the health of the body ?

You will take small occasion to raile, before you will hold your tongue. If you can charge the Bishop that euer he withdrew himselfe from Sermon or seruice by any such exercise, you might bee the bolder with him : but contrariwise it is wel knowen, that he and his whole familie doeth euery day in the weeke twice say the whole seruice, calling vpon God for them selues, the State, and the Queenes Maiestie, praying for her highnesse by that meanes deuoutly and heartily many times : I pray God you do the like. But, *oratio animæ maleuolæ non placet Deo :* The prayer of a malicious heart neuer pleaseth God.

Martin with his bitter stile of malicious *Momus* dipt in the gall of vngodlinesse, proceedeth in a shamelesse vntrueth touching the Bishops answere to the executors of *Allein* the Grocer, as though he should flatly denie the payment of a certaine debt, due to the sayde *Allein :* which is as true as all the rest of *Martins* writings is honest and sober. For bee it that at the first demaunde, the Bishoppe was somewhat mooued to heare his name to be in the Merchants bookes, which hee euer so precisely auoyded, that commonly he sendeth to them whom hee hath to doe with, warning them to deliuer nothing in his name, without his owne hand or ready money, vsed peraduenture some sharpe wordes in a matter that was so suddaine and so strange to him : Yet most certaine it is, that though not at that time, yet very shortly after, the debt was discharged, as shall be prooued, long before *Martins* railing booke was heard of or seene: ten pound excepted, which the sayde executors for a time respited. But this fellowe will trauaile farre before he will lacke matter to furnish a lye.

Another mountaine that he maketh of molehils (for such is all his blasphemous buildings) is, that one *Benison* a poore man, was kept in the Clincke I cannot tell howe long, vniustly without cause, &c. The trueth is this: *Benison* comming from *Geneua*, full fraught with studie of *Innouations*, and vtterly emptie of obedience, which *Beza* that learned Father had or might haue taught him, as by his Epistles appeareth, both to the Queene and the gouernors of the Church, set vp in *London* his shop of disobedience, being maried in a contrary order to the booke and vsage of the Church of *England*, abusing good M. *Foxe* as hee himselfe in griefe of heart after confessed. After that, the said *Benison* gathering conuenticles, and refusing to goe to his owne parish church, seeking to set al in combustion with schisme in the Citie, was long before the B. heard any thing of him, called before Sir *Nicholas Woodrofe* a graue Citizen, and the Recorder: who found him in such an humour, that they ment to haue sent him to prison. But because he was of the Clergie, they thought good to commit him to his Ordinarie, who trauailing with him most earnestly to bring him to the Church and become orderly, when he coulde profite nothing with him, sent him againe to the Sessions to the Lord Maior and the Iudges. After they had dealt with him, and could finde at his hands nothing but railing, they sent him againe to the Bishop, and he finding him in vnspeakable disobedience to her Maiestie and her Lawes, offered him the oath, which he contemptuously and spitefully refused. Which being certified according to order, hee was sent to the Queenes bench, and was condemned, and thereupon sent to prison. And this is that wonderful tragedie wherin this fellow so greatly triumpheth, wishing belike (as his whole Libell seemeth to desire) that no malicious schismatike should be punished for moouing sedition in the lande. But to this vnbrideled tongue, it may be said as the Psalme sayth, *Quid gloriaris in malitia tua? &c.* Where he courseth the Bishop of *London* with the lewde lying Epithete of *Dumbe Iohn*, fetched I cannot tell from what grosse conceite, either as willingly stumbling vpon

Dumbe for *Don*, or for that he preacheth not so oft, as hee and other of his crewe babbling in their verball sermons vse to doe, or from whence else I know not, vnlesse it please his wisedome to play with his owne conceite, and minister matter to the Prentises and Women of *London*, to sport himselfe in that pretie deuised and newe founde name. If the Bishop shoulde answere for himselfe, I knowe he might say somewhat after this sort: Good charitable *Martin*, howe olde are you? how long haue you knowen the man? what reports in the booke of Martyrs, in Master *Askams* booke of his Schoolemaster, and in some learned men that haue written from beyond the Seas, haue you heard of him? Master *Foxe* saith of him, that hee was one of the fiue, and now onely aliue, that stoode in the solemne disputations in the first of Queene *Mary*, with a hundred hauberdes about his eares: (the like whereof you threaten now him and others) in the defence of the Gospell, against all the learned Papists in *England*. For the which hee was driuen into banishment, and there continued for the space of fiue or sixe yeeres, visiting almost all Vniuersities in *Italie* and *Germanie*, hauing great conference with the most and best learned men: at the last being stayed at *Iany* an vniuersity erected by the dukes of *Saxonie*, and should, if he had not come away, had the Hebrewe lecture, which *Snepphinus* had, intertained by them to read in their said vniuersity both Greeke and Latin, in the company and with the good loue and liking of those famous men, *Flaccus Illyricus, Victorius, Strigellus, D. Snepphinus*, called *alter Luther*, with diuers others, where belike he was not dumb. And after comming home, was appointed among the famous learned men, to dispute againe with the enemies of the religion, the papisticall Bishops, and like, that if the disputations had continued, to shew him not ignorant in all the three tongues, as he wil yet, if *Martin Malapert* prouoke him too far, not to be dumbe. Is he dumbe because hee was the onely preacher in *Leicestershire* for a space, as the noble Earle of *Huntington* can witnesse? and by their two meanes, that shire, God be blessed, was conuerted and brought to that state that it is now in? which in true religion is aboue any other place, because they retaine the Gospell without contention, which fewe other places doe. And in *Lincolneshire* did he nothing? did he not first purge the Cathedral Church, being at that time a neast of vncleane birdes, and so by preaching and executing the Commission, so preuailed in the countrey (God blessing his labours) that not one recusant was left in the countrey, at his comming away to this sea of *London*? Is this to be dumbe? howe many Sermons hath hee preached at *Paules* crosse? sometime three in a yeere, yea, sometime two or three together, being an olde man, to supply some yonger mens negligence.

It is omitted, that Episcopomastix had a fling at the Bishoppe of *London* for swearing by his faith, wherefore he termeth him a Swag. What hee meaneth by that, I will not diuine: but as all the rest is lewd, so surely herein he hath a lewde meaning. It is to be thought, that the Bishop wil take profite hereby, being a man that hath diligently read *Plutarke, De vtilitate capienda ab inimico*. If it bee an othe, as this gentleman hath censured it, it is not to be doubted, but that he wil amend it: but if it were lawful, as it may bee for any thing *Martin* can say, to aske his brotherhood, what *Amen* signifieth, or whether it be an othe: then in his wicked and malicious wishes for the ouerthrow of the Clergie, how oft is he to be found to say *Amen*? for in the phrase of our speech, *by my faith* signifieth no more, but, *in very trueth, bona fide, in trueth, assuredly, id est, Amen*.

It is to be thought, that *Martin* misliketh to say by his faith, because a railing and slanderous spirit can haue no faith: for where Charitie is away (the soule of all good workes) there can be no faith. Read that of *Paul, Charitas non inuidet, non est suspicax, &c*. The contraries whereof swell in *Martin* as venemous humours in an infectious sore.

Among other their reproches, they affirme of the bishop of *Rochester*, that hee presented him selfe to a benefice. I doe not thinke it to be true, for that I know it can not be good in Lawe. If he hath procured a benefice in way of *Commendam* (as they call it) it is by lawe allowed, and hath bene done by other.

The bishop of *Lincolne* is knowen to bee learned and zealous in religion. There are few men towarde her Maiestie that haue preached in the court, either oftner times, or with more commendation, or better liking, as well before he was bishop, as since. It is therefore maruaile, that none in all this time could espie his inclination vnto corrupt and Papisticall doctrine, vntill the chickens of the scratching kite yong *Martinists*, got wings to flee abroad, and crie out vntrueths against euerie man that displeaseth them.

If the bishop of *Lincolne* had not euen of late shewed himselfe in the Commission Court, at the examination of some of them, he had now escaped this scratch of the lewde lying *Martin Marprelate*. What his wordes were I haue forgotten, and yet I heard them deliuered by a learned man that was present. For I did not then meane to deale in this cause, but they were nothing sounding to that which the Libell layeth downe. And the person considered at whose funerall hee preached, hee could not with comelinesse speake lesse in her commendation then he did, vnlesse they woulde haue had him as rash and furious as themselues, and to enter into Gods secrete iudgement, and openly to condemne her as a reprobate. God may work great matters in a moment.

THE bishop of *Winchester* is charged with certeine wordes vttered in two sermons the last Lent: the one in the Queenes Chappell, the other at S. *Marie Oueries* in *Southwarke*. The wordes of the challenge are these, Like a flattering hypocrite, he protested before God and the congregation, that there was not in the worlde at this day, nay, there had not beene since the Apostles time such a flourishing state of a Church, as nowe wee haue in England. Surely, if hee had vttered these wordes for the state of the Church appointed by lawe and order, not respecting the faultes of particular persons, it might in Christian duetie bee well defended. But it was not vttered in this manner, nor for the matter, nor for the time. The first part of those wordes hee doth not acknowledge at all, for they are purposely inserted to stirre enuie. Thus in deede it was deliuered: *As for the trueth of doctrine, according to the worde of God, for the right administration of the Sacraments, for the true worship of God in our prayer, layde downe in the booke of seruice: since the Apostles age, vnto this present age of the restoring of the gospell, there was neuer Church vpon the face of the earth, so nigh the sinceritie of*

Gods trueth, *as the Church of England is at this day*. These wordes with Gods helpe, he will iustifie to be true, vpon the daunger, not of his liuing only, but of his life also, against any man that will withstand it: and yet therein shall not shew him selfe either desperate Dicke, or shamelesse, impudent or wainscot faced Bishop, as it pleaseth the Libeller to rayle. Neither doth he thinke, that any learned man that fauoureth the Gospell, though he mislike some things and persons now in present vse, will reproue it. The Papists I know in deede doe detest the Assertion, and thinke their Synagogue blasphemed by it: No refourmed Church can iustly take offence at it. Where the bishop is burdened by this speech to excuse the multitude of *Thieues, Drunkards, Murtherers, Adulterers, &c.* that be in our Church: neither did his thought conceiue, nor his wordes include any such matter. But what doeth not malice, enuie, and spite vtter against the most innocent person that is? The bishop of Winchester hath openly more impugned the vices of this age heere in the Church of England, then the whole broode of them that are of the Anabaptisticall Conuenticles, and the residue of these Libellers. *Woe be to them* (saith *Esay* the Prophet)

Esay. 5. *that speak euill of good, and good of euill, and put light for darknesse, and darknesse for light, sweete for sowre, and* Psal. 120. *sowre for sweete.* Dauid had great cause to crie, *domine libera animam meam à labijs iniquis, et à lingua* Pro. 24. *dolosa.* And Salomon, *cogitatio stulti peccatum est, et abominatio hominum Detractor.* The deuise of a foole is sinne, and all men abhorre the backbiter or Slaunderer. If any man will reproue the Assertion before written, God willing he shall be answered, so that he rayle not.

This may be a sufficient aunswere to the vntruth fathered vpon the B. of Winchesters words, and that he is not for the same iustly tearmed Monstrous and flattering hypocrite, speaking against his owne conscience. But I see in these words the reproch not only of the B. but much more a malicious spite against this Church of England, and that so deeply setled in their hearts, that their eares cannot, without griefe, heare any good spoken of it. Therefore I thinke my selfe in Christian dutie bound, somewhat farther to followe this matter, and with some signification of thankfulnesse, to acknowledge and confesse those excellent blessings, which it hath pleased God, of his great mercies, to bestowe vpon the same, as well in King Edward the sixts dayes, as much more in her Maiesties reigne that nowe is: and first, to beginne with that which is the principall, that is, the sinceritie of doctrine, and all branches of true religion receiued, professed, taught, and established in this Realme. In which point, I thinke it very superfluous and needles for me to recite the particular branches, and to make a new catechisme, or to pen a new confession of the Church to England, seeing they both are so sufficiently performed, that (without enuy be it spoken) there is none better in any refourmed Church, in *Europe*. For a Catechisme, I refer them to that which was made by the learned and godly man *Master Nowel*, Deane of *Paules*, receiued and allowed by the Church of England, and very fully grounded and established vpon the worde of God. There may you see all the parts of true Religion receiued, the difficulties expounded, the trueth declared, the corruptions of the Church of Rome reiected. But this I like not in our church, that it is lawfull to euery man to set foorth a newe Catechisme at his pleasure. I read, that in the Primitiue church, that thing did great harme, and corrupted the mindes of many simple persons with foule errours and heresies. I see the like at this day: for thereby many honest meaning hearts are caried away to the misliking of our manner of prayer, and administration of Sacramentes, and other orders: whereby it is made a principall instrument to maintaine and increase discorde and dissention in the Church.

For a sound and true confession acknowledged by this our church, I refer them to that notable Apologie of the English church, written not many yeeres since, by that Iewel of England, late Bishop of *Sarisburie*. Wherein they shall find al partes of Christian religion confessed and proued, both by the testimonie of the canonicall scriptures, and also by the consent of all learned and godly antiquitie for the space of certain hundred yeres after Christ. For the integrity and soundnes, for the learning and eloquence shewed in the same apologie, they (that contemne that notable learned man because hee was a bishoppe) may haue very good testimonie in a little Epistle, written by *Peter Martir* vnto the said bishoppe, and nowe printed, and in the latter edition set before the same Apologie: where they shall finde that hee speaketh not for himselfe onely, but for many other learned men of the church of *Tygure*, and other places. Nowe, as this learned bishop doth acknowledge and confesse for this Church, all trueth of doctrine: so doth hee reprooue, condemne and detest all corruptions brought into the same, either by the church of *Rome*, or by any other auncient or newe heretikes, whome hee there particularly nameth: yea, and to the great comfort of all them that are members of the same church, and acknowledge the same confession, hee prooueth and euidently sheweth, that the testimonies of the Scriptures, whereon that confession is grounded, for the true interpretation of them, haue the witnes and consent of all the learned antiquitie, as I haue saide, for certaine hundred yeeres. Which I take to bee a very good comfort and confirmation to all honest consciences in these captious and quarelling dayes.

That which I meane, I will declare by some particulars. VVhat is more euident, certaine and firme for the article of the *person of Christ in his Godhead and manhood*, then those things that the auncient fathers decreed out of the canonical scriptures in the Councels of *Nice*, *Constantinople*, *Ephesus*, *Chalcedon*, and some others against *Arius*, *Samosatenus*, *Apollinaris*, *Nestorius*, *Eutiches*, and those heretikes that were tearmed *Monotholetes &c?* Therfore whosoeuer do teach contrarie to the determination of those councels (as some do in these daies) they do not iustly hold that principal article and foundation of Christian religion.

Moreouer, as touchiug the grace and benefite of Christ, the beginning whereof riseth from the eternall *loue* of God toward vs, and from the free *election* to redemption and eternall saluation, and proceedeth to our vse and benefit, by the dispensation of Christ once offered vpon the crosse, by effectual calling wrought by the holy ghost in preaching of the gospell, by our iustification, sanctification, and the gift of perseuerance and continuance in the faith, thereby in the end to obtaine resurrection and eternall life: touching (I say) this free grace of God (another principall ground of Christian religion) what could be, or can bee more certainly or abundantly layde dovvne out of the holy scriptures, then vvas determined in the councels of *Carthage*, *Mileuitane*,

Aurasicane &c. against the *Pelagians*, and other enemies of the free grace of God in Christ Iesu our Sauiour? Especially if you adde the writings of *August[ine]*, and other ancient fathers for defence of the same.

As to that which is necessary to bee knowen touching the true Catholique Church (a matter of great importaunce euen at this day) waht can bee more copiously or with more perspicuity declared, then is by that learned father *Augustine*, as well in other places, as principally in his bookes against the Donatists?

Likewise, for the matter of the Sacrament of the Lordes Supper, (if simple trueth coulde content men) what is more euident, then that doctrine, which hath bene layd down by the ancient fathers, *Iustine*, *Irenæus*, *Tertullian*, *Cyprian*, *Augustine*, *Theodorete*, and a number of other? For proofe whereof, I referre you to B. *Iewell*, in his worthy booke, wherein he answereth *Hardings* reply against his 27 questions, proposed at *Paules* Crosse, &c. I remember, touching this matter of the Sacrament, *Oecolampadius*, a man of great reading and godlines, saith of S. *August[ine]*. *Is primus mihi vellicauit aurem*. He did first put me in minde of the true vnderstanding of this Sacrament.

These foure principal Articles I haue laid downe for example, that the Christian Reader may the more easily perceiue what comfort it is to any Church, to haue the grounds of their faith and religion so established vpon the holy Scriptures, that for the interpretation of the same, they haue the testimonie and consent of the Primitiue Church, and the ancient learned Fathers. From which *Consent* they should not depart, either in doctrine, or other matter of weight, vnlesse it so fal out in them, that we be forced thereto, either by the plaine wordes of the Scriptures, or by euident and necessary conclusions following vpon the same, or the Analogie of our faith. Which thing if we shal perceiue, we ought, and safely may, take that liberty that themselues, and especially *Augustine* hath vsed, and requireth other to vse. *Nec Catholicis Episcopis, &c.* We must not consent (saith Augustine,) *so much as to Catholique Bishops, if they* De vnitate *be deceiued, and be of opinion contrary to the Canonicall* Eccle. cap. 10 *Scriptures.* Againe, *I am not tied with the authoritie* Contra Cres. *of this Epistle. For I haue not the writings of* con. lib. 2. ca. 32.

Cyprian in like estimation, as I haue the Canonicall Scriptures, but I measure them by the rule of the holy Scriptures. If I finde any thing in his writings agreeing to the Scriptures, I receiue it with commendation and reuerence: if otherwise, with his good leaue, I refuse it. The like you haue, *Epist.* 48. 111. and 112. *In Proœmio li.* 3. *de Trinitate,* and many other places. Othervvise, to reiect the testimonie of the ancient Fathers rashly, is a token of too much confidence in our ovvne vvits. It vvas noted as a great fault in *Nestorius,* and a chiefe cause of his heresie, that contemning the Fathers, hee rested too much vpon his ovvn iudgement. The like confidence drevv many learned men, and of great gifts, to be Patrons of sundry foule and shamefull errours. Hovv came it to passe, that after that notable councell of *Nice,* so many detestable heresies arose against the Deitie and the Humanitie of Christ, against the vniting of both natures, and the distinction of the properties of them? &c. but only out of this roote, that they contemned the graue sentences, interpretations, and determinations of those famous Confessors and great learned Fathers, as vvere in the same assembled, and had too much liking in their owne wits and learning. But *woe be vnto them* (saith *Esay*) *that are ouerwise in their owne conceite.* Vigilius in his first booke against *Eutyches* saith thus. *These cloudes of fond and vaine accusations are powred out by them chiefly, which are discased either with the sickenesse of ignorance, and of a contentious appetite: and while they being puffed vp with confidence of a proud stomacke, for this only cause they reiect the rules of faith, laid downe by the ancient fathers, that they may thrust into the Church their owne wauering deuises, which they haue ouerthwartly conceiued.* This sentence, I would our vncharitable accusers and troublers of the Church would well weigh and consider with themselues. Therfore (good reader) I protest for my selfe, and for the residue of this church, that we dare not in conscience, nor thinke it intollerable, with contempt to reiect the testimonies of antiquity in establishing any matter of weight in the Church. We leaue that to our *hasty diuines,* that in three yeeres study thinke themselues able to controll al men, and to haue more learning then all the Bishops in England: And for this cause will they giue no credit to ancient writers against their new found equality. For with them, it is a foule fault, once in a sermon to name an ancient father, or to alledge any testimony out of his works.

Nowe (good Christian Reader) seeing by the good blessing of God, we haue all parts of Christian fayth and Religion professed and taught in this Church, and the same grounded vpon the canonicall Scriptures, with the consent and exposition of the Primitiue Church and ancient Fathers: What a vaunting pride is it? (as *Cyprian* speaketh) what an vnthankefulnesse to God? what vncharitable affection toward the Church of their naturall Countrey, that they cannot abide any good to be spoken of it? pretending nothing but the priuate faultes and vices of some men, or the disagreeing from them in some orders and partes of Gouernement, which they will neuer be able to proue by the word of GOD to bee of necessitie. In other reformed Churches, whome they so greatly extolle, and would make paterne to vs, haue they not imperfections? Haue they not foule faults, and great vices among all sorts of men, as well Ministers as others? Surely, their worthiest writers and grauest Preachers doe note, that they haue. And if they woulde denie it, the world doth see it, and many good men among them doe bewaile it. I will not stay in the other blessings of God, wherewith hee hath adorned this Church. I shall haue occasion to speake somewhat more of it hereafter, and God send vs grace, that we may with true thankefulnesse acknowledge it. But this I may not omitte without great note of vnthankefulnesse towarde our mercifull God, which hath not only preserued, maintained and defended the State, but also appoynted this Church to be as a Sanctuarie or place of refuge for the Saints of God, afflicted and persecuted in other Countries for the profession of the Gospell: for whome I am perswaded wee doe fare the better at Gods hand. And I doubt not but in that respect, al reformed Churches in other places, feeling the blessing of God by vs, thinke reuerently of our State, and pray to God for vs, as all good men with vs ought to doe for them, that the true linke of Christian charitie may soundly knitte vs together in one bodie of right faith and Religion. If some fewe persons thinke amisse of our Church, I impute the cause therof onely to the malicious and vntrue reports made by some of our owne Countreymen vnto them. Which persons, if they did vnderstand the true State of this our

Realme, would thinke farre otherwise, as diuers of the most graue and learned writers haue already euidently declared. This also is not the least blessing of God, as well in the time of *K. Edward*, as in the reigne of our gracious Souereigne, that this Church hath had as ample ornaments of learned men, (*Rumpantur vt Ilia Momo*,) as the most reformed Churches in *Europe*, and farre more plentifully then some place, whose state they seeke to frame vs vnto. Only I except those excellent men, whom God had prepared in the begining to be the restorers of his Trueth, and doctrine of the Gospel in those parts: Namely we haue had *B. Cranmer, Ridley, Latimer, Couerdale, Hooper*, and diuers other, which were no Bishops, as *M. Bradford, M. Saunders, M. Rogers, M. Philpot, D. Haddon*, &c. Most of which, as they haue left good proofe of their learning in writing: so did they confirme the same with their blood in the ende. The like I may iustly say of them whome God hath sent to restore his Trueth since the beginning of her Maiesties reigne, (howsoeuer it pleaseth the Broode of the *Martinists* to deface them) as Bishoppe *Coxe, Pilkington, Grindall, Sands, Horne, Iewel*, &c. which haue good testimonie of their learning giuen them by as graue, learned, and zealous men, as any haue liued in this age, among whome for certaine yeeres they liued. A number of other haue proceeded out of both our Vniuerisities, which though *Martin Momus* wil say the contrary, deserue singular commendation for their learning, and haue declared the same to the worlde in answering and confuting the opprobrious writings of the common Aduersaries. In which their answeres (without enuie and displeasure be it spoken) there appeareth as sufficient learning, as doeth in the most workes at this time published by the writers of forreine Countreies. If Englishmen at this time so greatly dispraysed, were giuen with like paines to set forth the exercises of their studie and learning, as in other places they doe: they woulde drawe as good commendation of learning to their Countrey, as most other Churches doe. To which number of ours, I adde also some of these, whom certaine occasions haue caried away to the misliking of the present state of this Church: which I knowe haue receiued of God singular good giftes, which I pray earnestly they may vse to his glory, and the procuring the unity and peace of the Church, which our *Hastie Divines* of *M. M* his brood, seeke to breake and disturbe. This testimonie, I thought my selfe bounde in conscience to yeelde to that Church of my naturall Countrey, in which, and by which, through the mercy of our gracious God, I am that I am. The godly, I trust, will interprete all to the best: the residue I looke not to please.

    The B. of Winchester is further charged in this maner, He said that men might find fault, if they were disposed to quarrel, aswel with the Scriptures, as with the booke of common prayer. Who could heare this comparison vvithout trembling? Let the Libellers, whatsoeuer they are, remember, *Os quod mentitur, occidit animam*. At that time, in *S. Mary Oueries* church, in a large discourse, he did answere the obiections that many make at this day, against the booke of common praier, and toward the end vttered these words, *If it could be without blasphemy, they might picke as many and as great quarrels against the holy scriptures themselues. For euen the best writings are subiect to the slanderous malice of wicked men*. This assertion was found fault withall, by a Iesuite or Massing priest at that time in the Marshalsey, and therfore the B. the next Sunday following, expounded his meaning, and at large shewed, that that might be done, which beforetime was done by a great number: and that he was not so far beside himself, as to compare the booke of *common prayer* with the holy scriptures in dignity, trueth, or maiestie: He leaueth such blasphemous dealing to the *Papists*, the *Family of Loue*, and some other *Sectaries*: but he compared them in this (as it is before said) that the Scriptures themselues were subiect also to slaunderous and deprauing tongues, and yet not therfore to be reiected, whereof he recited sundry examples. *Celsus* that heathenish Epicure, (against whom *Origen* writeth) in his book [Lib. i. contra Celsum.] called *Verax*, doth powre out many railing and slaunderous reproches, not only against the holy Scriptures, but also against the course of Christian Religion: as that they receiued their religion and doctrine of the barbarous Iewes, that is, out of the bookes of *Moses* and the Prophets. The like did *Porphyrius* an other [Euseb. lib. 6. cap. 19.] Philosopher, and in his bookes reprooued the the Scriptures in many places: for hee wrote thirtie bookes against Christian religion. That scoffing sophister *Libanius*, and his scholler *Iulian* the Apostata, vsed the like blasphemies aggainst the Christian fayth, and the Scriptures, out of which it was prooued, as appeareth in sundrie aunceint Writers. Who knoweth not, that some Heretikes reiected the most part of the olde Testament, as false and fabulous? The *Valentiniane* Heretike, sayeth Tertullian, *Quædam legis et Prophetarum improbat, quædam probat, id est, Omnia improbat, dum quædam reprobat.* The *Marcionists* receiue onely the Gospell of *Matthewe*, the other they reiect. And likewise they admitte but two Epistles of Saint Paul, that is, to *Timothie* and *Titus*, and (as *Hierome* sayeth) to *Philemon*. *Tatian* also depraueth the Scriptures, reiecteth the Actes of the Apostles, and picketh sundry other quarrels against them. There was neuer any Heretike, but that to giue countenance to his opinion, he would seeme to ground it vpon the Scriptures. And what is that but wickedly to father lies vpon the Scriptures? And for this cause you know, the Papists think it no sure ground to rest vpon the scriptures onely, affirming blasphemously, that *the Scriptures are darke, vnperfect, and doubtfull, because they may be wrested euery way, like a nose of waxe, or like a leaden Rule.* Wherefore, Christian charitie and modestie woulde not thus maliciously and slaunderously wrest and wring the words of the Bishop, tending to a good and godly meaning.

Socr. lib. 1. cap. 9.
In Præscript.
Tertull.
Eusebius.
Euseb. lib. 4. cap. 28.
Epiphanius.
Theodor.

Of like trueth it is, that he burtheneth the Bishop of Winchester, to affirme that it was heresie to say, The preaching of the vvorde vvaw the onely ordinarie vvay to saluation, which he neuer thought, or spake, either then, or at any other time of his life. But in handling of that controuersie, *Penrie* spake things so strangely and obscurely, that he seemed to attribute that effect to the preaching of the word only, and not otherwise vsed by reading: And being vrged with that question, by occasion of reading the Scriptures in Churches, his answere was such, as he euidently shewed himselfe to meane, that that effect of saluation could not be wrought by hearing the word of God read, with some other wordes, giuing suspition of worse matter. And then in deede the B. rose not out of his place, (as these honest men doe carpe) nor spake in such cholerike maner, as they pretend: but quietly said, My Lord, this is not farre from Heresie. What were the words that *Penry* vsed, and especially moued the B. to speake, he doeth not at this time remember: but sure he is, they were as farre from that, which is laide down in the Libel, as falshood can be from truth. I wonder that men which professe God, yea, or that beleeue there is a God, can with open mouth so boldely povvre foorth such heapes of vntrueths. *Detractor abominabilis est Deo.* The counsell of the Prophet is good. *He that would gladly see good daies, let him refraine his tongue from* Psal. 34. *euill, and his lippes that they speake no guile.* The mouth of a *malicious man* (saith Ambrose) *is a deepe or bottomles* Epist. lib. 7. *pit. The innocent that is too easie of credit, doth quickly* Epist. 44. *fall, but he riseth againe. But the backebiting railer is by his owne craft cast downe headlong to confusion, in such sort, as he shall neuer recouer him selfe againe.* And Bernard, Super Cont. *Let not my soule be in company of backbiting tongues,* Serm. 24. *because God doth hate them, when the Apostle sayth, Backbiters are odious to God, Euerie one that backbiteth, sheweth himselfe voyd of charitie. Moreouer, what other thing seeketh he by deprauing, but that he whome hee backbiteth, may come in hatred and contempt with them among whom he is depraued? Wherfore the backbiter woundeth charity, in all that heare him, and somuch as in him lyeth, doth vtterly destroy him whome hee striketh with his tongue.*

As for the reproch of want of learning, hee will not striue much with them. The Bishoppe hath not vsed (God bee thanked) to vaunt himselfe of great learning. Neyther doth he disdaine to be accounted vnlearned of these men, which many yeares since contemned Bishoppe *Iewell* as a man of no deepe learning, and euen of late daies could saye that *Erasmus* was no Diuine. His praier is, that the small measure of knowledge, which it pleased God to giue him in the continuance of fiftie yeeres studie, may be imployed to the glorie of God, and the benefite of his Countrey. It is knowen fiue and fourtie yeres since, that he was Master of Art, and Student of Diuinitie, and disputed in that facultie:

since which time, hee was neuer drawen from that exercise of good learning. This is his greatest comfort, that since he was a yong man in *Magdalen Colledge* in *Oxford*, hee hath bene brought vp in the loue of the Gospell, and was reasonablie able to confirme his conscience, and to represse the aduersary, not only by the holy scriptures, but also by the writings of the ancient Fathers, and the best authors of this age since the renewing of the Gospell, as he hath many honest and learned men witnesses yet aliue. *M. Trauers*, whome they preferre before him, he knoweth not what he is. Hee neuer saw him to his remembraunce, but once, and that vvas at my Lord of *Canterburies*, in the presence of some honourable persons: at vvhich time the man shevved no great learning. Doctor *Sparke* is so vvell knovven to the Bishoppe of *Winchester*, and the Bishoppe to him, that hee cannot bee persvvaded that Doctor *Sparke* vvill affirme, that he did put the bishop at that time or anie other (as they terme it) to a *non plus*. But vvhatsoeuer hee vvill doe, if the one or the other, or they both, doe make anie bragge of a victorie then gotten (as I haue before sayde) surelie they doe greatlie forget themselues, and declare that *Ladie Philautie* did bleare their eies, and made that they could not see the right rules of modestie: especially considering, vvhat the vvitnesses vvere. and vvhat report they haue made thereof to the best of this Lande, vvhich hath not bene made vnknowen to the vvorld.

<small>Lib. epist. 1.
Epist. 3.</small> It is true that *Gregorie* sayth, *Superbia lumen intelligetiæ abscondit.* Pride daseleth the eies of a mans vnderstanding. And again, *Superbi &c.* Proud men <small>Moral 8.
Idem. 12.</small> when the[y] thinke themselues despised, fall by and by to railing. *Cyprian*, that reuerend and learned father, sayth notably. *An high and swelling heart, arrogant and proud bragging is not of Christ that teacheth humilitie, but springeth of the spirit of Antichrist.* I pray GOD these men may remember these lessons.

AS touching the Gouernement of the Church of England, now defended by the bishops, this I say. When God restored the doctrine of the Gospell more sincerely and more abqundantly then euer before, vnder that good young Prince, *King Edward* 6. at which time not the gouernours onelie of this Realme vnder him, but a nomber of other Noblemen and Gentlemen, were wel knowen to be zealous in the fauor of the trueth: by consent of all the States of this Land, this maner of gouernment that now is vsed, was by law confirmed as good and godly. The bishops and other of the clergy that gaue their aduise and consent to the same, were learned and zealous, *Bishop Cranmer, Ridley, Latimer*, and many other, which after sealed their doctrine with their blood, all learned, graue and wise in comparison of these yong Sectaries which greatly please themselues. *M. Couerdal* and *M. Hooper*, neuer thought to be superstitious or inclining to Antichristian corruption, were contented to vse the office, authoritie, and iurisdiction of bishops, the one at *Exeter*, the other at *Glocester*. *Peter Martir, Bucer*, and *Iohn de Alasco*, graue men, and of great knowledge and godlinesse, did liue in that state vnder the Archbishops and bishops that then were, and wrote to them most reuerendly, not refusing to giue them those Titles, that novve bee accompted Antichristian. The like the[y] did to other of late time. Reade the Preface of *Peter Martir*, set before his Dialogues against *Vbiquity*, and see what honourable testimonie hee giueth to bishop *Iewel*, and what titles he affoordeth him. To condemne all these as Reprobate and Pety Antichrists, were great rashnesse, and such impudencie as ought not in any Christian Church or common vveale to bee borne without punishment. When God had marueilously preserued for vs our gratious soueraigne *Queene Elizabeth*, and set her in her Fathers seat, being brought vp from her tender yeres, in the instruction of Gods trueth, shee tooke aduise of her most honourable Counsell, Nobles, and learned of the Realme, and especially such as were most forward in religion, and with consent of all the States of this Realme, by law receiued, confirmed and established the manner of Gouernment, and other orders of the Church novv obserued. The learned men that yeelded their advise and consent to the same, were those reuerend and godly persons, that came lately out of banishment, from the schoole of affliction, and could not so soon forget their Lord God, and the zeale of his trueth, namely, Master *Cox, Grindall, Sandes, Horne, Pilkinton, Iewell, Parkhurst,* and a number of other, who were after chosen to be bishops, and executed those offices, vvithout grudging or repining of any, vntill about the tenth yeere of her Maiesties raigne, the curious deuises beganne to bee more common. Since which time, by the countenauncing of some, they haue greatly increased in strange assertions, and novv be come almost to the highest. The reproches therfore that are giuen to this state by these Libellers, touch not onely the bishoppes, but the Prince, the councell, and the honorable, worshipfull, wise, and learned of the Realme.

As for this question of Church-gouernement, I meane not at this time to stand much on it. For let them say what they lust, for any thing that hath bene written hitherto touching it, it is sufficiently answered. Onely this I desire, *That they will lay downe out of the worde of God some iust proofes, and a direct commaundement, that there should bee in all ages and states of the Church of Christ, one onely forme of outwarde gouernement.* Secondly, *that they will note and name some certaine particular Churches, either in the Apostles time, or afterward, wherein the whole Gouernement of the Church was practised, onely by Doctours, Pastours, Elders, and Deacons, and none other, and that in an equalitie, without superioritie in one aboue an other.* If this be done soundlie and truelie, vvithout any vvresting or double vnderstanding of the places of Scripture: I protest they will shake that opinion that novve I haue of this present gouernement of the Church of *Englande.* Yet vnder correction (I vvill not say, that I knovv) but I am surelie perswaded, that they will neuer be able to doe it.

Moreouer, *I would wish them vnfaignedly to declare, whether all the Churches at this day reformed in Europe, where the light of the Gospell was first restored, and specially of* Saxonie and High Almaine, *haue this gouernement, which by these men is nowe required, and none other.* If they haue, it is a good preiudice for their cause: if they haue not, it is hard, that the example of two or three Churches shoulde ouerrule all the residue, in which the light of the Gospell beganne before them. And it may bee well sayde, *Did the Gospell beginne first with you?* VVee may not pull downe one *Rome* and set vp an other. Surely as graue learned men as most that haue written in this time, euidently affirme the contrary, and doe make good proofe of this proposition. *That one forme of Church-gouernement is not necessarie in all times and places of the Church, and that their Senate or Segniorie is not conuenient vnder a Christian Magistrate.*

In *Denmarke* they haue Bishops both in *Name*, and *Office*, as it appeareth in certaine Epistles of *Hemingius* vvritten to some of them. In vvhich he sayth: They are greatly troubled vvith continuall visitation of their Churches. In *Saxony* they haue Archbishoppes and Bishops in *Office*, but not in *Name*. For proofe heereof, I alleadge the testimonies of that learned man *Zanchius* in the Annotations vpon certaine parts of his confession. *In the Church of the Protestants* (saith he) *indeede they haue Bishops and Archbishops, which* Pag. 272. *chaunging the good Greeke names into ill Latine names, they call Superintendents, and generall Superintendents, &c.*

The same *Zanchius*, in the same his confession, hath these words, *By the same reason, those things that were* Pag. 170. *ordained in the Church touching Archbishops, yea, and the foure patriarches before the Counsell of Nice, may bee excused and defended.* These vvordes and some other were misliked by one famous learned man, vvho vvrote to *Zanchius* of the same. But *Zanchius* was so farre from altering his iudgement, that in the foresayde *Annotations*, hee vvriteth a large defence of it out of *Bucer, in Epist. ad Ephes.* vvhich is also founde in a little Treatise, vvhich the same *Bucer* hath vvritten, *De vi et vsu Ministeri*. And *Zanchius* in the same place shewed the reason vvhy hee is so grounded in that opinion. *I beleeue* (sayth hee) *that those things which were concluded and determined by the Godly Fathers assembled in the name of the Lord, with common consent and without contradiction to the Scriptures, proceede from the holie spirite of GOD: and therefore I dare not in conscience improoue them. And what is more certaine by the Histories, Councels and writinges of the Fathers, then that those orders of the Ministers, of which wee haue spoken, haue bene receiued and allowed by the common consent of Christendome? And I pray, who am I, that I should reprooue those thinges, which the whole church hath allowed? Neither durst all they that bee of our time*, (he meaneth the learned men of *Germany*) *reprooue the same*.

In the foresayde place of his *Annotations*, when he hath
_{Pag. 273.} spoken of the gouernement of the churches of *Saxonie*, he addeth touching other places, *Euen there where they haue neither the good Greeke names, nor the euill Latine termes: yet haue they certaine chiefe men, in whose hands well neere is all authoritie. Seeing then we agree in the things, why shoulde we haue controuersie about the names and titles?*

This man vndoubtedly knevve the gouernement of all the Churches in *Germany*. For hee had bene a reader and Teacher in diuers of them. He had bin in *Geneua*: he taught at *Argentine* eleuen yeres: After at *Clauenna* foure yeres: Again after that, at *Heidelberge* ten yeeres: And lastly, by *Cassimire* appointed at his town at *Newstade*, where yet he liueth an olde man, if God of late hath not taken him out of this world.

Those places of high *Almaine*, wherein most zealous preachers and learned men haue remained, and vvith vvhome
_{Vide Gualte-} in doctrine vvee most nighlie agree, haue not one
_{rum in 1. ad} maner of gouernement, nor formes of Discipline.
_{Cor. cap.}
_{5. &c.} In *Tygure* it is well knowen, they haue no Senate of Elders, nor thinke it tolerable vnder a Christian Magistrate: nor the Discipline by Excommunication, which they more mislike. I thinke it be not much differing at *Berne* (one of the greatest Churches) as I gather by *Aretius* in sundry places. At *Geneua*, and some other places, especially such as haue had their beginning from thence, they haue a gouernment not much vnlike that platforme, which is desired to be vvith us, and is novve in *Scotland*. I might say the like for some ceremonies and outward orders. In *Saxony* and at *Basile* they kneele at the Lords Supper. At *Tygure* they sit, and it is brought to them: In other places they go and receiue it, for the more expedition, as they passe.

The like libertie and diuersitie vse they in some other externall thinges, which I am not willing for some causes to lay dovvne in vvriting. All those Churches, in vvhich the Gospell in these daies, after great darkenesse, vvas first renevved, and the learned men vvhome God sent to instruct them, I doubt not but haue beene directed by the spirite of God to retaine this liberty, that in external gouernment, and other outward orders, they might choose such as they thought in wisedome and godlinesse to bee most conuenient for the state of the Countrey, and disposition of the people. Why then should this libertie that other Countries haue vsed, vnder anie colour bee wrested from vs? I thinke it therefore great presumption and boldnesse, that some of our nation, and those (vvhatsoeuer they thinke of themselues) not of the greatest vvisedome and skill, shoulde take vpon them to controlle the vvhole Realme, and to binde both Prince and people, in necessity of conscience, to alter the present state, and to tie themselues to a certaine platforme deuised by some of our neighbours, which in the iudgement of many wise and godly persons is most vnfit for the state of a Kingdome, or to be exercised vnder a Christian Prince that defendeth the Gospell, as in part, experience already hath taught in some. I pray God they looke not further, and haue not a deeper reach, then good subiects that loue their Prince and countrey, should haue.

Lastly, I would wish them (leauing the long discourses whereunto Doctor *Bridges* was drawen by some of their strange and intricate assertions) they woulde briefly without corruption lay downe his arguments and allegations, touching the supreme authoritie of the Prince, and the superioritie of bishops, and modestly, and soundly answere the same, not reiecting the testimonie of the ancient Writers and Historiographers, especially such as were within 400. yeeres after Christ, so farre as they may be *Testes temporum*. For if they shall otherwise deale, and seeke to shift off the matter with reproches, scoffes, and slaunders: they wil discredit their cause, and make good men thinke, that the spirit with which they are carried, is not the milde spirit of Christ, but the spirit of him that is condemned for the father of lying, murdering and slandering from the beginning.

The reason that mooueth vs not to like of this platforme of gouernement, is, that when wee on the one part consider the thinges that are required to be redressed, and on the other, the state of our countrey, people, and commonweale: we see euidently, that to plant those things in this Church, wil drawe with it, so many, and so great alterations of the State of gouernment, and of the lawes, as the attempting thereof might bring rather the ouerthrowe of the Gospel among vs, then the end that is desired. The particulars hereof in some fewe things, in steade of many doe here follow, and hath bene opened to you before, if reasonable warning would haue serued.

First, the whole state of the lawes of this Realme will be altered. For the *Canon law* must be vtterly taken away, with all offices to the same belonging: which to supply with other lawes and functions, without many inconueniences, wil be very hard. The vse and studie of the Ciuill law wil be vtterly ouerthrowen: For the *Ciuilians* in this Realme liue not by the vse of the Ciuill law, but by the offices of the *Canon law*, and such things as are within the compasse thereof. And if you take those offices and functions away, and those matters wherewith they deale in the *Canon Lawe*: you must needes take away the hope of rewarde, and by that meanes, their whole Studie. And matters of *Tithes, Testaments, and Matrimonie, iudgements also of Adulterie, Slaunder, &c.* are in these mens iudgements meere temporall, and therefore to bee dealt in by the temporall Magistrate onely: Which, as yet haue eyther none at all, or very fewe lawes touching those things. Therefore the Temporall and Common lawe of this Realme, must by that occasion receiue also a very great alteration. For it will be no small matter to apply these things to the Temporall lawe, and to appoynt Courts, Officers, and maner of processe and proceedings in iudgement for the same.

Beside this, the Iudiciall law of the Iewes, especially for such offences as are against the law of God, must bee brought into this Common weale. For to this opinion doe they playnely incline. For they say already flatly, that no Magistrate can saue the life of a blasphemer, stubborne Idolater, murderer, Adulterer, Incestuous person, and such like, which God by his Iudiciall lawe hath commaunded to be put to death. The same assertion must haue like authoritie for the contrarie, that is, that a Magistrate ought not to punish by death those offences that God by his Iudiciall law hath not appointed to be punished by death, and so may not our lawes punish theft by death, nor diuers other felonies: and so some of them haue openly preached. The lawes also mainteining the *Queenes supremacy in gouerning of the Church, and her prerogatiue in matters Ecclesiasticall*, as well Elections as others, must be also abrogated. Those lawes likewise must bee taken away, whereby *Impropriations* and *Patronages* stand as mens lawful possession and heritage. In these *Impropriations* and *Patronages*, as I doe confesse, there is lamentable abuse, and wish the same by some good Statute to bee remedied: so how the thing it selfe can vvithout great difficultie and danger be taken away, being so generall as it is in the state of this Realme, I leaue to the iudgement of the vvise and godly.

The lawes of *Englande* to this day, haue stoode by the authoritie of the three Estates: vvhich to alter now, by leauing out the one, may happily seeme a matter of more weight, then all men doe iudge it. If there vvere no more then this one thing, vvhich hitherto I haue spoken of, that is, the alteration of the state of all the lawes of this Realme: I thinke there is no vvise man but seeth what daunger may followe in these perillous times, not onely by fulfilling the thing, but also by offering to doe it.

It hath beene alwayes dangerous, to picke quarrels against lawes setled. And I pray God, that the very rumour hereof, spread by these mens bookes, haue not already bred more inconuenience, then without hurt will be suppressed: I may not put all that I thinke, in writing.

The fourme of finding of Ministers by Tithes, must with the Canon lawe be abolished. For it was not vsed in the gouernment of the Apostles time, nor a great many of yeeres after, and therefore may seeme Papisticall and Antichristian. There must bee some other order for this deuised. Which, vvith hovve great alteration it must bee done, and hovv hard it vvil be to bring to good effect, I thinke there is no man but he seeth: For the liuings of bishops and Cathedrall Churches, (whereat they carpe) though they were all that way bestowed, vvill not serue the third part.

If this gouernment, whereof they speake, be (as they say) necessary in al places: then must they haue of necessity in euery particular parish one Pastor, a company of Seniors, and a Deacon or two at the least, and all those to be found of the parish, because they must leaue these occupations, to attend vpon the matters of the church. But there are a number of parishes in *England* not able to find one tollerable minister, much lesse to find such a company. The remedy hereof must bee, to vnite diuers parishes in one, wherof this inconuenience wil folovv, that people in the countrey must come to Church, three, foure or fiue miles off: whereas now they that dwel in the same towne, can scarcely be forced by any penalties of Law orderly to come vnto the church, to seruice or sermons, so that they will growe to a barbarisme in many places.

Whereas it is required, that the people shoulde choose their Pastours, Elders, and Deacons: it is greatly to be feared, that it wil be matter of schisme, discord and dissension in many places: or that one or two busie heads shall leade the residue to what purpose they will, to the great disquieting both of the Church and of the common weale. Examples heereof did commonly appeare in the olde Churches, while that manner of Election did continue, as the Ecclesiasticall histories in many places doe declare. And that inconuenience caused Princes and bishops so much to intermeddle in that matter. The common people through affection and want of right iudgement, are more easily wrought by ambitious persons to giue their consent to vnworthy men, as may appeare in all those offices of gaine or dignity, that at this day remaine in the choice of the multitude, yea, though they be learned.

Men doe knowe by experience, that Parishes, vpon some priuate respect, do send their Letters of earnest commendations for very vnfitte and vnable persons: whereby it may bee gathered, what they would do, if the whole choise were in their handes, especially, being so backwardly affected toward the Trueth of Religion, as a great part of men are. They will aunswere (perhaps) that they shall bee ouerseene by the Pastours neere about them in a particular Synode, and forced both to bee quiet, and also to make more fitte elections. But who seeth not what matter of trouble this will bee, when vpon the occasion almost of euery Election, they must haue a particular Synode? And if the Parish will not be ruled (as surely many will not) then must they be excommunicated, and appeale made vnto the Prince and Magistrate. And that which passeth nowe vvith quietnesse, and with a little amendment may be well vsed, shall be continuall occasion of broile and trouble, whereto this nation is more inclined vpon light causes, then any other.

Moreouer, that which is most of all pretended for this manner of common Election, that they may knowe their Minister, and thereby haue the better liking of him, cannot possibly bee brought to passe, vnlesse they will imagine, that euery parish shall haue within it selfe a Schoole or Colledge, where those shall bee brought vp, that shall bee preferred to the Ministerie among them. But howe possible that is to bring to passe among vs, let any man iudge. If their Ministers shall come vnto them from the Vniuersities or other schooles, they shall haue as little acquaintaunce with them, as nowe they haue, and farre greater occasion of partiall suites, then nowe there is. So that inconueniences by this meanes shall bee increased and not remedied.

That euery parish in England may haue a learned and discreete minister, howsoeuer they dreame of perfection, no man is able in these dayes to deuise, how to bring it to passe, and specially when by this change of the clergie, the great rewards of learning shall be taken away, and men thereby discouraged to bring vp their children in the studie of good Letters. Furthermore, who seeth not howe smal continuance there shall be in the Vniuersities, to make men of any profound knowledge, when the very necessity of places, shall drawe men away before they come to any ripenesse? the effect whereof, is partly perceiued at this day already, and much more would be, if their deuise should take place.

Touching the inconuenience of Discipline by excomunication onely, which they so much cry for, how it will bee of most men contemned, and of how small force it wil be to bring to effect any good amendment of life, some learned men of this age in their workes set foorth to the worlde, haue at large declared. I let passe, that experience teacheth, that men of stubburnnesse will not shunne the company of them that bee excommunicated, and then must they bee excommunicated for keeping of company with them, and so will it fall out, that more will be excommunicated, then in Communion: whereof what deformities and inconueniences will arise, *S. Augustine* doeth teach vs. The loosenesse of these dayes requireth Discipline of sharper Lawes by punishment of body and danger of goods: which they doe, and will more feare, then they will excommunication. And, God bee thanked, (if men would be contented with any moderation) we haue a very good manner of discipline by the ecclesiasticall commission, which hath done, and doth daily much good, and would do more, if it were more common, and men would take more giltlesse in the cause. There folowed two or three, much like to schollers: their names were *Dolus, Fraus, Insidiæ*. These clapped their Master on the backe to encourage him. And because Master *Martin* will be a gentleman, he had a *treader* before him, an olde fellowe: his eyes were fierce, his face thinne and withered, his whole countenance much like to one pined away with a melancholy and fretting furie. His name was *Liuor*, that is, *cankred malice*, or enuie: A little behinde followed *dolefull Dame repentance* in mourning apparell, and looking backe with shame and teares, goeth to meete *Lady Trueth*, comming somewhat after. In the toppe of the table this sentence was written, *Who so euer slaundereth honest men, shall come to iust punishment*. In the lower part is this, *Nothing can be safe from the backebiting tongue*. Rounde about was this written, *Beware thou neyther slaunder nor giue ear vnto the Backebiter. Flee slaundering both with thine eares, and with thy tongue. Hee that giueth fayre countenance and light eare, encourageth a Backbiter*. If *Martin* that delighteth so much in himselfe, woulde discreetely beholde this Table, I trust hee would diminish some part of his follie. But for that it liketh *Martin*, not onely to be a false accuser, but also a rash and credulous Iudge with his long Asses eares receiuing euery vntrueth that is tolde him, he may beholde himselfe in all the partes of the Table. The best aduise that I can giue you, is out of *Chrysostome*. *Let discretion and truth sit as Iudges ouer your owne soule and conscience. Bring foorth before them, all thine offences. Lay downe what punishment is due for euery of them. Say continually this vnto thy selfe, Howe durst thou do this? How durst thou do that? &c. If thy conscience will refuse this, and prye vpon other mens faults, say vnto her, Thou sittest not here as Iudge of other, but to answere for thy selfe. What matter is it to thee, if this or that man offend: looke to thine owne steps, blame thine owne doing, and not others.* To the description of a Detractor or Backebiter, are these properties. First, he is malicious, and studieth to hurt others, and sometimes purposely doeth hurt himselfe, the sooner to hurt other. Secondly, his soule and life is lying. Thirdly, he is an hypocrite and a Dissembler, and pretendeth a zeale of iustice and pietie, to colour his malice. Lastly, he is a Serpent byting secretly, and fleeth knowledge. These properties learne by the complaintes of

Hom. Ad. Matth.

Dauid in sundry of his Psalmes, *Deliuer me O Lord, from the naughtie, and from the wicked man, which deuiseth euill in his heart. They haue sharpened their tongues like Serpents: the poison of Aspes is vnder their lippes. The mouth of a backbiter is full of cursed speaking: vnder his tongue is sorowe and griefe. He lyeth in waite in secrete places to destroy the innocent. He lyeth lurking as a Lyon in his denne, to rauish the poore. He falleth downe and humbleth himselfe, that the poore may fall into his nette.* Reade the tenth Psalme, and diuers other. The residue of their malicious and more then ruffianly railings together with Histrionical mockes and scoffes, too immodest for any Vice in a play, are not meete for any honest man to meddle with: and therefore are returned ouer to the Libellers themselues, as vnfallible tokens of that spirite, with which they are ledde to these outragious dealings. But it is nowe time to answere those quarrels that are made generally against all Bishops.

Obiection.

But let vs see what is layde downe against the Bishops and chiefe of the Clergie. First is, that they are exceeding couetous, and set to sale the libertie of the Gospel, and the vse and Discipline of the Church, like Simoniakes and Prelates of the Church of Antichrist: yea, that in Simonie and sale of the Gospell, they are nothing behinde the Bishop of Rome. *The obiection of the couetousnesse and Simonie of Bishops.*

Answere.

Surely, this is a grieuous and an horrible accusation in the eares of any christian Magistrate: and if it be found true, the offendours not worthie to liue in this Common wealth: Or if it be false and slaunderous, the Accuser not meete to escape vnpunished. The example of the slaundering of the Ministers of the Church, is a matter more dangerous, then in these daies it is esteemed. But as touching the thing it selfe, I am of opinion, that no man of meane learning, or any experience, hauing regarde of his credite, would vndertake to iustifie such an accusation in the hearing of any honest man. For, this I dare say, and vpon hazard of that is most deere vnto mee in this world wil proue, that where the state of this our Church of England doth leaue to an euill disposed B. one occasion of the practise of Simony, and couetous giltlesse in the cause. There folowed two or three, much like to schollers: their names were *Dolus, Fraus, Insidiæ*. These clapped their Master on the backe to encourage him. And because Master *Martin* will be a gentleman, he had a *treader* before him, an olde fellowe: his eyes were fierce, his face thinne and withered, his whole countenance much like to one pined away with a melancholy and fretting furie. His name was *Liuor*, that is, *cankred malice*, or enuie: A little behinde followed *dolefull Dame repentance* in mourning apparell, and looking backe with shame and teares, goeth to meete *Lady Trueth*, comming somewhat after. In the toppe of the table this sentence was written, *Who so euer slaundereth honest men, shall come to iust punishment*. In the lower part is this, *Nothing can be safe from the backebiting tongue*. Rounde about was this written, *Beware thou neyther slaunder nor giue ear vnto the Backebiter. Flee slaundering both with thine eares, and with thy tongue. Hee that giueth fayre countenance and light eare, encourageth a Backbiter*. If *Martin* that delighteth so much in himselfe, woulde discreetely beholde this Table, I trust hee would diminish some part of his follie. But for that it liketh *Martin*, not onely to be a false accuser, but also a rash and credulous Iudge with his long Asses eares receiuing euery vntrueth that is tolde him, he may beholde himselfe in all the partes of the Table. The best aduise that I can giue you, is out of *Chrysostome*. *Let discretion and truth sit as Iudges ouer your owne soule and conscience. Bring foorth before them, all thine offences. Lay downe what punishment is due for euery of them. Say continually this vnto thy selfe, Howe durst thou do this? How durst thou do that? &c. If thy conscience will refuse this, and prye vpon other mens faults, say vnto her, Thou sittest not here as Iudge of other, but to answere for thy selfe. What matter is it to thee, if this or that man offend: looke to thine owne steps, blame thine owne doing, and not others*. To the description of a Detractor or Backebiter, are these properties. First, he is malicious, and studieth to hurt others, and sometimes purposely doeth hurt himselfe, the sooner to hurt other. Secondly, his soule and life is lying. Thirdly, he is an hypocrite and a Dissembler, and pretendeth a zeale of iustice and pietie, to colour his malice. Lastly, he is a Serpent byting secretly, and fleeth knowledge. These properties learne by the complaintes of

Hom. Ad. Matth.

Dauid in sundry of his Psalmes, *Deliuer me O Lord, from the naughtie, and from the wicked man, which deuiseth euill in his heart. They haue sharpened their tongues like Serpents : the poison of Aspes is vnder their lippes. The mouth of a backbiter is full of cursed speaking : vnder his tongue is sorowe and griefe. He lyeth in waite in secrete places to destroy the innocent. He lyeth lurking as a Lyon in his denne, to rauish the poore. He falleth downe and humbleth himselfe, that the poore may fall into his nette.* Reade the tenth Psalme, and diuers other. The residue of their malicious and more then ruffianly railings together with Histrionical mockes and scoffes, too immodest for any Vice in a play, are not meete for any honest man to meddle with : and therefore are returned ouer to the Libellers themselues, as vnfallible tokens of that spirite, with which they are ledde to these outragious dealings. But it is nowe time to answere those quarrels that are made generally against all Bishops.

Obiection.

But let vs see what is layde downe against the Bishops and chiefe of the Clergie. First is, that they are exceeding couetous, and set to sale the libertie of the Gospel, and the vse and Discipline of the Church, like Simoniakes and Prelates of the Church of Antichrist : yea, that in Simonie and sale of the Gospell, they are nothing behinde the Bishop of Rome. *The obiection of the couetousnesse and Simonie of Bishops.*

Answere.

Surely, this is a grieuous and an horrible accusation in the eares of any christian Magistrate : and if it be found true, the offendours not worthie to liue in this Common wealth : Or if it be false and slaunderous, the Accuser not meete to escape vnpunished. The example of the slaundering of the Ministers of the Church, is a matter more dangerous, then in these daies it is esteemed. But as touching the thing it selfe, I am of opinion, that no man of meane learning, or any experience, hauing regarde of his credite, would vndertake to iustifie such an accusation in the hearing of any honest man. For, this I dare say, and vpon hazard of that is most deere vnto mee in this world wil proue, that where the state of this our Church of England doth leaue to an euill disposed B. one occasion of the practise of Simony, and couetous

oppression of the people, that the B. of Rome had fourtie.
For a taste hereof, I referre the meaner learned to the common places of *Muscul. cap. Quare coniugium ministris ademptum.* The better learned, I know, are better able of themselues, to make further declaration out of their own lawes, decrees, and registers, commonly read of all them that are desirous to know the trueth, and not by ignorance, to exaggerate infamie, by false and vniust reportes. Yea, the very histories of this Realme can witnesse, that by Simony and couetous oppression, the bishops of Rome haue had yeerely out of this Realme more money, then at that time the reuenevv of the Kings crowne did extend vnto, or at this day (as I thinke) al the bishopricks in England be worth. For *Mat. Paris,* vvriteth, that in the time of king *Henry* the 3. the *Pope* had yerely out of this Lande 60000. markes: vnto which if you doe adde his like dealing in *Germanie* and other countreyes, you shall perceiue the value to bee inestimable. And surely I am of that hope, and in my conscience I thinke it to bee most true, that all the Bishops of this lande, by Simoniacall practise and couetous oppression, do not gaine the hundred part thereof. And if it do rise to that value, it is a great deale too much: yea, if it be one penie, it is wicked, and by no good man ought to bee defended, and much lesse by them to be practised. I hope well of all, although I vvil not take vpon mee to excuse all: But for some, I assuredly knowe, and in my conscience dare depose, that since they vvere made bishops, they haue not vvittingly gained that vvay, one twentie shillings. Therefore in equalling the bishops of England in the practise of Simonie with the Pope of Rome, there must needs be great oddes in the comparison, and the whole speech may vvell be called *Hyperbole,* that is, an vncharitable amplification, surmounting all liklihood of honest and Christian trueth.

Obiection.

But somewhat to giue countenance to an euill slaunder, it will be sayde, that the Bishop of Rome practized Simonie by al meanes that he had, and our bishops, by as many as they haue

Answere.

Oh, a vvorthy reason. Is this to iustifie so shameful a

slaunder of the church of God, vnder a christian Princes gouernment? Is that Christian Preacher and Bishop, (if any such be) that vseth Simoniacall practise in two or three points of smal importance, and little value in grieuousnesse of offence before God and the vvorlde, to be equalled to the head of Antichrist, and the principal enemy of the Gospel, practizing the same in a thousand of great weight and vnestimable value? I can not but wish more charitable hearts to them that will take vpon them the zeale and profession of the Gospell. Let sinne be blamed, euen in them that fauour the word, and chiefly the Clergie: but yet so, as trueth will beare, and modestie with Christian charitie doeth require, lest in much amplifying of small offences, you become instruments, not only to discredit the parties blamed, but also to ouerthrow the doctrine that they teach. There ought to be great difference betvvene Christian Preachers, and vvriters inueighing against Antichrist and his members enemies of the Gospell, and zealous professors, blaming and reprouing the faults of their owne Bishop and Clergie in the estate of a church by authority setled. The one part is kindled with an earnest zeale and detestation of the obstinate patrones of errour and Idolatrie: the other shoulde bee mooued onely with a charitable sorowe and griefe, to see Preachers of the trueth, not to declare in life that, which they vtter to other in doctrine. They that by humane frailtie offend in blemish of life only, are not with like bitternesse to bee hated, harried, rated and defaced, as they that with obstinate and vnrepentant hearts, offend both in life and doctrine, and to the face of the worlde shewe themselues aduersaries of the truth. Christ after one maner blameth the Scribes and pharises, and after another he reproueth the ignorance, the dulnesse, the ambition and carnall affection of his owne Disciples that follovved him. But I pray you, let vs consider the particular proofe of this generall accusation, and odious comparison. Surely they are so trifling, that I am ashamed to stay vpon them, and yet I must needes speake a word or two of them. The Church of England retayneth a good and necessarie order, that before the celebration of marriage, the Banes should be asked three seuerall Sabboth dayes.

Answers to generall [Bp. T. Cooper. Jan. 1589.

The first proofe of Couetousnesse. Dispensing with Banes.

Obiection.

This order (saith the aduersarie and accuser) is by Dispensation abused, and by our Bishops solde for money.

Answere.

The order I thinke very good and meete to bee obserued in a Christian Church, and not without good cause to be altered: and yet doth it not beare any necessitie in Religion and holinesse, whereby mens consciences should be wrung or wrested. But I wil demaund of the accuser, whether there be not some cases, wherein, the circumstances being considered, this matter may bee dispensed withall among Christians? And if there be (as no reasonable man can deny) then I aske further, whether there be any lavve in this Church of England, vvhereby, with the authoritie of the Prince, it is granted, that a Bishop may in such conuenient cases dispense with this order? And if there be such lawe of the Church and of the Realme: I marueile, how it can be counted Simonie, or couetous selling of the libertie of the Gospell, to dispense with it.

Obiection.

Yea, but if the order bee good, why is it not kept vnuiolably? if it be euill, why is it solde for money?

Answere.

The order is good, no man can deny it, or without good cause alter it: but there is no external order so necessary, but that authoritie may in some considerations lawfully dispence therewith. It was a good order and commandement of God, that none but the Priests should eat of the shew-bread,
1. Sam. 22. and yet in a case of necessitie, *Abimelech* the hie Priest, did dispense with *Dauid* and his company in eating the same bread. The external obseruation of the Sabboth day was a good order, and a commaundement streightly giuen *Maccab.* by God: and yet we read that the Iewes in necessity did breake it, and fought on the Sabboth day. And *Marke. 2.* Christ himselfe defended his Disciples, that on *Matt. 12.* that day did bruise Corne and eat it. Therefore by lavvefull authoritie, such orders may bee dispensed with, and not deserue iust reproofe, much lesse the crime of Couetousnesse and Simonie.

Obiection.

Yea, but the dispensations are solde for money: for some haue for writing, and other for sealing, and my Lord for granting &c.

Answere.

By as good reason may they accuse any Iudge, or chiefe officer in this Land, of extortion and bribery: because his Clearkes and vnder officers take money for the writing and dispatch of Processes, Writs, and other like matters, whereof happily some small portion commeth to the Iudge or chiefe officer himselfe, and the same also warranted, and made good by the lawes of this Realme. If either Ecclesiasticall Ministers or other officers and Magistrates, shall by extortion wrest more, then by order is due: there lieth lawfull remedie and sharpe punishment for the same. And in all societies and common weales that euer haue bene, aswell among Christians as other, it hath beene counted lawfull, that the Ministers to higher officers, aswell Ecclesiasticall as other, should haue lawfull portions and fees allowed them for such thinges vvherein they trauell. Therefore, howe this may bee imputed to Bishoppes as Simonie, and sale of Christian libertie, I see not.

Obiection.

They will say, Dispensations for Banes, for greedinesse of money, are graunted more commonly then they shoulde be.

Answere.

If that be true, I praise it not, I defend it not, I excuse it not: and I thinke the fault more in inferiour Officers, then in bishops themselues. But in whome soeuer the faulte be, that cannot be so great and hainous, that bishoppes of England may iustly be accounted Antichristian Prelates, Petie Antichrists, Sub-vice-Antichrists &c. as some in the heate of their zeale, doe tearme them. But God, I trust, in due time, vvill coole their heate with the spirite of mildenesse and gentlenesse. If many bishops haue gained by this kind of Dispensation, I maruaile. Surely I knovve some, that neuer receiued pennie, in that consideration, but haue giuen strait charge to their inferiour officers, neuer to dispense with that matter, but vpon great and weighty cause: and such order is now generally taken. But (good Christians) here is the griefe, that moueth all this grudge: that euill persons, vvhen, either to cloke their whoredome, or to preuent another of his lawfull wife, or some other like purpose, will marry without orderly asking in the Church, they be for the same conuented and punished by the magistrate. This they be grieued at, and count it great extremitie: for, because they see the lawfull magistrate, vpon good considerations somtime to dispense with this order, they thinke it as conuenient for them without leaue, of their owne heads to vse the same, to the satisfying of their vnlawfull lust, or other lewde affection. For such is now the state of this time, that whatsoeuer an Officer, specially Ecclesiasticall, may do by lawful authoritie, the priuate subiect thinketh he may doe the same, at his owne will and pleasure. And if he be brideled thereof, why then it is Lordlinesse, Symonie, Couetousnesse, and Crueltie. And I pray God, the like boldenesse growe not towarde other Officers and magistrates of the Common weale also. Surely, we haue great cause to feare it: for the reasons whereon they ground their doings, may be applied as well to the one, as to the other.

Obiection.

Another Argument of coueteousnesse in bishops is farre worse, as it is said, then the former:

The second proofe of couetousnes forbidding of Marriage.

that they prohibite marriage at certaine times, most contrary to Gods worde: that is (say they) a Papisticall practise, to fill the Cleargies purse: yea it is a doctrine of Antichrist, and of the deuill him slefe, prohibiting Marriage euen in Lay men, contrarie to S. Paules word,

Heb. 13. who sayth, Marriage is honorable in all persons.

Answere.

Surely, for my part I confesse, and before GOD and the worlde protest, that in my conscience I thinke, that whosoeuer forbiddeth marriage to any kinde of men, is tainted with the corruption of Antichristian doctrine, and hath his conscience seared with an hot iron, bearing the mark of the beast spoken of in the *Apocalypse:* but I am clerely resolued

Apoc. 13. that the Bishoppes of England are free from anie touch of that opinion, and doe account it no lesse then a token of Antichrist noted by *Daniel*, to prohibite lawfull Matrimonie. Their doctrine openlie taught and preached, and the practise of their life doth shevve it to be so, that no man vnlesse hee bee blinded with malice, will impute that error vnto them. Who seeth not, that by exercise of mariage in their owne persons, they cast themselues into the displeasure and misliking of a great nomber, in that onely they be maried, contrarie to the corruption of the Popish and Antichristian Church? Wherefore, I pray you (good Christian readers) weigh and consider with your selues, what vnchristian and heathenish dealing this is toward the ministers of God, of purpose onely to deface them, and bring them in misliking by sinister interpretations, to cast vpon them the filth and reproch of that corrupt doctrine of Antichrist, which most of all other they doe impugne in their teaching, and withstand in their dooing. Is there feare of God in those hearts that can do this?

Obiection.

Why? (they will say) It is euident that Mariage is prohibited by them at certaine times of the yeere, and thereby occasion giuen to weake and fraile persons, to fall into whordome and fornication, or to burne in their consciences with great danger of their soules.

Answere.

Vndoubtedly this must needs be thought a captious and rigorous interpretation, to say that a stay of mariage for certaine daies and weeks, is an vnchristian forbidding of mariage, and worthy so grieuous blame, as is cast vpon bishops for it. For then it is a *Popish disorder also, and Antichristian corruption, to stay marriage for three weekes, vntill the Banes bee asked*: for in that space, light and euill disposed mindes, may easily fall to offence. And yet this order both is, and ought to bee accounted of them, a godly and necessary order in the Church.

Obiection.

They will answere, that it is Popish and superstitious, to tye the order of Marriage vnto any time or season, more then other. For the thing beeing good and lawfull by the worde of God, why shoulde it bee (say they) assigned to any time or place? There is no place more holy then Paradise was, nor no time so good as was before Adam fell by his disobedience, &c.

Answere.

I aunswere, if any man appoint Marriage to bee vsed at this or that time and place, for conscience sake, or for holinesse, as though the time or place coulde make the thing either more or lesse holy, surely I must needs condemne him as superstitious, and cannot thinke well of the doing, though all the Bishoppes in England shoulde affirme the contrary. For to make holy, or vnholy, those things that God hath left free, and bee of them selues indifferent, is one of the chiefe groundes of all Papisticall corruption. But I suspect no bishop in this Realme to be of that iudgement, and I dare say there is not. A thing left by Gods lawe free and indifferent, may be accounted more conuenient, comely, and decent, at one time and place, than at another: but more holy it cannot bee.

All meats are free at all times by the law of God: *for nothing is vnclean that is received with thanksgiuing: neither doeth any thing that goeth into the mouth defile a man.* And yet because it is now a Positiue law in this common weale, not for holinesse, but for orders sake: it is not so comely and conuenient for an Englishman to eate flesh on Fridayes and Saturdayes, or in the Lent, as it is at other times.

Obiection.

Heere they will crie and say, that both the one lawe, and the other is superstitious and naught, and proceeded both out of the Popes mint, and there were coyned, and had their beginning, and therefore that the Bishops doe wickedly, and like to popish prelates, that so retain in the Church and common weale, the dregs of Antichristian corruption.

Answere.

This is the voice and opinion of them only, which think not any thing tollerable to be vsed, that hath bin vsed in the church before time, were it of it selfe neuer so good. These will haue no Font, but Christen children in basons: They wil weare no caps nor surplices: many of them wil not vse the old pulpits, but haue new made: they will not accept a collect or praier, be it neuer so agreeable to the word of God. I maruaile, that they vse the Churches them selues, then which, nothing hath bin more prophaned with superstition and idolatrie. They should do that *Optatus Mileuitanus* writeth, that the Donatists were wont to do, that is, when they obteyned a Church, which before had beene vsed by Catholikes, they woulde scrape the walles therof, and breake the Communion tables and cups. But it may appeare, that the learned father *August.* was not of that opinion. For in his epistle written to *Publicola,* a question was mooued vnto him, whether in destroying the idoles temples, or their groues, a Christian might vse any part of the wood, or water, or any other thing that did apperteine vnto them: His aunswere was, that men might not take those things to their priuate use, least they run into suspicion, to haue destroyed such places for couetousnes: but that the same things might be imploied in *pios et necessarios vsus.* But I recite not this to defend that lawe, whereby mariage for a time is forbidden. For I thinke it not a matter of such necessitie, neither is it so greatly pressed, as they pretend. I thinke there is no lavv remaining, that is so little executed, as that is.

The other law of forbearing flesh on Fridayes, in Lent, and other dayes, for the state of our countrey I thinke very conuenient, and most necessarie to be vsed in Christian policie. I woulde to God those men, that make so small accompt of this lavve, had heard the reasons of the grauest, wisest, and most expert men of this realme, not only for the maintenance of this Law, but also for some addition to be made vnto it. How God hath placed this land, there is no reasonable man but seeth: The Sea are our vvalles, and if on these vvalles vve haue not some reasonable furniture of ships, we shal tempt god, in leauing open our countrey to the enemy, and not vsing those instruments, which God hath appointed. There is no state of men, that doth so much furnish this realme with sufficient numbers of mariners for our nauie, as fishers do. And howe shall fishers be maintained, if they haue not sufficient vtterance for those thinges, for which they trauell? And hovve can they haue vtterance, if euery dainty mouthed man, vvithout infirmity and sicknesse, shall eat flesh at his pleasure? They cannot pretend religion, or restraint of Christian libertie, seeing open protestation is made by the lawe, that it is not for conscience sake, but for the defence and safetie of the realme. Therefore this crying out against this lawe, is not onely needlesse, but also vndiscreete and factious.

Obiection.

But there bee other matters that more nighly touch the

The crime of making vnlearned Ministers. quicke, and if they be true, can receiue no face of defence. They make lewd and vnlearned Ministers for gaine. they mainteine pouling and pilling courtes: they abuse the Churches discipline, &c.

Answere.

As touching the first, if they make lewde Ministers, it is one great fault: if they do it wittingly, it is farre a more heinous offence: if they do it for gaine, it is of all other most wicked and horrible, and indeede should directly proue deuilish simonie to be in them. That some lewd and vnlearned ministers haue bene made, it is manifest: I will not seeme to defend it: I woulde they had had more care heerein, that the offence of the godly might haue beene lesse. And yet I knowe, all their faults in this are not alike, and some haue smallie offended heerein. And in them all, I see a certaine care and determination, so much as in them lieth, to amend the inconuenience that hath risen by it. Which thing, vvith professours of the Gospell, shoulde cause their fault to bee the more charitably borne, least they seeme not so much to haue misliking of the offence, as of the persons them selues, for some other purpose, then they will bee openly knowen of. But if they shoulde doe, as they be (I trust) vniustly reported of, that is, to make lewde and vnlearned Ministers for lucre and gaine: truely, no punishment could be too grieuous for them. Which way that should be gainefull to Bishops, I see not.

The Clarke or Register, I knowe, hath his fee allowed for the writing of letters of Orders: but that euer Bishop did take any thing in that respect, I neuer heard, neither thinke I, that their greatest enemies be able to proue it vpon many of them. Therefore this may goe with the residue of vncharitable slanders. Or if there hath bene any one such euil disposed person that hath so vtterly forgot his duetie and calling, that eyther this way, or any such like, in making of Ministers hath sought his owne gaine and commoditie: it is hard dealing, with the reproch thereof to defame the innocent, together with the guiltie, and to distaine the honestie of them that neuer deserued it. There is no Magistrate in this land so sincere and vpright in his doings, but that by this meanes his honestie and good name may be defaced.

Obiection.

It will be sayd that all this is but a glose or colour, to hide and turne from you those great crimes that you are iustly charged withall. For the world seeth, and all men crie out against you, that you, to the great hurt and hinderance of the Church, vphold and maintaine an vnlearned ministrie, and will not suffer any redresse or reformation to be made therin. Hereby commeth it to passe, that the people of God be not taught their duetie, eyther to God, or to their Prince: but, by their ignorance, are layde foorth as a pray to Sathan. For, by that occasion, they be ledde away to euill with euery light perswasion that is put into their heads, either against God or their Prince, so that it may bee iustly thought that all those mischiefes that of late haue fallen foorth, haue sprung out of this onely roote, aswell in them that haue slid backe and reuolted from religion, as in those that haue conceiued and attempted the wicked murthering of our gratious Prince, and bringing in of a stranger to sit in her royal seate. You are therefore the principall causes of all these mischiefes.

Answere.

This is surely a grieuous accusation: but God, I trust, will iudge more vprightly, and regard the innocencie of our hearts, in these horrible crimes laid to our charge. These accusers, to satisfie their misliking affection towarde our state, not onely suffer themselues to bee deceiued with false and captious reasons, but dangerously also seeke to seduce other. Logicians, among other deceitfull arguments note one principally, *A non causa vt causa*, that is, when men, either to praise, or dispraise, doe attribute the effects of either part to some things or persons, as causes therof, which indeed are not the true causes. Which false reasoning hath done great harme at al times, both in the Church of God, and in common weales. After the ascension of Christ, when God sent his Apostles and other holy men to preach the Gospell of our saluation in Christ, and the same was among men vnthankfully receiued: God did cast sundry plagues and punishments vpon them, as *dearth and scarcitie, famine and hunger, the pestilence, and sundry other diseases, warre and tumult, earthquakes and great deluges in sundry places*. The causes of al this, very slanderously and blasphemously they imputed to Christian Religion, and therby raised those dreadful persecutions, which at that time were exercised against the Christians.

This errour was the cause that Saint *Augustine* wrote his

notable worke *De ciuitate Dei*, and that *Orosius*, by the counsell both of Saint *Hierome* and Saint *Augustine*, wrote his historie: wherein he answereth this false argument, and sheweth that God in all times, had sent the like plagues for the sinnes and offences of mankinde, and for the reiecting of his word and trueth.

In the fourtie foure Chapter of *Ieremie*, The Iewes deceiue themselues with the like argument, to confirme their conceiued superstition and idolatrie. *But we will do* (say they) *whatsoeuer thing commeth out of our owne mouth: as to burne incense to the Queene of Heauen, and to powre out drinke offrings vnto her as we haue done, both we and our Fathers, our Kings and our Princes in the Cities of Iudah, and in the streetes of Hierusalem: for then had we plentie of victuals, and were well, and felt no euill. But since wee left off to burne incense to the Queene of Heauen, and to powre out drinke offerings vnto her, we haue had scarcenesse of all things, and haue bene consumed by the sword and by the famine.* In these words you see, to the hardening of their owne hearts, they attribute the good gifts of God to their idolatrie, and their dearth and trouble to the preaching of *Ieremie* and other Prophets, which indeede were not the true causes therof. In like maner reason rebellious subiects in common weales, when they seeke to make odious the Princes and gouernours vnder whom they liue, vniustly imputing to them the causes of such things, wherwith they finde themselues grieued.

_{Walsingham.} So reasoned the rebels in the time of King *Richard* the second, against the King, against the Counsell, and chiefe Nobilitie of the Realme, against the Lawyers, and all other States of learning, and therefore had resolution among them, to haue destroyed and ouerthrowen them all, and to haue suffered none other to liue in this Realme with them, but the Gray Friers onely.

Seeing therefore this maner of reasoning is so perillous, it behooueth all them that feare God, and loue the trueth, and will not willingly be caried into errour, to take diligent heed that they be not abused herewith. And so I pray God they may doe, which at this time so earnestly seeke to make odious the state of the Clergie of *England*, imputing to them the causes of those things, which they most detest and abhorre.

For if they will see the trueth, and iudge but indifferently, they shall finde that there is no such vnlearned Ministerie, as they complaine of: neither such want of preaching, as may iustly prouoke the wrath of God, to send such plagues and punishments vpon vs, as they recite. This I dare iustifie, that since *Englande* had first the name of a Christian Church, there was neuer so much preaching of the word of God, neuer so many in number, neuer so sufficient and able persons to teach and set forth the same, as be at this day, howsoeuer they be defamed and defaced. There be, I confesse, many vnlearned and vnsufficient Ministers: but yet I take it to bee captious and odious, in respect of them to name the whole Ministerie vnlearned or ignorant. For the simplicitie and charitie of Christian iudgement, doth giue the name of any Societie, according to the better part, and not according to the worse.

There were in the Church of *Corinth*, many euill persons, aswell in corruption of doctrine, as wickednesse of life: and yet Saint *Paul* noteth that Church to bee a reuerend and holy congregation. The Church of Christ militant heere in earth, hath alwayes a great number of euill mixed vvith them that be good, and oftentimes the worse part the greater: yet were it reprochfull and slaunderous to call the Church wicked. In like sort may it well bee thought vncharitable, to call the ministerie of the Church of *England* ignorant, when that (thankes be to God) there bee so many learned and sufficient preachers in this land, as neuer were before in any age or time, and the same adorned with Gods excellent good giftes, and comparable to anie other Church refourmed in *Europe*. If men would cast so curious and captious eyes vpon the Ministers of other countries, and note the blemishes and imperfections in them, as they doe in our owne: I am perswaded (vnder correction) they would not thinke so meanely of the state of the Ministerie of *England*, as they doe. But this is the generall disease of vs Englishmen, to haue in admiration the persons and states of other foreine countreys, and loath their owne, bee they neuer so commendable or good. I speak not this, to note with reproch any refourmed Church in forreine countries, or to diminish the commendations of those excellent gifts, which it hath pleased God plentifully to poure downe vpon them, as the first renuers and restorers of the Gospel in this latter age, to vvhome, in that respect, we owe great loue and reuerence:

But yet they see and acknowledge, that they haue imperfections, and cannot haue churches in this world without blemishes. Notwithstanding it is not free among them, no not for the best learned, or of greatest authoritie, in publike speech or writing, to vtter those things which may tend to the generall reproche of their Church or common weale, as it is commonly vsed with vs at this day: Or if they doe, they are sharpely dealt withall for the same. For, as wise gouernours, they see, that such doings is the very seede of dissention, discorde, and faction, the verie pestilence of all Churches, commonweales, and societies. Wherefore in most Churches, they doe tollerate some imperfections setled by order, at the beginning, least by change of lawes, there should bee greater inconuenience.

Obiection.

Yea but all their Ministers are learned and able to teach.

Answere.

Of that I doubt: and in some places, by good testimony I know it not to be true. That is easie to be had in a free Citie, that hath no more congregations, but those that be within the Citie, or within a fewe villages about, which is not possible, in so great a kingdome as this is, replenished with so many Villages almost in euery place, as scantly you haue two miles without a Tovvne or Village inhabited.

And yet, that men doe not conceiue euill opinion of the Bishops, for that which can not bee remedied: it behooueth the vvise and godly to consider, that the state of this Church is such, as of necessitie there must be some of very meane abilitie, in comparison of that perfect rule of a Minister that S. *Paul* requireth.

It is well knowen, as it is before recited, that there be a number of parishes in this Realme, the liuings whereof are so small, that no man sufficiently learned, will content himselfe with them. In some one meane shire there bee aboue foure score Chappels to be serued, onely by Curates, with very small stipends. To place able men in them, is vnpossible: For neither sufficient number of learned men can be had, nor, if there could, woulde they be contented to be to such places appointed. And to leaue those parishes and places vnserued of common prayer, and administration of the Sacraments, were an inconuenience as great as the other part: For it bringeth men to an heathenish forgetfulnes of God. To ease this matter by combinations and ioyning of many parishes together (as some deuise) besides other inconueniences, the thing is not in the bishops authoritie, nor possible for him to doe. Euery parish hath a sundry patrone, which wil neuer bee brought to agree to that purpose, and to forgoe their patrimonie and heritage. Now to attempt the matter, by making a law for that purpose, would bee occasion of so great troubles and alterations, as would draw with them more inconueniences, then would stand with the safe state of this common weale, as the wiser sort doe see, and were easie for me to declare, if it were pertinent to this matter here to lay them downe in writing. The only remedie that necessitie beareth, is, to tolerate some of the meaner sort of Ministers, hauing carefull consideration, so much as diligence can doe, that the same may be of life and behauiour, honest, and godly and such at the least, as may bee able to instruct the parish in the Catechisme. And surely, I hope, by the care of the bishops, that they haue already vndertaken, this thing wil be, either altogether, or in a good part brought to effect ere long time passe.

Obiection.

But some will say, that all this is but a cloake of colourable reason to hide an vnexcusable fault. For that no necessity can excuse a man, to breake the law of God: and Gods holy commandement is vttered by Saint Paule, that among other properties, a Minister shoulde 1. Tim. 3. be *Aptus ad docendum*, that is, able to teach, and therefore no bishoppe can be borne with, in making an vnlearned Minister. For he may not do euill that good may come thereof.

Answere.

For answere heereunto, it cannot be denied, but the rule which Saint *Paul* giueth, is an exact rule, and 1. Tim. 3. such an absolute description of a Minister, as is Tit. 1. according to Christian perfection: and therefore that all Ministers ought to bee correspondent to the same: And so much as they want thereof, they lacke of their perfect state. Yea, and ecclesiasticall gouernours shoulde carefully see, so much as humane frailtie and the miserable state of this worlde wil suffer, that all Ministers of the church of God be such. And when they doe faile heerein, they offend, and goe from that perfection that the worde of God requireth. But yet I doubt not, but God of his great mercie in Christ our Sauiour will gratiously consider, that he hath to doe with flesh and bloud, and that euen his best children liue not here in an heauenly state, but in a miserable and wretched worlde, and specially when he seeth, that they offend not of negligence or malicious wickednesse, but are carried with the necessitie of this earthlie frailtie. For if God shoulde measure all thinges done in his Church by the perfect rule of his worde, who should be able to stand before him? We may not therefore, either condemne other, or esteeme our selues condemned before God, if through the frailtie of the worlde, we be not able to frame all things in his Church to such perfectnesse, as his holy worde appoynteth.

As the description of a Minister, deliuered by Saint *Paul* to *Timothie* and *Titus* is perfect, so doth it containe many branches and propeities to the number of (I thinke) twentie or aboue : As, that he must be vnreproueable, the husband of one wife, watching, temperat, modest, not froward, not angrie, one that loueth goodnesse, righteous, holy, harberous, apt to teach, holding fast the wholesome word according to doctrine, able to exhort with wholsome doctrine, and conuince them that say against it, not giuen to much wine, no striker, nor giuen to filthie lucre, gentle, no quarreller, not couetous, one that can rule his owne house, keeping his wife and children in honest obedience, not a yong scholler least he be puffed vp with selfe liking, well reported of, graue, not double tongued, holding the mysterie of the faith in a pure conscience.

If they wil admit no Ministers as lawfull, but such as shall haue fully all these properties : Surely they will cut from Churches the greatest part, or all the Ministers that they haue. Euen that one propertie which they so greatly call vpon, as of all other most necessarie, that is, that hee shoulde be apt to teach : that is, as Saint *Paul* expoundeth himselfe, to be sufficiently able to teach them that be willing, and to conuince the aduersarie : If it be pressed to the extremitie and rigour thereof, it comprehendeth so much, as it will exclude a great many of Ministers and Preachers, which in their measure doe good seruice in the Church of God.

The best writers that euer I did reade vpon that, say, That to the performance of the same, a man must haue readie knowledge in the Scriptures, the vnderstanding of the tongues, the reading of the ancient Fathers, and histories of antiquitie. If a great many of them woulde looke into their owne bosomes, and measure themselues by this rule of sufficiencie: they woulde not iudge so rigorously of other, nor be so rash to condemne them.

We see in the Scriptures, that God sometime beareth with breach of his commandement, falling by the necessitie of our fraile life. God gaue in charge, as before is sayde, that none shoulde eate of the Shew-bread, but the Priests: And yet in necessity *Dauid* did eat of it, though he were no Priest. [Exod. 29.] [1. Reg. 21.]

The *Machabies* fought on the Sabboth day contrary to this commandement, *Thou shalt keepe holy the Sabboth day*: and yet it is not read, that God was therfore displeased with them, or tooke punishment of them, though the Scripture mention, that one without necessitie gathering stickes on the Sabboth day, was stoned to death. [Num. 15.]

Christ himselfe may seeme to giue the reason for their defence, when he saith, *The Sabboth was ordeined for man, and not man for the Sabboth.* [Mar. 2.]

Yea, in a morall commandement of God touching mariage, we see God to vse a maner of dispensation, in respect of the frailtie of mans nature. The Scripture saith precisely, *Quos Deus coniunxit homo ne separet :* and yet in the lawe, wee finde this dispensation or qualifying thereof. *When a man hath taken a wife, and maried her, if she finde no fauour in his eyes, &c. then let him make a bill of diuorcement, and put it in her hand, and send her out of his house.* [Deut. 24.]

Of this merciful bearing of God with the breach of his commaundement, Christ sheweth the reason, *Math.* 19. saying in this wise. *For the hardnesse of your hearts God suffered you to put away your wiues, but from the beginning it was not so.*

Heere wee learne that our gratious and mercifull God, for the shunning and auoiding of a greater mischiefe among stubborne people, suffered his seruaunt *Moses* to giue foorth a more fauourable interpretation of his iust and perfect Lawe, and to suffer diuorcements in such cases, as the right and rigor of his iustice in it selfe, had forbidden.

This haue I written, not of purpose to incourage men to breake and alter the Lawes and ordinances of God, but rather to comfort those consciences, which in this case may bee troubled, and to put away that opinion, wherewith some are led to thinke that that Congregation is not worthie the name of a Christian Church, nor meete wherein a good Christian man shoulde abide as Minister, where all things are not reformed, to the perfect rule of Gods holy word.

Surely the auncient Fathers of the primitiue Church do not seeme to be of that iudgement. For they did all finde fault with manie enormities in their time, as well in outward ceremonies, as corruption of life, yea, and in some point of doctrine also: and yet it is not read that they did therefore separate themselues from the Churches, or thinke that they coulde not as faythfull Ministers serue in them.

Saint *Augustine* sheweth of himselfe, and of Saint *Cyprian* very notably, as in many places, so chiefely against the *Donatists* who were infected with that errour: but most plainely of all other places, *De Baptismo contra Donatistas, Lib.* 4. *Cap.* 9. Where at large he disputeth this question: which place is worthie diligent reading and consideration.

<small>Aug. de baptis. contra Donatist: lib. 4. cap. 9.</small>

Cyprian had blamed the Bishops and Ministers in his time, <small>Cypr. de lap.</small> of *Couetousnesse, Extortion* and *Vsurie*. And yet sayth Saint *Augustine*, Cyprian *writeth vnto* Antonianus, *that before the last separation of the wicked and the Godly, no man ought to separate himselfe from the vnitie of the Church, because of the mixture of euill persons. What a swelling pride is it* (saith hee) *what a forgetting of humilitie and mildnesse, when a vanting arrogancie, that he can thinke himselfe able to do that which Christ woulde not permit to his Apostles, that is, to separate the weedes from the Corne?* &c. Yea, and *S. Paul* himselfe as before I haue said, iudgeth the Church of *Corinth*, an honorable and blessed Church of God, though there were in the same not onely some blemishes and imperfections, but many great and enormious faultes. Wherefore, to returne againe to my purpose, though our Bishops through the necessitie of time, neither at the beginning had, nor now can haue perfect good Ministers in euery parish within their charge: I see no cause, why they may not vse such as with their best diligence they may haue, especially if they order the matter so, as the fault be not in their owne negligence or corruption.

That you may the better conceiue, that an vnlearned Ministery for want of preaching of the Gospel, is not the cause of the backesliding and reuolting of so many in these dayes, nor of sundry other inconueniences imputed to the same: you shall easily vnderstand, if you will call to your remembrance, that when there were fewer preachers and lesse teaching by great oddes, then of late yeres hath bene, the people did not reuolt as now they doe. There is therefore some other cause, if we will with vpright mindes looke into it. There were fewer preachers and lesse teaching in the dayes of that King of blessed memorie *Edward* the sixt, and yet did not the people then reuolt, as nowe, although the reformation of the Church was then but greenely settled. They had the same imperfection and want of Ministers, which we haue now, and that in greater measure: in so much as they were faine to helpe out the want with reading of Homilies, as you know. Which deuise, although it be greatly misliked and inueighed against in these dayes, as intollerable: yet did that reuerend and learned father *M. Bucer* highly commend the same, and shewed his good liking thereof, willing moe Homilies to bee prepared for that purpose. And what were they that were then Preachers, and in the state of gouernment of the Church? Surely such persons as did diligently obserue those orders in outwarde thinges, which the Bishops nowe, for feare of further inconuenience, desire and studie to maintaine. In the first ten yeres of her Maiesties most gratious reigne, there was little or no backsliding from the Gospel, in comparison of that now is: yet was there not then so much preaching, by the halfe, nor so many Preachers in the Church of England by 1000. as now there are. And since that time (I speake of good experience, and better knovvledge then gladly I vvould) that in diuers places vvhere there hath bene often preaching, and that by learned vvnd graue men, there haue bene many that haue reuolted, and litle good effect declared among the residue. You vvil aske me then, vvhat I thinke to be the true cause thereof? Surely, the causes are many: but I vvill note vnto you onely two or three, that bee of greatest weight. First, to haue the fruites of the Gospell setled in the consciences of men,

The causes why an vnlearned Ministerie is not the occasion of backe sliding &c.

The first cause why the Gospel prospereth not so well heere.

and declared in their liues: It is not sufficient to haue often and much preaching, but also to haue diligent and reuerent hearing. Though the Preachers be neuer so learned and discreete, if it be not heard as the worde of God, it is to no purpose. But in these days, as in all other, men be easily induced to disburthen themselues, and lay the whole fault vpon the Ministers and Preachers.

Obiection.

Oh, say they, if wee had good and zealous Bishoppes, and godly Preachers, such as the Apostles were: vndoubtedly, this doctrine of the Gospell woulde haue had better succcesse, and would more haue preuailed in mens hearts. For they are not zealous, nor seeme to bee mooued with the spirite of God: therefore it cannot be, that they should moue other.

Answere.

Though this reason seeme somewhat plausible to some kinde of men, and to be of great force to excuse the common people: yet I aduertise all them, that haue any sparke of the feare of God in their hearts, that they take heede of it, and beware, that, to their own great danger, they be not caried away with it. For it hath bene seldome or neuer heard or read, that the people of God among whom true doctrine hath bin preached (as the Lorde be thanked it hath bene with vs) did euer vse such allegations for their ovvne excuse and defence. It hath bene alwayes the pretence of the reprobate and wicked, to colour their owne obstinacie, and contempt of Gods word, when they were offered the light of the Gospell and called to repentance. But that these kinde of men may not flatter and deceiue themselues: I let them vnderstande, that the Scriptures in no place teach them, that the offences and faults of the Ministers, are always the only cause, why the word of God doth not take place in mens hearts. It is more commonly, and almost alwaies imputed to the *waywardnesse, vnthankfulnesse,* and *obstinacie* of the people that heare it. Therefore it were good for all sortes of men, of what calling soeuer, to looke into their own bosomes, and carefully to consider, whether the fault thereof be not in themselues. For they know right vvell, that the master may bee learned and diligent, and yet the scholer not thriue, by reason of his own dulnesse. The Physition may bee honest and skilfull, and the obstinate Patient make light of

his wholesome counsaile. The seede may be good, and the seede sower a painefull and skilfull husbandman, and yet the fruite not to bee answerable to his trauel, because of the naughtinesse and barrennesse of the ground. This our Sauiour Christ teacheth vs in the parable of the Seede-sovver. *Matth.* 13. *The Sower* (sayeth he) *went foorth to sowe his seede, and some fell in the high way,* that is to say, into the hearts of them that vvere continually trampled with wicked and vngodly cogitations, so that the seede could not sinke into their hearts, but by those birds of the deuill, vvas carryed avvay vvithout fruite. *Some fell into stonie ground,* that is, into such hearts as wanted the good iuice and moysture of Gods holy spirite : and therefore when the heate of persecution ariseth, or some great temptation assaulteth them, their zeale is withered, and they reuolt from the trueth. *Some fell into bushie ground,* that is, into the mindes of them, that were troubled with the cares of the worlde, with the loue of riches and with the pleasures of this life, which wholly choked vp the good seede of the Gospell of Christ, so that it could not in any wise prosper and bring foorth fruite. Heere you may perceiue, that for one fourth part of good grounde, that yeeldeth fruite of the doctrine of God, there are three greater parts of euill ground, wherein it nothing at all prospereth. But in these our dayes amongst vs, we haue a fourth sort of men, which obstinately at al refuse to heare the word of God, and do shut vp their eares, not only against preaching, but against priuate exhortation also. If there were lesse store of these euill grounds in this land at this day, vndoubtedly wee shoulde see more successe of the Gospell, and more ample fruite of our teaching then nowe we doe. It were good for men to looke that these quarrellings at other mens liues, bee not one of the *coardes of vanitie* that *Esay* speaketh Esay. 5.
of. *Woe bee to them* (sayth God by his holy Prophet) *that drawe on iniquitie with coardes of vanitie, and sinne, as it were with a Cart-rope,* that is, Woe bee to them, that imagine excuses and coulours, to nouzell and mayntaine them selues in contempt of Gods worde, and vvant of repentaunce. Let men take heede of such dealing, that such *Coardes of vanitie* pull not on iniquitie so fast, that it draw them to the vtter contempt of God and his trueth. Example whereof is seene at this day, in too many, to the griefe of all good mens

hearts: For the schoole of *Epicure*, and the Atheists, is mightily increased in these daies. The like effect *Esay* noteth to haue fallen out among the Iewes, at that time. For this hee maketh them to say in derision of the preaching of the Prophets, *Let God make speede, and hasten his worke, that wee may see it. Let the counsell of the holy one of Israel drawe neere, and come, that we may knowe it.* And in like maner dealeth the wicked in *Ieremie* Chapter 5. *They haue denyed the Lorde, and sayde, It is not hee. Tush, the Sworde and the Plague shall not come vpon vs, neither shall we see it. The threatnings of the Prophets are but winde, and the true word of God is not in them. They vtter their owne fantasies, and these things shall come vnto themselues.* Euen with like contempt and derision, many at this day abuse the Preachers of Gods worde. *When we lay before them the terrible threatnings of Gods wrath and indignation, if they reuolt from the trueth of the Gospell, or suffer the same to be betrayed into the handes of the enemie, saying, that God will forsake them: that he will take his defence from them: that he will set his face against them: that he will bring strangers vpon them to destroye their countrey and possesse their great lands and goodly buildings:* Oh, say they, These Preachers make great outcries: they put strange expectations into the peoples heads: they are vndiscreete: they medle with matters, which do not appertaine vnto them: if matters go amisse, the greatest fault is in themselues. But I haue sufficiently spoken of this maner of intertaining of Ministers alreadie, and shall speake of the same hereafter

The second, and in deede a chiefe cause of backsliding and reuolting, is the schisme, faction and dissention, which for the space of these fifteene or sixteene yeeres, hath exceedingly growen, betweene the Ministers and Preachers of England. For the like hath in all ages bene a cause to many, of falling, both from the trueth of God, and to wickednesse of life. *Basile* speaking hereof, saith, *Ob hæc rident increduli, fluctuant qui modicæ sunt fidei, ambigua est fides ipsa.* The effects of this schisme hath beene (as in part I haue declared in other parts of this treatise) First, that not only in sermons publikely, but also in common table talke priuately, yea, and in writing and treatises spredde abroad into all mens handes wickedly, vehement and bitter inuectiues haue beene made against the bishops and other Preachers

The second cause of backsliding.

of the Church of England, to the discredite not onely of their persons, but also of the doctrine which they haue taught. Yea, the whole state and gouernment of this church, the Liturgie and the booke of Common prayer, and the administration of the Sacramentes established by Lawe and authoritie, the externall rites and ceremonies layde downe onely for order sake, haue beene publikely misliked, depraued and condemned, as directly contrary and repugnant to the worde of God. Men haue not onely deliuered foorth these inuectiues against the whole state of our Church, and all the partes thereof: but in the face of the worlde, against Lawe, against authoritie, haue taken vpon them to alter all thinges according to their owne pleasure : VVhich dealing, you may bee sure, can not bee without great offence of an infinite nomber, as the worlde euidently seeth it hath beene. Moreouer, many persons, both vndiscreete and vnlearned, because they will not bee accompted *Dumbe dogs*, haue taken vpon them to preach without license or triall: and entring into discussing of matters nowe in controuersie betweene vs and the aduersarie, haue handled them so coldly, nakedly, and vnperfectly, that many haue bene greeued to heare them, and some brought it in doubt of their consciences, which neuer doubted before. Many strange Assertions, either plainly false, or as Paradoxes, true in some rare and extraordinary sense, haue beene by sundry persons, and some of them well learned, vttered and taught, to the troubling of many mens mindes, and specially such as were not able to reach to the depth of them. As for example, that it is a grieuous offence to kneele at the receiuing of the Communion. A gentleman of good countenaunce hath affirmed to my selfe, that hee woulde rather hazard all the land hee had, then be drawn to kneele at the Communion. An heauie burthen to lay vpon a mans conscience, for an external gesture. The doctrine of *the Lords Supper*, hath bene so slenderly taught by some, that a number haue conceiued with themselues, that they receiue nothing but the external elements, in remembrance that Christ died for them. And these their cogitations haue they vttered to other to their great misliking. Priuate baptism, yea and publike also, if it be ministered by one that is no preacher, hath bin so impugned, as it if were no sacrament at al: whereby questions haue bin raised by sundry persons, what is become of them that were neuer baptised otherwise: Or whether it were not necessary, that all such persons, as are certainly knowen, not to haue receyued any other baptisme, then that was priuately done, ought not to be baptised againe, because the other is esteemed as no Sacrament?

The article of the common Creed touching Christes descension into hell, contrary to the sense of all ancient writers, hath beene strangely interpreted, and by some, with vnreuerent speeches flatly reiected. These and a number of such other, haue vndoubtedly bred great offence, and wounded the hearts of an infinite number, causing them partly to reuolt to Papistry, partly to Atheisme, and neglecting of all Religion, as is seene by the liues of many, to the exceeding griefe of all them that feare God and loue his trueth. As I haue talked with many Recusants, so did I neuer conferre with any that would vse any speech, but that he hath alleadged some of these offences to be cause of his reuolting. And some haue affirmed flatly vnto me, that in seeking to presse them to come to our Church and seruice, we doe against our owne consciences, seeing our most zealous preachers (as they be taken) openly speake and write, that as well our seruice, as the administration of the sacraments, are contrary to the word of God. I beseech Almightie God of his great mercie, that hee will open the eies of them, which thus eagerly haue striuen against the present state of this Church, to see what hurt and hinderaunce hath come to the profession of the Gospell, by these vncharitable and needelesse contentions. And vndoubtedly, if God moue not the heartes of the chiefe Rulers and Gouernours to seeke some ende of this Schisme and faction, which nowe renteth in pieces this Churche of England: it cannot be, but in short time for one Recusant that now is, wee shall haue three, if the increase of that number, which I mention, be not greater. For I doe heare and see those things, that it grieueth my heart to consider. What hurt and trouble Satan hath at all times raised in the Church of God by occasion of dissention and discorde, mooued not onely by heretikes and false teachers, but also by them, which otherwise haue beene good and godly Christians: the Ecclesiasticall Histories doe euidently declare. What should I recite the Schisme between the East and West Churches, for the obseruation of the feast of Easter, which continued a great number of yeeres, and grevv to such bitternesse, that the one excommunicated the other? What shal I say of the Schismes and grieuous contentions in the East Church, and especially at *Antiochia*, and *Alexandria*, between *Paulinus* and *Flauianus*? *Lucifer* and *Eusebius*? the *Meletians* and *Eustathians*? all at the beginning good Christians, and imbracing true doctrine? And yet did they with great troubles, eschewe one the others Communion, as you may reade in *Epiphanius lib.* 2. *Theodor. lib.* 1. *cap.* 8. &c. *Socrat. lib.* 1. *cap.* 23. *Sozom. lib.* 2. *cap.* 18. for the space of 80. yeres and aboue. I omit the great strife betweene *Chrysost.* of the one part, and *Theophilus*, *Cyrill* and *Epiphanius*, on the other, for the burning of *Origens* bookes. They were all good and learned bishops, and wee doe worthily reuerence their memory: yet fell this matter so foule among them, that because *Chryost.* woulde not consent to the burning of *Origens* bookes, *Theophilus* and *Cyrill* woulde scantly euer acknowledge him to be a lawfull Bishop. I mention not a great number of other like factions, which grew in the same age, to the trouble and hinderance of true Christianitie, as many godly and learned men did then complaine. And sundrie graue authours which haue written in this our time, and before, iudge, that these wayward contentions in the East Church, were the chiefe causes that brought vpon them afterward, the heauie wrath of God that tooke his Gospell from them, and cast them into the tyrannie of *Saracens* and *Turkes*, as we haue seene now these many yeeres. A notable example to vs (good Christian Readers) to take heede in time, and earnestly to pray vnto God, that he will so blesse vs with his holy Spirite, *that we may be all like minded, hauing the selfe same loue, being of one minde and of one iudgement, that nothing be done among vs, through strife and vaine glory, but that in humblenesse of minde, euery one will thinke of other better then of himselfe,* that wee may grow together in one heart and minde, against the common aduersarie to the glory of God, and the promoting of his gospel, the safety of our gracious Prince, and naturall countrey. Of such discord in the church, *S. Basile* grieuously complaineth, *When I was growen* (saith he) *into mans age, and often going into strange Countries fel into troubles, I obserued and found, that in other Artes there was great concord and agreement betwene them that were the chiefe of those Artes and Sciences: Onely in the church of God, for which Christ died, and vpon which he had plentifully powred downe his holy spirit, I saw great and vehement discord, aswell among themselues particularly, as in things contrarie to the holie Scriptures. And that which is most horrible, I saw them that are the chiefe of the Church so drawen asunder in diuersitie and contrarietie of opinions, that without all pitie, they did most cruelly teare in pieces the flocke of Christ, so that if euer, now it is verified that the Apostle speaketh, From among your selues shall rise men speaking peruerse things, that they may draw Disciples to follow them.*

The third cause and the principall of all other is, *that the* The third cause of reuolting. *ramping and roaring Lion that goeth about seeking whom he may deuoure,* and watching all occasions to doe mischiefe in the Church of God, hath taken the opportunity of this Schisme and diuision among our selues. And therefore euer since that began, he hath not ceased from time to time, out of his scholes and Nurceries, to sende into this realme fit instrumentes for that purpose, Iesuites, Massing-priests, and Seminary men, and such other of our own nation, as haue bin purposely by them corrupted: which beeing armed with some shew of learning, but specially with readines of tongue and boldnes of speech, with some outward shevv of holines in wordes, haue mightily preuailed against the subiects of this realme, taking commonly reasons of perswasion, from the discord that is among our selues, as by particular dealings with them I haue learned. The indeuours of these men haue taken the greater effect, by one perswasion, which they principally haue vsed: which is, that they haue put into their minds a certain expectation of a speedy alteration and change to be, not only in religion, but also in the state of the realme. Their reasons haue beene, that all the Princes Catholike in Christendom, were entred into league by all means that might be, to depose our gracious Soueraigne Queene *Elizabeth*, and to set vp in her place the Queene of *Scots* when she liued: and then woe be to them that should be found in this land, to remaine in the fauour and liking of the Gospell of Christ, which they blasphemously call horrible schisme and heresie, which would bee reuenged to the vttermost. To worke this deuise, they vvere let to vnderstand, vvhat plots and meanes were made, hovv easie, hovv likely, hovv certaine to come to passe within fevv yeres, yea, moneths, yea, dayes. For they confirmed the hearts of all them that bend to their persvvasion, with all hope that might be : In so much that I knovv some, that within these tvvo yeeres were very forward in religion, and not onely heard Sermons diligently, but also vvere at sundry conferences, for their better confirmation: yet vvithin fevve Moneths, vvith the certaine persvvasion of this expectation, were cleane caried away, and so remaine peruerse and obstinate Recusants, vvith the example thereof shaking the consciences of many other. In these their vvicked and deuilish practises against God and his trueth, and against the state of this lande, they were not a litle imboldened by slacke and remisse dealing toward them. The lawes were not executed : the aduauntage was giuen to some, that did fauourably compound with them.

Hereby I knowe by good experience, that much harme hath bene done in diuers places. They haue also comforted and imboldened themselues in this, that mercie and fauour shoulde bee shevved them. For this they can say, that our Christian Princes and Magistrates, especially such as be Protestants, by their owne doctrine, should shewe mercie and clemencie, chiefly in matters of conscience. But vvhat a malicious hypocrisie is this, to call vpon Christian Magistrates for mercie and fauour, and they themselues in the mean time, breath nothing but crueltie and blood in their hearts? I graunt mercie becommeth a Christian Gouernour, but not without seueritie of Iustice. For seueritie stayeth a greater nomber, then mercie and fauour allureth, as (*August.* saith) *Sicut meliores sunt quos dirigit amor : ita plures* De Correct. *sunt quos corrigit Timor.* The greater part is alwayes et Gratia. the worst : therefore Magistrates must take heede, that mercie bee not turned into crueltie : For as *August.* saith, there is *Misericordia puniens et Crudelitas parcens.*

Obiection.

Faith (say they) is the gift of God, it cannot be forced by any punishment : by hardnesse and extreme dealing men may be made hypocrites, but not religious : yea, they adde further, that the Apostles vsed no such helpe of Princes power to bring men to the faith, or to pull them away from errour.

Answere.

But these and such other like their Allegations, are contrary to the word of GOD, and iudgement of all the ancient learned Fathers, and specially Saint *Augustine*, who chiefly dealt against the *Donatists*, in this, and other opinions. Reade the thirteenth and seuenteenth of *Deuteronomie*, and see howe straightly God giueth charge for the punishment of them that seduce other from the true worshippe of God. In *Exodus* he sayeth, *Qui immolat Dijs alienis, præterquam Domino soli, exterminetur.* Hee that offereth vnto any other gods, saue vnto the Lord, &c. In the *Nombers*, he that brake the Sabboth day, was stoned to death, that his example might not seduce other. *Paul* in the *Act.* of the Apostles, by the power of God, strooke blind *Elymas* the magitian, withstanding the truth of God. *August.* in the 11. *Tract.* vpon *Iohn*, disputing against the *Donatists*, by the example of *Nabuchodnosor*, exhorteth christian princes to vse sharp punishment against such persons, as contemne Christ and his doctrine. *If king Nabuchodnosor* (saith he) *gaue glory to God, because hee had deliuered the 3. yong men from the fire, and gaue vnto him so great glory, that he made a decree throughout all his empire, which comprehended so many kingdoms: how should not our kings be mooued, which knowe not onely three yong men to be deliuered out of the fire, but themselues, and all other faithful persons deliuered from the eternall fire of hell? especially when they see Christ thrust out of the minds of christians, and when they heare it saide to a christian, Say thou art no christian. Such offences will they commit, but yet such punishments will they not suffer. For vnderstande you what they do, and what they suffer? They kil mens soules, but they are afflicted but in body: They worke to other eternal death, and they complaine that they suffer temporal death. &c.* Againe, the same *Aug. De vi coercend. Hæreticis ad Vincent. Epist.* 48. writeth in this sort, *My opinion was at the beginning, that none should be forced to the vnitie of the church, but that we should endeuour to deale by the worde of GOD, by disputation, by reasoning, and perswading, least happily of those which wee knewe to be open Heretikes, wee shoulde make counterfaite Christians: but this mine opinion was not ouercome with the wordes of them that reasoned against mee, but by the experience of them, which shewed mee examples to the contrarie. For first mine*

Deut. 13. and 17.

owne Citie of Hippo was obiected against mee, which was wholly carried away with the opinion of the Donatistes, and yet through feare of the Emperours lawes was turned to the Catholike vnitie. Which Citie, we now see so to deteste that pernitious errour, as if it had neuer bene among them. And likewise diuers other cities, were namely rehearsed vnto mee, so that by experience I learned, that my former iudgement was not right.

The first Christian Emperor Constantine vvriting to his Lieutenant *Taurus*, *It hath pleased mee* (sayth hee) *that in all the places and cities, all the Temples of the idoles should presently be shut vp, and all wicked persons forbidden to haue access vnto them. Our pleasure further is, that all men shoulde forbeare their sacrifices. If any such wickednesse shalbe committed, let them be beaten downe with the reuengement of the sword, and their substance to be seised vpon, and brought into my Treasurie: And in like maner the gouernours of Prouinces to be punished, if they neglect to execute the same.*

But I will make no longer discourse herein. Such as doe doubt hereof, and desire to be better satisfied, I referre them to a Treatise which Maister *Beza* hath written for that matter. I haue tarried the longer in this part, for that I am desirous to let the indifferent christian reader vnderstand, that it is but an affectionate iudgement of some, when they impute the only cause to be in bishops, why there is in these daies so great back-sliding from the Gospel, and so great mischief deuised against the Prince and the State. It appeareth their mindes are blinded with affection, that they cannot see the trueth.

AN other crime laide against Bishoppes, is, that they maintayn pilling and pouling, and (as some in despite terme them) bawdie courtes. If they maintayne courtes for the administration of Iustice, in such things as are within their charge: they doe, as I am perswaded by Gods law they may doe, and as by the lawes of this Realme, and state of this Church they ought to doe. But if they mayntaine pouling in their Courtes, that (in deede) is worthy blame, and by no pretence can bee salued. For, as al Magistrates ought to deale vprightly, and without corruption: so principally, such as be Spirituall, and of the Church of God.

The quarrel of maintayning poulling Courts.

But howe is it prooued, that Bishops maintaine pouling Courtes? Surely, I knowe not: For they doe not lay it downe in particulars. If they did, I thinke the matter might easily be answered with good reason.

It may bee they thinke, the vnder-Officers take money and bribes, where they should not: For that is polling and extortion. If it bee so, it is euill, and not to be suffered, and vpon proofe, the Lawe appoynteth sharpe punishment. Though it bee true that they surmise in this case, that Officers are so corrupt: it is one thing to say, The Officers vse pouling and another to say, The bishop maintaineth a pouling Court.

A bishop may haue an euill Officer, whome yet he will not maintaine, no nor suffer, if hee knewe it, and be able to redresse it. I am in perswasion, there is no bishop in this Realme, but if it be complayned of, and proofe made vnto him, that his Officers take more then is prescribed by order and law that they may doe, but wil mislike with the thing, and doe his best to see it redressed: Or if hee will not, I fauour not their State so much, but that I could wish him to be punished himselfe. But if a bishops Officers shall be counted to poule, when they take no more then the ordinary fees and dueties by Lawe allowed, and the bishop, when he beareth with the same, shal bee called a maintainer of a poulling Court: this is a matter in a slaunderer to bee punished, and not a fault in a bishoppe to be blamed. By this meanes all the Courtes in *Englande* may bee defamed and called poulling Courtes, and the Officers or Iudges, vnder whose authoritie they stande, may be prerooued as maintayners of poulling Courtes. Bee it, that there is vnlawful taking in many Courts of this Realme, as happily there is in some by greedie Officers: were it therfore the duetie of christian and godly Subiects, to spread libels against the Prince or chiefe gouernours, as maintainers of corruption, briberie, and poulling?

An hard matter it is, in so corrupt times, for anie Magistrate, to warrant the doinges of all inferiour Officers: I pray God this making of exception to Courtes and Officers, goe no further then to the officers of bishops and of the Cleargy. Whatsoeuer they pretend, the very root of the matter is this: The whole State Ecclesiasticall, by the loosenesse of this time, is growen into hatred and contempt, and al inferiour subiectes disdaine in any point to bee ruled by them. And therfore when they be called, conuented and punished for such things, wherein they haue offended, or be brideled of that they would doe disorderly: they grudge at it, their stomackes rise against it, and thinke all that is done to be vnlawful, though it be neuer so iust. And because they are not able otherwise to be reuenged, they crie out, that they be cruel and pouling Courtes.

Obiection.

To cut off the whole matter, it will be said, that by the word of God it is not lawfull for bishops to haue such Courtes, nor to exercise such iurisdiction.

Answere.

Yet truely I must answere, that it is lawful for christian subiects to obey it, and vnlawful for them to kicke and spurne against it, seeing it standeth by authoritie of the Lawes, and of our christian and gracious Prince, by whom God hath sent to vs, and doeth continue with vs, the free course of his Gospell. But why may not a Bishop exercise iurisdiction, and haue a Court to iudge, determine, and ende matters? Surely Saint *Paule* saieth to *Timothie, Against a* 1 Tim. 5. *Priest or Elder, receiue no accusation, vnder two or three witnesses.* Here is an accuser: Heere is a person accused: heere are witnesses examined: here is a iudgement and deciding of the matter: therefore here is an exercise of iurisdiction, and a manner of a Court.

They will say, It was not Timothies Court onely, but ioyntly exercised with the residue of the Elders, that had the Gouernment.

Vndoubtedly, there is no such thing there in that place. The words are directed to *Timothie* onely: the adioyning of some other, is but the interpretation of some fewe: vpon which, to builde the necessity of a doctrine in the Church of Christ, is but hard dealing, and not sufficient to ground mens consciences vpon. And yet here note you, that by this place it is euident, that ecclesiasticall persons may haue, and vse iurisdiction.

To proue that bishoppes may not alone exercise iurisdiction, they adde Christes saying, *Matthew* 18. *If thy brother offend thee, goe and tel him his fault between thee and him alone. If he shall heare thee, thou hast wonne thy brother: but if he will not* heare thee, take yet with thee one or two : *if he will not heare then*, Dic Ecclesiæ, *tell it to the Church.*

Here (say they) we are willed to tell the Church : but the Church cannot be vnderstanded to be one person, as the Bishop, or such like.

First I answere, that by the consent of most Interpreters, that place speaketh not of the exercise of publique iurisdiction, but of a charitable proceeding in priuate offences. And Christes large discourse, which immediatly following he maketh vnto *Peter*, touching the forgiuing of them that doe offend vs, doth very euidently iustifie that meaning. If some do interprete the place otherwise (as I haue before said) Christians should not build thereupon a general doctrine of necessitie.

It will be asked what Christ meant when he said *Dic Ecclesiæ*. As some interprete it, he meant, *Tell the Gouernours of the Church :* After some other, *Tell it openly in the Church or congregation, as Hierome* saith, *Vt qui non potuit pudore saluari, saluetur opprobriis,* that is, *that hee which could not be saued by shame, might haue his saluation wrought by reproch.* For a great thing it is to one that hath any feare of God, to haue reproch in the face of the Church.

And to this interpretation, the most of the ancient writers agree.

Obiection.

They will reply, that at that time there were manie Presidents as it vvere, and gouernours of the Church, together vvith the chiefe Ministers in euery Congregation.

Answere.

I graunt it was so: But it doth not follow thereupon, that it is a commaundement, that for euer in all places and times, it should be so. I am not of that opinion, nor euer was any of the auncient writers, no more are sundry learned men of great credite at this time, *Quod vna semper debet esse œconomia Ecclesiæ,* that is, that the externall gouernement of the Church, should alwaies, ahd in all places be one, and specially by a College or company of Elders. When Christ sayd, *Tell the Church,* there was as yet no Christian church established: but Christ tooke his speech according to the state of the Iewes Church that then was, as in another place he saith, *If thy brother trespasse against thee, leaue thine offering before the altar.*

If they will gather by the former speech, *Tell the Church*, that of necessitie, they must haue a company of Elders, as then was in the Iewes church: why, let them make like collection of the latter, that of necessitie there must be altars in the church of Christ: the absurditie whereof will bee greater, then any good christian man will easily receiue.

Obiection.

They will say, the Apostles afterward, and the Primitiue Church did practise the same.

Answere.

That is not yet proued: but let them struggle while they that lust, they shall neuer find a commandement in the scriptures, charging that it should for euer be so. It were too great a bridle of christian liberty in things external, to cast vpon the church of Christ. So long as the church of God was in persecution vnder tyrants, it might well seeme to be the best and fittest order of Gouernment: But when God blessed his Church with Christian Princes, the Scriptures doe not take away that liberty, that with the consent of their godly magistrates they may haue that outwarde forme of iurisdiction, and deciding of Ecclesiastical causes, as to the state of the Countrey and people shall be most conuenient. And that libertie haue diuers reformed churches, since the restoring of the Gospell, vsed.

Now, as when other Churches in their externall order of Gouernment, differ from ours, we neither do, nor ought, to mislike with them: so if ours differ from theirs, retaining still the sinceritie of the gospel and trueth of doctrine, I trust they will euen as charitably thinke of vs.

If any desire further aunswere in this controuersy of Church gouernment, I referre them to the reply of D. *Bridges*, vntill they haue with modesty and grauitie answered his booke.

It is obiected also against Bishops, that they abuse Ecclesiasticall Discipline. I take Ecclesiasticall Discipline to consist in reproouing, correcting and excommunicating such as be offendors in the Church. And I thinke their meaning is here, that bishops and their officers abuse *Excommunication*, in punishing therewith those persons, which obstinately and with contempt refuse, eyther to appeare, when *[The crime of abusing Ecclesiastical Discipline.]*

they bee called to aunswere their offences: or when they appeare, disobey those orders and decrees by Ecclesiasticall officers appoynted. Howe this part of Church Discipline was abused by the Pope, it is well knowen: and that hee made *Excommunication* an instrument to bring the neckes of Emperors and Princes, vnder his girdle, and to make the whole world subiect to him. For this was almost the onely meane, whereby he became so dreadfull to all men, and got to himself so great autoritie. The perpetual course of the histories, euen such as were written by his owne Parasites, and chiefly of this Realme of *England*, declare this to be most true. For trial hereof, reade the historie of *Thomas Becket*.

But I thinke no man is so caried with the misliking of our Bishops, that he wil accuse them, in this sort to abuse *Excommunication:* seeing by their preaching they haue bin principall instruments to ouerthrow the same in the Church of *Rome*.

They can not say, that any Bishoppe of this Church, euer since the restoring of the Gospell, indeuoured to excommunicate the Prince and gouernours, of purpose to make them subiect to their authoritie in the Church. And happily that may bee a fault, yea and a great fault that is found with them in these dayes, that they doe not so, and constraine the Prince and Rulers to doe that, which by perswasion they will not doe.

But howe expedient this maner of *Excommunication* is for this time, I leaue to the wise and godly to consider. Sure I
<small>Tygure.</small> am, that some of the most zealous Churches reformed haue it not, nor thinke it tollerable. And yet such a maner of *Excommunication* it is, that many striue at this day to haue brought into the Church, vnder the name of *Discipline*.

But how easily it would grow to abuse, and what danger it might bring in this state of time, I thinke there is no wise man that doeth not foresee: vnlesse it be such, as to bring their purpose to passe, and to settle their deuise in the Church, thinke no danger to be shunned.

As for the *Excommunication* practised in our Ecclesiasticall Courtes, for contumacie in not appearing, or not satisfying the iudgement of the Court: if it had pleased the Prince, and them that had authority to make Lawes for the gouernment, to haue altered the same at the beginning, and set some other order of processe in place thereof: I am perswaded the

Bishops and Clergie of this Realme would haue bene very well contented therewith.

Gualter a learned man of the Church of *Tygure*, writing vpon the first to the *Corinthians*, hauing shewed the danger of this other *Excommunication*, speaketh of a maner of ciuile discommuning, vsed in that Church: Which, or the like good order, deuised by some godly persons, if it might bee by aucthoritie placed in this Church, without danger of further innouation, I thinke it would be gladly receiued to shunne the offence that is taken at the other, and yet surely, vnder correction, the Lawe of alteration would breede some inconuenience.

But the perpetual crying of many to haue a mutation of the whole state of the Clergie, and a number of other thinges in the Church beside, (which must needes draw with it a great alteration in the state of the Realme also) maketh the Prince and other Gouernours to bee afrayde of any mutation. For they knowe what danger may come in these perillous dayes by innouations: And if they shoulde once beginne, things are so infinite, that they can see no ende of alterations. Therefore seeing wee haue a Church setled in a tollerable maner of reformation, and all trueth of doctrine freely taught and allowed by the autoritie of this Realme, yea, and the aduersaries of trueth by lawe repressed: they thinke it better to beare with some imperfections, then by attempting great alterations, in so dangerous a time, to hazard the state both of the Church and of the Realme. And the like toleration in some meane things, I vnderstand, vpon like consideration hath bene vsed in other Churches reformed beyond the Seas.

Obiection.

An other crime is obiected, not onely against Bishops, but against all other of the Clergie, that is,

Ambition and greedie seeking after liuings and promotions. If a benefice fall voyde (say they) then rideth he, then writeth hee, then laboureth he, then inquireth hee, who can doe most with the Patrone. And if he be a Lay-man, then at the least, a reasonable composition will serue: And if the Bishop haue the gift, then Master Chancellor, or Master Steward, or my Lords Secretarie, or my Mistresse his wife, must helpe to worke the matter.

The quarrell of ambition, and seeking of liuings.

Answere.

Doe you not see, how this malicious spirite passeth ouer all the good gifts, that God hath in these dayes bestowed on a number of learned men, to the great ornament of this land? and of purpose onely to deface the Church, taketh holde of those imperfections and blemishes, which the corruption of mans nature, specially in so perillous times, and so large a Church, must needes worke in a number? Well writeth *Basile, Quemadmodum vultures &c. As vultures or carren Rauens flye away to stinking carcasses and passe ouer many sweet medowes, and many sweete sauouring places: And as the flies shun the whole and sounde places of the body, and rest onely vpon scabs and soares, out of which they suck matter to nourish them: euen so the enuious, malitious, and backbiting spirite, passeth ouer all the ornaments and worthy commendations of the liues of men, and carpeth and biteth at those things that he findeth worthy blame.*

[marginal note: De inuidia.]

This Realme of *England* neuer had so many learned men, nor of so excellent gift in deliuering the word of God: It is the greatest ornament, that euer this church had. For my part, surely, I doe reuerence and maruell at the singular giftes of God that I see in manie. But these thinges bee wincked at, and passed with silence, and the ambitious doings of some few, brought in, as matter to discredite the whole number of Preachers.

Diogenes, seeing the cleanly furniture of *Plato* his house, got vp vpon his bed, and trampled on it with his dirtie feete, saying, *Calco fastum Platonis*, that is, *I contemne and tread vnder my feet the pride of* Plato. *True it is*, quoth *Plato, sed alio fastu, with another pride-woorse then mine.* So these men, in rebuking ambition, reach at an higher authoritie and power, then any bishop in *England* hath or will vse.

Ambition, I knowe and confesse, is very wicked, and hath euer bene a perillous instrument of the deuil to make mischief. By this he drew our first parents to the disobedience of the commandement of God, perswading them not to be content with that happy state that God had placed them in. By this he incensed *Corah, Dathan,* and *Abiram* with other, to rebel against *Moses* and *Aaron*. By this he thought to ouercome Christ, when he sawe hee could not preuaile by other meanes. By this he hath always raysed discorde, dissention, rebellion, warre and tumult, not onely to the troubling and disquieting, but to the shaking and ouerthrowing almost of all common weales that euer haue beene, and thereby also hath wrought the murther and destruction of an infinite number of the creatures of God. By this he hath from time to time raised many schismes and heresies in the Church of Christ. By this, vndoubtedly I thinke he worketh no small euill nowe at this day, in this our church of *Englande*. But what then? Doe they thinke, that if the bishoppes landes, and the rich liuings of the Cleargie be taken away, that they shal extinguish *Ambition* in the heartes of the Ministers? Was there no *Ambition* in the church before that bishoppes had lands, or before Preachers had so large liuinges? No man can so thinke, but they that are ignorant of the Ecclesiasticall histories. What was the first roote of the troublesome schisme of the *Donatists*? Whereof sprang first the heresies of the *Nouatians* at *Rome*? What gaue the first occasion of the pestilent heresie of the *Arians*? What maintayned and continued it? was it not *Ambition*, and seeking of preheminence? But what shoulde I number vp anie more examples? Fewe schismes and heresies in the church, but had their beginning out of this roote. And many knowe, that a repulse of a dignitie desired, was the first cause that our schisme brake foorth, and hath so eagerly continued. Surely, though I confesse, that I see and knowe in our Church more corruption that way, then I am gladde to beholde, and so much especially in some kinde of Ministers, as I praie GOD by some sharpe order may bee diminished: yet this I dare stande to iustifie, that all the enemies of the bishoppes, and better sort of the cleargie, shall neuer be able to proue, notwithstanding the daunger of this corrupt time, that there is at this day in this Realme, such heauing and shoouing, such canuasing and woorking for bishoprikes and other Ecclesiasticall liuinges, as I will declare vnto them to haue beene in the ancient time aboue a thousand yeeres since, in the best state that euer was in the Church, from the Apostles age vnto this time. That there is no *Ambition* vsed among vs, (as I haue saide) I dare not affirme: but surely, if there be anie, there can be no *Ambition* on the one part, but there must bee corruption on the other: therefore let them look vnto themselues, that haue authoritie to bestow the liuings. The best sorte of the Ecclesiasticall liuings are in the disposition of the Princes authoritie. And those honorable that haue to doe therein, and are counsailers to her Maiestie, be not so vnwise, but they can espy Ambition in him that sueth and laboureth for them. And if they doe perceiue it, they are verie greatly to blame, if they suffer it to escape without open shame, or other notable punishment, and thereby bring suspition, eyther vpon themselues, or vpon those that bee about them.

As for the corruption in bestowing other meaner liuinges, the chiefe fault thereof is in Patrones themselues. For it is the vsuall manner of the most part of them (I speake of too good experience) though they may haue good store of able men in the Vniuersities, yet if an ambitious or greedie Minister come not vnto them, to sue for the benefice, if there be an vnsufficient man, or a corrupt person within two shires of them, whom they thinke they can drawe to any composition for their owne benefit, they wil by one meanes or other finde him out. And if the bishop shal make courtesie to admitte him, some such shift shall be found by the law, either by *Quare impedit*, or otherwise, that whether the bishop will or no, he shall be shifted into the benefice. I know some bishops, vnto whom such sutes against the Patrones haue beene more chargeable in one yeere, then they haue gained by all the Benefices that they haue bestowed since they were bishoppes, or I thinke will doe, while they bee bishoppes. They haue iniurie therefore, to bee so openly slaundered in the face of the worlde. If there bee any bishoppe that corruptly bestoweth his liuinges by sute of Maister Chauncellor, or Maister Steward, or anie other: looke what punishment I woulde haue any lay-man in that case to sustaine, I would wish to a bishop double or triple.

Obiection.

But now I must come to that which toucheth bishops most nighly, that is,

The obiection, that the Bishops bee carnall and worldly disposed. that they be carnally disposed, and not euangelically, and this their affection and corruption they shew to the worlde, by hoarding of great summes of money, by purchasing lands for their wiues and children, by marrying their sonnes and daughters with thousands, by increasing their liuings with flockes and heards of grased cattell, by furnishing their tables with plate and guilded cups, by filling their purses with vnreasonable fines and incomes, &c.

Answere.

Wee heare in this place an heape of grieuous offences, and indeed, if they be true, wel worthy such lamentable outcries, as are made against them. But the godly must consider, that where lauishing tongues and pennes be at libertie, to lay forth reproch without feare of correction or punishment, that the best men in the worlde may be slandered and brought in danger, especially where through enuie and malice men haue conceiued displeasure against any State.

Eustathius, a godly and chaste Bishop, by conspiracie and false suggestion of certaine Heretikes and Schis- matikes, was not accused onely, but uniustly also condemned of adulterie, and by the Emperor *Constantine* cast into banishment, into a Citie of *Sclauonie*. *Cyrillus* a good and learned father, Bishop of *Hierusalem*, and an earnest patrone of the true faith of Christ, was by the heretike *Acasius*, and his friends in the Court, accused to the Emperor *Constantinus*, that he had imbezeled the Church goods, and had solde to a player of Enterludes, a rich garment, giuen to the Church by his father. [Theod. Lib. 1. cap. 20.] [Soz. Lib. 4. cap. 26. Socr. Lib. 2. cap. 30.]

This false accusation so much preuailed, that the good Bishop was for it deposed &c. I noted you the like before of that blessed man *Athanasius* and other, and might bring a great number of examples, out of the Ecclesiasticall histories and writers. For it was the vsuall practise of all such as did endeuour to furnish any heresie or Schismaticall faction, were they of the Clergie or Laitie, by all meanes they coulde, through infamie and discredite, to pull downe such as did withstand their euil and troublesome attempts in the Church, and not onely to raile at them, and to deface them with false and vniust reports, but also to draw to their reproch their best and most Christian doings: as the charitable dealing of *Cyrill*, was so wrested, that it brought him to great danger. And surely I cannot but feare, that the deuill is euen now in hatching of some notable heresies, or some other hid mischiefes, which hee woulde bring foorth, and thrust into the Church of England, and therfore prepareth the way for the same, by defacing and discrediting the best learned of the church, that both would and should resist them. This we see already in that peeuish [Athan. Apol. 2.]

faction of the *families of the loue*, which haue bin breeding in this Realme the space of these thirty yeeres, and now vpon confidence of the disgracing of the state of Bishops, and other Ecclesiasticall Gouernours, haue put their heads out of the shell, and of late yeeres, haue shewed themselues, euen in the Princes Court. The like I might say of the *Anabaptists* and other Sectaries, as bad as they.

As touching this present point of the accusation of Bishops, I haue to admonish the godly reader, that in Christian charitie and wisedome they consider, aswell, what diuers of those persons which now be Bishops, haue bene before time: as also, in what state they are nowe in this Realme, and howe they are beset on euery side with aduersaries and euill speakers of diuers sortes, and then to weigh with themselues, whether it bee likely that all is true, which is vttered against them, or rather that for despite and displeasure, many things are spoken falsly and slanderously, and many other meane and small blemishes amplified and exaggerated to the worst, more then trueth.

That those which nowe be, or of late haue bene Bishops in this Church, shoulde be so carnally and grosly giuen ouer to the world and the cares therof, as they are by some defamed: my heart abhorreth to thinke, neither will the feare of God suffer me to iudge it to be true. I see what they are presently in all trueth of doctrine: I see how earnestly and zealously they teach and defend the same in their preachings: I see howe carefully they beate downe the grosse superstition of Antichrist and his ministers: I call to remembrance, that of late yeeres, in the time of persecution, when the most of them were in state well able to liue, that they were contented for the freedome of their consciences, and that they might enioy the doctrine and liberty of the Gospel, to forsake their liuings, to leaue their friendes, to hazard their liues, to bee accompted Traitours, and to sustaine all those miseries and troubles, that might followe vpon banishment, and casting out of their Countrey.

And I see nothing in them, if God, as wee by our vnthankefulnesse daily deserue, should cast the like scourge vpon this Realme againe, but that they would be most readie to do the same, although happily prosperitie in the meane time may drawe them to some offences. May any Christian heart then conceiue of them, although there be faults in them moe then the worthinesse of their office requireth, that they be so carnally and fleshly giuen ouer to the world, as the immodest accusations of many their aduersaries do make them? Mans nature is corrupt and fraile, and therfore may fal to much euil: but that so many learned men trained in the scoole of the Crosse, and continuing in teaching and preaching of the trueth, should be so vtterly caried away from God, I can not beleeue, and I trust, God shall giue some euident token of the contrary. If there now be, or before time haue bene such, as haue giuen iust occasion in such things, as they are accused of: I cannot but blame them, and wish to the residue more feare of God, and care of their calling. I neuer entred into other mens hearts to see their consciences: I neuer looked into their Cofers to see their treasures: I neuer was desirous to be priuie of their secret doings. I must therfore by what I see, heare, and know, iudge the best.

He that shall charitably consider the state of Bishops, as they are by the authoritie of the Prince and lawes of this Realme, will not thinke it impietie in them, against the time of neccessary seruice of their countrey, to haue some reasonable summe of money before hand, gathered in honestie, and iust vsing of their owne. But if they hoarde vp heapes, either for greedinesse and loue of riches, or of perswasion to put their trust in them in time of affliction, as they are reported: surely their offence cannot be excused.

As touching their purchasing of lands, I haue not heard much. The greatest value that euer I heard of, doth scant amount to one hundred pound: and that in very few, scarce to the number of 3. persons. Which in them, that so long time haue enioyed so large benefit of liuing, may seeme no great matter, especially toward the relieuing of their wiues and children.

Obiection.

They will say perhaps, that Preachers shoulde not bee so carefull for their children, nor Bishops ought not to make their wiues Ladies.

Answere.

If any looke to leaue them like Ladies in wealth and riches, they are to blame: but moderatly to prouide for their wiues and children, I thinke them bound in conscience, especially in this vncharitable, vnkind, and vnthankfull world. For we may see the wiues and children of diuers honest and godly Preachers, yea, and of some bishops also, that haue giuen their blood for the confirmation of the Gospel, hardly to scape the state of begging, euen among vs that professe the Gospel, to our great and horrible shame. The sight whereof, I thinke, doth moue some bishops, and other Ecclesiasticall persons, to bee the more careful for their wiues and children, that they may haue some stay after their time, and not to bee turned to liue vppon Almes, where charitie and Christian consideration is so cleane banished. Ecclesiasticall persons are not as other parents are. For so soon as they depart this life, or otherwise bee put from their liuing, because they haue no state but for life, their wiues and children without consideration are turned out of the doores. And if in their husbandes time they haue not some place prouided, they hardly can tel how to shift for themselues. And surely experience teacheth mee so much, that I must needs bewaile and lament the pitiful case of diuers honest matrons, and poore infants, which in my knowledge, at the death of their husbands and fathers, haue beene driuen to great hazard and distresse. And this causeth, that most honest women, of sober and good behauior, are loath to match with ministers, though they be neuer so wel learned, bicause they see their wiues so hardly bested, when they are dead. They that are not mooued with this, haue but colde zeale toward the Gospel.

And seeing the case is so among vs in this realme: as he is worse then an heathen by S. *Paules* iudgement, that in his life time doth not prouide for his familie: so surely hee cannot escape the blame of an vnkinde husband, or vnnatural parent, that hath not some care of his wife and children, after his time.

I write not this to defend the peruerse or couetous affection of any, neyther doe I thinke that there be manie such in this church. Diuers I knowe, that when God shall call them, will leaue so litle, as their children, as I think, must commend themselues only to the prouidence of God. And therefore it is not well, that the fault of a fewe (if any such be) should bee taken as a matter, to discredite the whole calling.

But surely, they that murmure so greatly against the moderate prouision of the wiues and children of Ecclesiasticall persons, and turne that as matter of haynous slaunder vnto them : let them pretend what they will, it may be suspected, they scantly think wel of their marriages : Or if they doe, the very Papistes themselues are more fauourable and charitable Aduersaries to Preachers, then they are. For seeing the state of our Church alloweth Ministers to be married, they think it to stand with godly reason also, that they should in honestie prouide for their wiues and children.

Diuers persons of other calling, by the exercise of an office onely in fewe yeeres, can purchase for wife and children many hundreds, and all very well thought of : But if a bishop, that by state of the lawe hath the right vse of a large liuing many yeeres, doe purchase one hundred Markes, or procure a mean Lease for the helpe of his wife and children, it is accompted greedie couetousnesse, and mistrust in the prouidence of God. I woulde it were not spite and enuie, with greedie desire of bishops Liuinges, that caused this euill speeche, rather then their couetous and corrupt dealing. They feare that all will be taken from themselues.

As touching that bishops are blamed for taking of vnreasonable Fines, and furnishing their Cupboardes with siluer vessel and plate, I trust euery charitable man, that hateth not the present state, may easily see what is to be answered. To take Fines for their leases and landes, is as lawful for them, by the word of God, and by the law of this Realme, as for any other christian subiect, that hath possessions. And likewise, to haue plate or siluer vessell, their condition beeing considered, is a thing indifferent, and not worthy so great reproch or biting speech as is vsed. If they had not such furniture, it is likely a great number woulde thinke euil of it, and in another sort blame them as much for it. But if they take immoderate Fines, or let vnreasonable Leases, to the grieuing and burthening of their poore and honest Tenants : or if they pompously auaunce themselues, and set their glory in the gorgious plate and gay furniture : I am so farre from defending that abuse that I will bee as ready to blame them, as any man. And so much do I mislike such dealing in them, as I would wish those that can be found faultie in these thinges, by the Princes and Gouernours to bee examined and tryed, and vpon iust and lawfull proofe of their offences, to be punished according to their demerits ; And, if the weight

Of taking of Fines, &c.

of matter so required, to be deposed, for the example of other, and better set in their places. But if that trial were made, as some faults perchance might be found vnworthy their calling: so I am in hope, they would not appeare so great and so grieuous, as to the discrediting of their doctrine, should deserue so heinous and bitter exclamations, and so reprochful Libels, as are giuen abroad against them. Faults, in al states, and specially of ministers, would be examined, tried, iudged and punished, by the lawe and ordinary Magistrates: and not an vnchristian loosenesse and liberty left to vnquiet and vngodly subiects, either by euil speeches, or vncharitable writings to slander them, and bring them into hatred and misliking. The example wherof may grow to great danger, and hath bene counted perillous in all common weales, and much more in the Church of God.

But, I pray you, what is meant by this disgracing of bishops, and other chiefe ministers of the church? For what purpose are their liues in such sort blazed? to what ende are their doings so defamed? Why is their corruption, their couetousnesse, their Simony, their extortion, and al other vices, true or false, laide abroad before mens eyes? Why is the perfect rule of their office and calling, according to the patterne of the Apostles time, required at their hands onely? Is God the God of Ecclesiasticall Ministers alone? Is he not the God of his people also? doth he require his word to be exactly obserued of bishops and ministers alone? doth he hate vice and wickednes in them alone? Or doth he lay downe the rule of perfect Iustice to them only, and not comprehend in the same all other states of his people, as well as them? Yes truely, I thinke no Christian is otherwise perswaded.

Obiection.

Perhaps they will say, that all other States do wel, and liue according to their calling. The word of God is sincerely euery where imbraced: Iustice is vprightly in all places ministered: the poore are helped and relieued: vice is sharpely of all other men corrected: there is no corruption, no couetousnesse, no extortion, no Simonie, no vsurie, but in the Bishops, and in the Clergie. There are no Monopolies in this Realme practised to the gaine of a fewe, and the vndoing of great multitudes, that were wont to liue by those trades. All courtes be without fault, and voyde of corruption, sauing the Ecclesiasticall courts onely. All officers are vpright and true dealers sauing theirs. None other doe so carefully and couetously prouide for their wiues and children. They onely giue the example of all euill life.

Answere.

I would to God it were so : I would to God there were no such euils as are recited, but in them : Yea, I woulde to God there were no worse then in them, on condition that neuer a Bishoppe in England had one groate to liue vpon. The want surely of the one would easily be recompensed with the goodnesse of the other.

What then is the cause that Bishops and Preachers haue in these dayes so great fault founde with them? Forsooth it followeth in the next branch of a certaine Accusation penned against them.

Obiection.

They have Temporall landes, they haue great liuings, They are in the state of Lordes &c. The Prince ought therefore to take away the same from them, and set them to meane Pensions, that in pouertie they may bee answerable to the Apostles, and other holy Preachers in the Primitiue Church : whereby the Queene may bring 40000 markes yeerely to her Crowne, beside the pleasuring of a great many of other her faithfull subiects and seruants. *The principall cause why the Bishops be so depraued.*

Answere.

This is the end, why Bishops and other chiefe of the Clergie are so defaced, why their doings are so depraued, why such common obloquies is in all mens mouthes vpon them raised, that is to say, that the mindes of the Prince and Gouernours, may thereby be induced to take away the lands and liuings from them, and to part the same among themselues, to the benefite (as some thinke) and to the commoditie of their Countrey and common weale. But it behooueth all Christian Princes and Magistrates to take heede, that they bee not intrapped with this sophistrie of Satans schoole. This is that Rhetorike that he vseth, when he wil worke any mischief in the Church of God, or stirre vp any trouble or alteration of a state in a common weale.

First by defaming and slandering, he bringeth the parties in hatred and misliking, and when the peoples heads be filled therewith, then stirred he vp busie and vnquiet persons to reason thus :

They be wicked and euil men : they are couetous persons: they oppresse the poore : they pill other to inrich themselues : they passe not what they doe, so they may grow to honour and wealth, and beare all the sway in the countrey. Therfore bring them to an accompt : let them answere their faults : pul them downe : alter their state and condition : let vs no more be ruled vnder such tyrants and oppressours : we are Gods people as well as they. *Did not he deale thus in Corah, Dathan, and Abiram? did he not by them, charge the milde and gentle Gouernour Moses, and his brother Aaron, the chosen Priest of God, that they tooke too much vpon them? that they lifted themselues vp aboue the congregation of the Lord, and behaued themselues too Lordly ouer his people? that they brought the Israelites out of a land flowing with milke and honie, of purpose to worke vnto themselues a dominion ouer the people, and to make them to perish in the wildernesse?* By this meanes they so incensed the hearts, not onely of the common people, but of the Noblemen also, that they led a great number with them to rebell against *Moses* and *Aaron*, and to set themselues in their roomes and offices. In like maner, and by like policie, hath hee wrought in all common weales, in all ages and times, as the histories doe sufficiently declare.

Nomb. 16.

In this Realme of England, when the lewde and rebellious subiects rose against *K. Richard* 2. and determined to pull downe the state, and to dispatch out of the way the counsellers, and other Noble and worshipfull men, together with Iudges, Lawyers, and al other of any wise or learned calling in the Realme: was not the way made before, and their states brought in hatred of the people, as cruell, as couetous, as oppressours of the people, and as enemies of the Common weale, yea, and a countenance made vnto the cause, and a grounde sought out of the Scriptures and word of God, to helpe the matter ?

At the beginning (say they) when God had first made the worlde, all men were alike, there was no principalitie, there was no bondage, or villenage : that grewe afterwardes by violence and crueltie. Therefore, why should we liue in this miserable slauerie vnder these proud Lords and craftie Lawyers ? &c. Wherefore it behooueth all faithfull Christians and wise Gouernours, to beware of this false and craftie policie. If this Argument passe nowe, and be allowed as good at this time against the Ecclesiasticall state: it may be, you shall hereafter by other instruments, then yet are stirring, heare the same reason applied to other States also, which yet seeme not to be touched, and therefore can be content to winke at this dealing toward Bishops and Preachers. But when the next house is on fire, a wise man will take heed, least the sparkes thereof fall into his owne. He that is authour of all perillous alterations, and seeketh to worke mischief by them, will not attempt all at once, but will practise by little and little, and make euery former feate that he worketh, to be a way and meane to draw on the residue. For he seeth all men wil not be ouercome with all temptations, nor will not be made instruments of all euill purposes, though happily by his colours and pretenses he be able to deceiue them in some. The practise hereof, wee haue seene in this Church of England, to the great trouble and danger thereof. At the beginning, some learned and godly Preachers, for priuate respects in themselues, made strange to weare the *Surplesse*, *Cap*, or *Tippet*, but yet so, that they declared themselues to thinke the thing indifferent, and not to iudge euil of such as did vse them. Shortly after rose vp other, defending that they were not thinges indifferent, but distayned with Antichristian idolatrie, and therefore not to bee suffered in the Church. Not long after came forth an other sort, affirming that those matters touching Apparell, were but trifles, and not worthie contention in the Church, but that there were greater things of farre more weight and importance, and indeede touching faith and religion, and therefore meete to be altered in a Church rightly refourmed: As *the booke of Common prayer, the adminstration of the Sacraments, the gouernment of the Church, the election of Ministers*, and a number of other like.

Fourthly, now breake out another sort, earnestly affirming and teaching, that we haue no Church, no Bishops, no Ministers, no Sacraments: and therfore that all they that loue Iesus Christ, ought with all speede to separate themselues from our congregation, because our assemblies are prophane, wicked, and Antichristian.

Hus haue you heard of foure degrees prepared for the ouerthrow of this State of the Church of England.

Now lastly of all, come in these men, that make their whole direction against the liuing of bishops, and other Ecclesiasticall ministers :

<small>Against the rich Liuings of Bishops.</small> that they shoulde haue no Temporal landes, or iurisdiction : that they shoulde haue no stayed liuings or possession of goods, but onely a reasonable Pension to finde them meate, drinke, and cloth, and by the pouertie of their life, and contempt of the world, to be like the Apostles. For (say they) riches and wealth hath brought all corruption into the Church before time, and so doth it now.

Answere.

Nowe is the enemie of the Church of God come almost to the point of his purpose. And if by discrediting of the Ministers, or by countenance of gaine and commoditie to the Prince and Nobilitie, or by the colour of Religion and holinesse, or by any cunning he can bring this to passe (as before I haue signified) hee foreseeth that learning, knowledge of good letters, and studie of the tongues, shall decay, as wel in the Vniuersities, as other wayes, which haue bene the chiefe instruments to publish and defend the doctrine of the Gospel, and to inlarge the kingdome of Christ : And then, of necessitie, his kingdome of darknesse, errour and heresie must rise againe, and leaue this land in worse state, then euer it was before.

But to perswade this matter more pithily, to couer the principal purpose with a cloake of holinesse, it is saide, and in very earnest manner auouched, and that by the word of God, that neyther the Prince can giue it them, nor suffer them to vse it, without the danger of Gods wrath and displeasure : nor they ought to take it, but to deliuer it vp againe into the Princes hand, or els they shal shew themselues Antichristian Bishops, vaine glorious, and lucres men, not ashamed, professing God to continue in that drossie way, and sowre lump of dough, that corrupteth the whole Church, and brought out the wicked botch of Antichrist. &c.

This doctrine (as it is boldly affirmed) God himselfe hath vttered, Christ hath taught, his Apostles haue written the Primitiue church continued, the holy Fathers witnessed, the late writers vphold, as it must forsooth bee prooued by the whole course of the scriptures of the olde and new Testament.

But (good Christians) be not feared away with this glorious

countenance, and these bigge wordes of a bragging champion. I trust you shall perceiue, that this doctrine is neither vttered by God, nor taught by Christ, nor written by his Apostles, nor witnessed by ancient writers, nor vpholden by learned men of our time: but that it is rather a bolde and dangerous assertion, vttered by some man of very small skill, countenanced with a few wrested Scriptures, contrary to the true meaning of God the father, Christ his sonne, and of his holy Apostles, and a little shadowed with vaine allegations of writers, either of no credite, or little making to the purpose. And surely, how great and earnest zeale, how vehement and lofty wordes so euer the vtterer of this assertion vseth: it may be suspected, that either he is not himself soundly perswaded in true religion, or if he be, that of simplicity, negligence or ignorance, he was abused by some subtile and crafty Papist, that woulde sette him forth to the derision of other, to thrust out into the world, and openly broach this corrupt and daungerous doctrine.

Wherfore it were good, that they which wil take vpon them to be the furtherers of such new deuises, should better looke to their proofe and witnesses, vnlesse they will seeme to abuse al men, and to thinke that they liue in so loose and negligent a state, that nothing shal be examined that they speake, but that al things shal be as easily receiued, as they may be boldly vttered. But I trust, those that haue the feare of God, and care of their soules, wil not be afraid of vaine shadowes, nor by and by beleeue all glorious brags, but take heed that they be not easily led out of the way, by such as wil so quickly be deceiued themselues.

I do not answere their vaine Arguments, because I feare that any discreet or learned man wil be perswaded with them: but because I mistrust, that the simple and ignorant people, or other that be not acquainted with the Scriptures, by the very name and reuerence of the word of God, will be carried away, without iust examination of them.

To descend something to the consideration of the matter, marke, I pray you, the Proposition that is to be proued. It is not, that they may bee good bishops and ministers of the Church, which haue neither glebe nor temporal lands to liue on: It is not, that there were in the primitiue church, and now are in sundry places, churches well gouerned, which haue not lands allotted vnto them: It is not, that the Apostles had no lands, nor any other a number of yeeres after Christ: For these points, I thinke no man wil greatly stand with them. But this is the Assertion.

Obiection.

No prince or magistrate by Gods word may lawfully assigne lands to the ministers of the church to liue on, but ought to set them to pensions: Nor any of the Ecclesiasticall state can by the Scriptures enioy, or vse any such lands, but shoulde deliuer them vp to the Prince, &c.

Answere.

Looke, I pray you, vpon this Assertion, and consider it well. Doe you not see in it, euen at the first, euident absurditie? Doe you not see a plaine restraint of christian liberty, as bold and as vnlawfull a restraint as euer the Pope vsed any? Do you not espy almost a flat heresie, as dangerous as many branches of the Anabaptists errors? It is no better then an heresie to say, that by the word of God it is prohibited for Ministers to marry. It is no better then an heresie to affirme that Christian men, by the lawe of God, may not eate fleshe, or drinke wine. Saint *Paule* doth _{1. Tim. 4.} consecrate these to be *Doctrines of Deuiles*, and therefore not of the Church of God: and the Primitiue church _{Theodoret.} doeth confirme these to bee heresies in *Saturninus*, _{Epiphan.} _{Clem. Alex.} *Marcion, Tatian, Montane,* and many other. And I pray you, what doth this Assertion differ from the other, when it is said, It is not lawful for Ecclesiastical persons to _{Gen. 3.} haue temporal lands to liue vppon? As marriage is the ordinance of God, and left free by his word to all men: As meates and drinkes are the good creatures of our God, and to be vsed of all such as receiue them with thankesgiuing: so are landes, possessions, money, cattaile, the good gifts of God, and the right vse of them, not prohibited to any of his people: For to their benefite he ordained them, as his good blessings. Christ by his death made vs free from all such legall obseruations. Therefore S. *Paul. Colos.* 2. *If ye be dead with Christ to the iudgements of the worlde, why are you ledde with traditions, Touch not, Taste not, Handle not, which all doe perish in abusing?* This boldnesse to bridle Christian libertie, and to make it sinne and matter of conscience, to vse the creatures of God, was the very foundation of al Papistical and

Antichristian superstition. Vpon this foundation was builded the holinesse in vsing, or not vsing of this, or that maner of apparell: in eating or forbearing these or those kindes of meates: in obseruing this or that day, or time of the yeere: in keeping this or that externall forme of life, with 1000. like inuentions and traditions of men. Neither do I thinke euer any errour did greater harme in the Church, or brought more corruption of doctrine then that did. Therefore I am sorie to see some in these daies, to leane so much to that dangerous stay, for the helpe of their strange opinions in things externall. For, what doe men meane when they say, It is not lawfull for a Christian man to weare a square Cappe, to vse a Surplesse, to kneele at the Communion? What (I say) doe they but bridle Christian libertie, and to the burden of consciences, make sinnes where GOD made none? And in like maner, hee that sayeth, It is wicked and not lawfull, that Bishops, Preachers, or Ecclesiasticall persons shoulde haue any temporall landes to liue vpon, hee seemeth to finde fault with the creature of God. For, that Bishops may haue liuing allowed them, is not denied: but to liue by landes, that (say they) is sinne, and prohibited, and therefore the temporall lands and glebe must be taken from Bishops and [o]ther Ministers.

This doctrine notwithstanding, must be proued and iustified by the Scriptures, and first by the ordinance of God himselfe in the olde testament. In the *Numbers*, when God had declared to *Aaron* what portion he shoulde haue to liue vpon, hee addeth: *Thou shalt haue no inheritance in their land, neither shalt thou haue any part among them. I am thy part, and thy inheritance among the children of Israel. Behold, I haue giuen the children of Leui all the tenth of Israel to inherit, for the seruice which they serue in the Tabernacle.* And againe after, *It shalbe a law for euer in your generations, that among the children of Israel, they possesse no inheritance.* And in Deut. 10. *the Lord separated the tribe of Leui, &c. Wherefore the Leuites haue no part, nor inheritance with their Brethren, but the Lorde is their inheritance, as the Lord thy God hath promised them.* In the 14. Chapter, and in the 18. and in diuers other parts of the law, and in *Iosua* 14. *Moses gave inheritance vnto two tribes and a halfe, on the other side of Iordan, but vnto the Leuites hee gaue no inheritance among them.* Vpon these

(Bishops must haue no lands.)

(Numb. 18. The answere to the obiection of the lawe and ordinance of God.)

testimonies, the application and conclusion is inferred in this maner.

Obiection.

Here it may bee seene what liuing God appoynted his Priestes to haue: not landes and possessions, but tithes and offerings. Seing then God denied it to his Priestes, it is not lawfull for our Priestes. Whose Priestes are they? If they be Gods Priests, it is not there permitted: If they be Antichrists priests, what doe we with them?

Answere.

As this reason may haue some small shew or likelihoode to the ignorant: so I am sure, they that haue trauiled in the Scriptures, and any thing vnderstand the state of Christianitie, will marueile to see this application of the Texts and the conclusion inferred. Shall the Ministers of the Church of God, nowe in the time of grace, by necessitie be bound to those orders that were among the Iewes appoynted for Priestes and Leuites by *Moses*? Will they bring the heauie yoke and burthen of the Law againe vpon the people of God, after that Christ hath redeemed vs, and set vs free from it? Will they haue Aaronicall and sacrificing Priestes againe to offer for the sinnes of the people? When it was in derision asked, Whose Priests ours are, if they be not Gods Priests? giuing signification that they be the Priestes of Antichrist, it may be right well and truely answered, that they are the Priestes of Gods holy blessed, and true Church, and yet that they are not such sacrificing Priests of God, as are mentioned in those places, nor in any way bounde to those thinges that they were, the morall Lawe of God onely excepted.

Obiection.

It is obiected to our Bishops and Ministers, that in their Landes and possessions, they reteine the corruption of the Romish Church.

Answere.

But I marueile to see them which so boldely controll other, to builde their assertions vpon the ruinous foundations of the Synagogue of Antichrist. As I noted a little before, that they layde their grounde vpon the restraint of Christian libertie: so nowe they settle it vpon the imitation of the legall and Aaronicall priesthood, as the Church of *Rome* did.

The aduersaries build vpon Popish foundations.

Whence (I pray you) came the massing apparel, and almost all the furniture of their Church in censing and singing and burning of Tapers ? their altars, their propitiatorie sacrifice, their high Bishop and generall head ouer all the Church, with a number of other corruptions of the Church of God, but onely out of this imitation of this Aaronical priesthood and legall obseruations ? Surely, while they thus vphold as good, the wicked foundations of the Synagogue of Sathan, they shall neuer so purely builde vp the Church of Christ, as they woulde bee accounted to doe. They may seeme to be in a hard streight, that to batter down the state of the Church of *England*, must craue ayde of Antichrist, to set vp a fort vpon his foundation.

The learned fathers of the primitiue Church, did, so much as they coulde, striue to be furthest off from the imitation of the Iewes, and of the Aaronicall priesthood, in so much that they woulde needes alter not onely the Sabboth day, but also the solemnizing of the feast of Easter : And shall the Lawe of the Leuites, and maner of their liuing bee layde downe to vs as a patterne of necessitie, which the Prince must followe in reforming her Church, or else the priestes thereof shall not be the priestes of God, but of Antichrist ? Is there no more reuerence and feare of the maiestie of Gods Prince and sacred Minister, then by such grosse absurdities to seeke to seduce her ? If this bee a conclusion of such necessitie, then let them goe further : for by as good reason they may.

God sayeth to *Aaron, Thou shalt not drinke wine, nor strong drinke, thou, nor thy sonnes that are with thee, when yee* Leuit. 10. *goe into the Tabernacle of the Congregation, least yee dye. Let it bee a Lawe for euer throughout your generations.*

In another place commaundement is giuen to the Priestes, *That they may not eate of that which is rent of wilde* Leuit. 22. *beastes.* And in the same chapter, *If the Priests daughter be marryed to any of the common people, shee may not eate of the hallowed offerings : but if shee be a Widowe, or diuorced from her husbande, and haue no childe, and is returned into her fathers house againe, she may eate of her fathers meate, as she did in her youth, but there shall no stranger eate thereof.* In the 21. of Leuiticus it is sayde, *Speake vnto the Priests the sonnes of Aaron, and say, Let none bee defiled by the dead among their people.* And a litle after, *Let them not make baldnes vpon their head, nor shaue off* the locks of their beard. And againe, *Let him take a Virgine to wife: but a widowe, a diuorced woman, or a polluted &c. shall he not marry.*

Now if the obseruation of the orders appointed by God to the Priests and Leuites of the olde Law, be a thing so necessary in the church of God: Why, *then the Ministers of the Gospell may not drinke wine or strong drinke: they may not suffer their daughters married forth, if they come vnto their houses, to eate any of the tenths and oblations, whereby they liue: they may not come nigh a dead body, nor burie it: they may marry no widowes, but maydes onely.* And so likewise shall you bring in by as good authoritie, infinite numbers mo of Leuiticall orders into the Church, and make it rather like a superstitious Synagogue, as the Popes church was, then like a sincere and vndefiled Church of God, as you would pretend to doe.

But let vs descende further into this allegation, and see howe they ouerthrowe themselues in their owne purpose. If vpon this proofe it be so necessarie, that bishops and other Ministers shoulde not liue by Lands: then, as the negatiue is necessarie in the one branch, so is the affirmatiue in the other. When God hath sayd, *Thou shalt haue no inheritance in their land,* he addeth: *Beholde, I haue giuen the children of Leui all the tenth of Israel to inherite for the seruice, which they doe. &c.* Then it is of necessitie by the Lawe of God, that bishops and Preachers shoulde liue vpon Tenthes and offerings, neither may this order be altered by any authoritie.

And here is another errour of the Papists, that Tenths and offerings are in the Church *Iure diuino,* by the lawe of God, and not by any positiue Law of the Church. Thus we see that these men are not able to stand to their positions, but they must ioyne arme in arme with the Papists, in their greatest and grossest errors. And if it be of necessitie, that Ministers must liue by Oblations and tithes, and no otherwise: how can the Prince by Gods lawe take away their Landes, and set them to meere pensions in money? Or if Princes haue libertie by the Lawe of God, according to their discretions, to appoynt the liuings of Ministers, by pensions of money, contrary to the order that God hath prescribed his Priests in his law: why haue they not like authoritie by the same worde of God, (if they see it conuenient for the state) to allot vnto them some portion of temporall Landes, and much more, to suffer and beare with that order, beeing already settled in the Church? By this it appeareth, that the assertion of the aduersaries doeth not hang together in it selfe, but that the one part impugneth and ouerthroweth the other.

But mee thinkes these men deale not directly, but seeme to hide and conceale that which maketh against them. For in the same place of *Iosua*, by vvhich they vvill prooue, that bishoppes and Ministers may not haue any possession of Landes, because hee sayth, *To the Leuites he gaue no inheritance among them,* Immediatly he addeth, *Sauing Cities to dwell in, and the fieldes about the Cities, for their beastes and Cattell.* And in like manner, *The Lorde sayde to Moses, Commaund the children of Israel, that they giue vnto the Leuites of the inheritance of their possession, Cities to dwell in. And yee shall giue also vnto the Cities suburbes harde by their Cities rounde about them, the Cities they shall haue to dwell in, and the Suburbes or fieldes about their Cities for their cattell, and all manner beastes of theirs. And the Suburbes of the Cities which you shall giue to the Leuites, shall reache from the wall of the Citie rounde about outwarde a thousande cubites. &c. And you shall measure on the East side two thousande cubites, and on the West side two thousande cubites. &c.* In the twentie one Chapter of *Iosua*, The number of these Cities is mentioned, *And the lot came out of the kinred of the Caathites, the children of Aaron the Priest, which were of the Leuites, and giuen them by lot out of the tribe of Iuda, Simeon, and Beniamin, thirteene Cities. And the rest of the children of Caath had by lot of the kinreds of the tribe of Ephraim, Dan, and halfe the tribe of Manasses, tenne cities. And the children of Gerson, had by lotte out of the kinred of the cities of Isachar, Aser, Nepthaly, and the other halfe of the tribe of Manasses in Basan, thirtcene cities. And the children of Merari, by their kinreds, had out of the Tribes of Ruben, Gad and Zabulon, twelue cities. The whole number therefore of the cities assigned to the Leuites in the lande of Iurie, amounted to fortie eight.*

Nowe I would demaund of indifferent Christians, that vvere not obstinately set to maintaine an euill purpose, Whether the state of inheritance without rent, of fortie eight Cities in one Region, no bigger then England, with the fieldes almost a mile compasse, may bee thought in trueth, to bee temporall possessions or no? Surely I thinke there is no man so wayward, that will denie it to be most true.

Wherefore, eyther the worde of God must bee found vntrue, (which is blasphemie to thinke) or els that boulde assertion, that is made of the contrary, is found vaine, and the argument to prooue it, false and deceitfull. They that had to their portions fortie eight Cities, with the fields thereof, did not liue by tithes and oblations onely.

You see therefore (good Christians) how they vnderstand the Scriptures, and in such immodest and confident maner, take vpon them to be masters and controllers of other: and by how sleight allegations and absurde arguments they seeke to leade men into error, euen in great and vveighty matters, without feare of God himselfe, or reuerence of his people with whome they deale. God blesse them with more grace of his true, milde, and humble spirite, that they runne not so headlong, to the daunger of their owne soules, and the trouble of the Church of Christ.

And for the better vnderstanding heereof, let vs consider, what state the Leuites had in this Lande that was allotted vnto them. They might sell, and alienate it, but not to any other Tribe or familie, but to some of the same familie, whereof they were.

The Lawe therein saith, Leuit. 25. *Notwithstanding, the Cities of the Leuites, and the houses of the cities of their possession, may the Leuites redeeme at all seasons. If a man purchase of the Leuites, the house that was soulde shall goe out in the yere of Iubile. But the fields of their Cities may not be soulde, for it is their possession for euer.*

And yet we read that the Prophet *Ieremie* bought a peece
Iere. 32. of land of *Hananael* his Vncles soone, which I take to bee, because *Ieremie* was his next of kinne, to vvhome by Lavve after him it shoulde come: So that *Hananael* soulde onely the interest of his life time.

Thus, by the way you may note, that buying and purchasing of such ground as was lawfull to them, was not prohibited to Gods Priests in the olde law.

Obiection.

Happilie they will say, That although they had some temporall Landes, yet it vvas in comparison of the large inheritaunce of the other

Tribes, but a small portion: And as the Ministers of God, they liued meanely and porely vpon it.

Answere.

But they that rightly consider and weigh the quantitie and largenesse of the Lande of Promise, not being (as I thinke) so large as this Realme of *England*, shall perceiue, that the same being diuided into twelue partes, according to the twelue Tribes, that eight and fourtie Cities, with the fieldes about them, onely for the tribe of *Leui*, was a portion, although not so big, yet not much inferiour to the residue, although the one part had their liuing together, and the Leuites had theirs disparkled in sundry partes of the Countrey. To which, if you adde Gods part, that is, the oblations, the first fruits and the tenthes of their fruites, and cattell beside, you shall perceiue, that the Priestes, Leuites, and Ministers of the Temple of God were not left in meaner or poorer, but rather in as good or better state, then any of the other Tribes. Which thing vndoubtedly God did of his gratious prouidence, not that his ministers should by wealth wax wanton and proud, but that by that meanes, they might be of more authoritie with his people, and not beeing drawen away by the necessitie of care howe to liue, they might more freely and quietly attend vpon the seruice of God in the Temple and other places. Wherefore these places of the Law of *Moses*, were not fitly alleadged to prooue, either, that the Ministers of the Church should haue no temporall possessions, or that they should by stipends of money liue in poore or base condition.

It pleased God, that the Leuites shoulde not haue their portion lying together, as the other had, but to bee sparkled among all the Tribes of that nation, that they might the better instruct the people of all partes, in the Lawe and ordinaunces of almightie God, as their office and duetie was. But if the value of their portion, together with the first fruites and tenths bee considered, you shall perceiue it was nothing inferiour to any of the best.

They that had not some peculiar drift and purpose in their heades, which by all meanes, right or wrong, they will further and confirme, but did sincerely, and with good conscience, seeke the true meaning of the spirit of God in the holy scriptures, out of these testimonies of the Lawe of God: might haue gathered a right and wholesome instruction, profitable not onely to Ministers of the Church, but to all other good and faythfull Christians, to whom these places appertain, as well as to bishops and Ministers.

For as *Aaron* the high Priest in the Lawe, was the figure of the true high Priest Christ Iesus our Sauiour: so the inferiour Priestes and Leuites seruing in the temple of God, represent vnto vs all other faithfull and elect of God, whome hee hath chosen vnto him, to serue him as his peculiar heritage, and in steed of the first begotten of mankinde. To this interpretation alludeth S. *Peter*, speaking, not to Priests alone, but to the whole Church of God, and number of the faithfull. *You are* (saith he) *a chosen generation, a royall priesthood, an holy nation.* This exposition S. *August.* confirmeth, *As for the Priesthoode* (saith he) *of the Iewes, there is no faithfull man that doubteth, but that it was a figure of the roiall Priesthood that should be in the Church. Whereunto all they are consecrated, which appertaine to the mysticall body of the most high and true Prince of Priestes, as Peter also witnesseth.*

Bede also writeth very euidently to the same purpose. *By the name of Priesthood in the Scriptures, figuratiuely is vnderstoode, not onely Ministers of the Altar, that is, Bishops and Priestes: but all they which by high and godly conuersation, and by excellencie of wholesome doctrine, are profitable, not to themselues onely, but to many other, while they offer their bodies as a liuelie and holy Sacrifice well pleasing God.* For Peter *spake not to Priests on[ly] but to the vniuersall Church of God.* Nowe, if this bee true, the right and sincere doctrine, that is to be taken out of the testimonies of the law of God, is this, that as the Preestes and Leuites had not a like portion of inheritance allotted vnto them, as the residue of their brethren had, but God onely whome they serued, was their portion: so all faithful Christians, being of the true Priesthoode of God, must not thinke they haue any allotted portion in this worlde, but God onely is their portion, to whome they must cleaue, and heauen to bee their inheritaunce after which they must seeke, according as S. *Paul* saieth, *Wee haue heere no abiding Citie, but wee seeke for one in Heauen. Wee be as pilgrimes and straungers in this earth.*

Therefore if wee bee risen with Christ, wee shoulde seeke those thinges that be aboue, where Christ our portion sitteth at the Co.3. right hand of God the Father, and our whole heart shoulde be fastened vpon thinges aboue, and not on earthly thinges. This instruction, as nighly and as deepely toucheth all Christians, as it doth Bishops and Ministers of the Church of God.

But countenaunce must bee giuen to this quarrell against bishops, and this strange Assertion must bee confirmed by the Prophets also, euen as aptly alledged as the other places before mentioned.

And first they beginne with Esay. *His watchmen are all blinde, they haue altogether no vnderstanding, they are all dumbe dogges, not being able to barke, they are sleepie, sluggish, and lie snorting, they are shamelesse dogges that neuer are satisfied, the shepheards also haue no vnderstanding, but every man turneth his owne way, euery one after his couetousnesse with all his power.* Out of *Ieremie* also, are alledged these wordes. *I wil giue their wiues vnto aliens, and their fields to destroyers: for from the lowest vnto the highest, they followe filthie lucre, and from the Prophet to the Priest, they deale all with lies.* The Prophet *Ezechiel* also is brought in, to helpe this matter, where hee terribly thundreth against negligent, naughtie and corrupt shepheards, that deuoure the flocke and feed it not. *Thou sonne of man, prophecie against the Shepheards of Israel, woe bee vnto the Shepheardes of Israel, that feede themselues: shoulde not the Shepheardes feede the flockes? yee eate vp the fat, ye clothe you with the wooll, the best fedde doe you slay, but the flocke doe you not feede, the weake haue you not strengthened, the sicke haue you not healed, the broken haue you not bounde together, &c. but with force and crueltie haue you ruled them.* Wise and discreete christians, that in iudging of things feare to be deceiued, and looke to the direct proofe of that which is in controuersie, will marueile to see these testimonies alleadged, to the ende before prefixed; that is, that bishops may not enioy any temporall Landes. For there is nothing in these places of the Prophets that toucheth it. But if the ende vvere onely to make an inuectiue against the negligent, corrupt, and couetous liues of bishops, or other Ministers: indeede these allegations

Esai. 56. Allegations out of the Prophets for the same purpose.

Ierem. 8.

Exech. 34.

might seeme not altogether to be vnfit for the purpose: And happily that is it that is especially intended, by such meanes to make them contemptible and odious. And yet this is no sincere handling of the Scriptures, to apply those places to the particular blaming of some one sort of men, which the spirite of God directeth against many. Who being acquainted with the Scriptures, knoweth not, that by the wordes *Watchmen* and *Shepheards,* in the Prophets, are meant not only bishops, Priests, and Leuites: but also Princes, Magistrates and Rulers? Vpon the place of *Ezechiel* aboue recited, *Hierome* saith: *The speech is directed to the Shepherds of Israel: by which we ought to vnderstand, the Kings, the Princes, the Scribes and Pharises, and the Masters of the people.* And againe vpon these words, *The fat they did eate,* by a *metaphore* (saith hee) *the Prophet speaketh to the Princes, of whom it is said in another place, Which deuouremy people as it were bread.* Yea, when God himselfe saith in this same place of *Ezechiel, with force and crueltie haue ye ruled them:* It may euidently appeare, that he speaketh not there to ecclesiasticall ministers onely, but to Princes, Iudges, and rulers also, which sucke the sweete from the people of God, and do not carefully see to their defence, and godly gouernment, but suffer them to bee spoyled of their enemies, and to wander from God, and his true worship. But what should I seeme to proue that, which all learned knowe to bee most true? The spirite of God speaketh to the same purpose by these Prophets vnder figuratiue wordes, that he doeth by other Prophets in playne speeche. *O yee Priestes* (sayeth *Osee*) *heare this O yee house of Israel, giue eare O thou house of the King: Iudgement is against you, because you are become a snare in Mispath, and a spread nette in Mount Thabor,* that is, you, as hunters lay wayte to snare the people, and to oppresse them by couetousnesse, extortion, and briberie: and your corrupt manners is as a nette to take other in, by your euill example. And likewise sayth *Micheas, Heare this O yee heads of the house of Iacob, and yee Princes of the house of Israel: they abhorre iudgements and peruert equitie: They build vp Sion with blood, and Hierusalem with iniquitie. The heads thereof iudge by rewardes, and the Priestes thereof teache for hire, and their Prophets prophecie for money.* These bee the ordinarie voyces of the holy Ghost, vttered by the Prophets, in sharpe

and earnest reproouing, not onely for the people for their
wicked reuolting from God, but also, yea and that chiefly, for
the Princes, Rulers, Magistrates, Iudges, Bishops, Pri[e]stes,
ministers and other, whome God hath set in place of
gouernment. For God hath appoynted them, as Shepheards,
as guiders, and Patrons of his people, to direct them, to
keepe them, to defend them in his true worship, and right
seruice, and, if they will bee wandering from him, eyther by
errour in Religion, or by wickednesse in life, to instruct and
teach them, and by all meanes that may bee, to call them
home againe: or if they vvill not bee ruled, by authoritie to
bridle and restraine them, yea, and by punishment to correct
them. Now if the watchmen and Shepheards, that is, the
guiders and rulers of the people, whether they bee Ciuill or
Ecclesiasticall, shall waxe ignorant, and vnskilfull of their
dueties, shall become negligent and carelesse of their charge,
shall be giuen ouer to voluptuousnesse and pleasure of the
world, or to couetousnesse, bribery, and extortion, to iniurie,
violence and oppression, and in their gouernment seeke their
owne pleasure and commoditie, and nothing regarde, either
the benefite of the people, or the glory of God : then (I say)
these speeches of the Prophets lie directly against them,
and may well bee vsed to declare the wrath of God towards
them. But what maketh this to the purpose pretended?
how hangeth this reason together? God by the Prophets
earnestly reproueth the gouernours, aswell of the Church as
of the commonweale, for their wickednesse, couetousnesse,
and extortion : therefore bishops, and ecclesiasticall ministers
may not by the word of God enioy temporall lands and
possessions. Or this, God blameth the priestes of the olde
lawe for couetousnesse : therefore the bishops of the church
of Christ may haue no Landes and possessions. They that
wil be perswaded with such reasons, wil easily be caried away
into error. If it were certaine, and did of necessitie followe,
that all they, which haue great liuings and possessions, must
needes bee couetous : then happily this reasoning might bee
of some force. But I thinke there is no reasonable man that
wil graunt it, and therefore this reasoning is without all
reason. The Priests and Leuites, as themselues confesse,
had no great lands and lordships, and yet wee finde them
often in the Prophets accused and blamed for couetous-

nesse: therefore it is not the want of temporall lands and liuings, that can bring a poore hearte and contented minde, voide of couetousnes. We see often as couetous and greedie hearts in meane mens bosoms, as in the greatest landed Lordes in a whole Country. And on the contrary part, wee finde in them that haue verie great possessions, as humble, and as contented mindes, and as farre from the affection of couetousnesse, as in the meanest man that is.

_{Neither doth pouerty bring a contented mind: neither great possessions causeth couetousnes.}

Iob was of great wealth and possessions, and yet wee reade not that hee was euer blamed for couetousnesse: Yea hee beareth witnesse of his owne free heart and liberality, and sayth, *Hee neuer set his heart vpon Gold, nor saide to the wedge of Golde, Thou art my hope, nor reioyced of beeing rich, nor because his hande had founde abundance, &c.* *Abraham* also was rich, and God had blessed him with great possessions, and yet surely his heart was farre from the loue of money.

_{Iob. 31.}

Ioseph had no small possessions, and was in place of honour, and yet fewe in the meanest state or degree did euer keepe a more humble heart, or put lesse delight in honour and riches then hee did. I might say the same of *Dauid*, though a king, and of *Daniel*, though in very high estate, and in great authoritie, and as it may bee thought, in liuing proportionable to the same. When Christ in the gospell had saide, that it was *as vnpossible for a rich man to enter into heauen, as for a Camell to goe through the eie of a needle*, and his Disciples had wondered at that saying, hee aunswered: *That which is with man impossible, is possible with God.* Albeit mans corrupt nature, as it is generally giuen to all ill, so it is chiefely inclined to couetousnesse, and delight of the worlde: Yet the good grace of Gods holy Spirite doeth so guide the hearts of his faythfull, that in the midst of greatest abundaunce of his plentifull blessings, they can retaine the feare of God, and contempt of the worlde. Wherefore, it is great rashnesse and presumption, to condemne all them to bee giuen ouer to couetousnesse and delight of the worlde, whom they see by the state of the Commonweale, or by the goodnesse of the Prince, or by any other lawfull and iust meanes to haue landes and possessions, or wealth and riches, according to their

<sub>Matt. 19
Mar. 10.
Luke 18.</sub>

state. Such persons as so rashly deeme of other, may seeme rather to bewray the sicknesse and ill disposition of their owne mindes, then to iudge truely of them, whome in such case they condemne. It is the pouertie and humblenesse of Spirite and minde, it is not the pouertie and Matth. 5. basenesse of outwarde estate and condition, vnto the which Christ imputeth Gods blessings. If couetousnesse be *a desire to haue, for feare of want and scarcitie,* as some learned men haue defined it; then is a poore estate to a corrupt minde a greater spurre to couetousnesse, then lands and plentie of liuing can bee. Before that bishops and Ministers had any Landes assigned vnto them, yea, vvhen they were yet vnder the Crosse of persecution in the time of *Cyprian*: Serm. de lapsis August. de bap. lib. 2. Not much more then 200. yeeres after Christs ascension. vvee reade that hee findeth great fault with many bishops, which leauing the care of their charge, went from place to place, vsing vnlawfull meanes to get riches, practising vsurie, and by craft and subtiltie getting other mens lands from them.

In like maner complaine *Hierome, Augustine, Chrysostome, Basile,* and other aunciert Writers, and Histories of their time. Yea, in the Apostles time wee see some giuen ouer to the worlde, and ledde away vvith couetousnesse, when Ministers as yet liued onely vpon the free beneuolence of the people. Wherefore, it is not pouertie, or a lowe and contemptible state in the face of the worlde, that can bring a satisfied and contented Spirite. And surely I am of this opinion, that a poore and straight state of liuing in the Ministerie, especially in these dayes, vvoulde bee a greater cause of euill and inconuenience in the church, and a more vehement temptation to carry avvay their mindes from the care of their Office, then nowe their ample and large liuings are. I coulde, and will (when God shall giue occasion) declare good reason of this my opinion: which for some considerations I thinke good at this time to lette passe.

If our bishops and other chiefe of the Cleargie, beeing nowe in the state of our Church, by the prouidence of God, and singular goodnes of our Prince so amplie prouided for, be so vnthankfull vnto God, and so giuen ouer to the worlde, as they are bitterly accused to bee: surely their fault must needes bee the greater, neyther will I, or any other that feareth God, in that poynt excuse them, but pray to God (if there bee any such) that these odious reportes spredde vpon them, may bee a meanes to put them in remembraunce of their duety, and to amend. But vndoubtedly (good Christians) I speak it with my heart, mee thinketh I doe foresee at hand those dayes, and that time, when GOD of his iustice will both condignly rewarde our vnthankfull receiuing of his Gospell, and contempt of his Ministers, and also giue to them iust occasion to declare vnto their aduersaries and euill speakers, that they are not such bond-slaues of the world, nor bee so lead away captiue with the lusts of the flesh, as they are defamed. Yea, I thinke, this crosse of contempt, slaunder and reproch, that nowe is layd vpon them, is Gods fatherlie admonition to warne them : and as it were a meane to prepare them to that day that is comming ; which day vndoubtedly will bee *a day of wrath, a day of trouble and heauinesse, a day of vtter destruction and misery, a darke and glo[o]my day : a cloudie and stormie day, a day of the trumpet and of the alarme against* ^{Sophon. 1. 2.} *the strong cities. On that day will the Lord search Hierusalem with Lanthorns, and visite them which continue in their dregges, and say, Tush, the Lorde will doe no euill. Therefore their goods shall be spoiled, their houses shall bee laide waste, they shall build gay houses, and not dwell in them, they shall plant vineyardes, but not drinke the wine thereof. In that day the Lord will visite the Princes, and Kinges Children, and all such as weare gay cloathing, and all those that leape ouer the thresholde so proudly, and fill their Lordes house with robberie, and falsehoode. On that day God will bring the people into such vexation, that they shall goe about like blinde men, and all because they haue sinned against the Lord, and contemned his worde.* Wherefore, I most heartily pray vnto God, that we altogether, both Prince and people, honourable and worshipfull, ecclesiasticall and lay persons, preachers and hearers, may ioine together in the faythfull remembrance of that day, and to consider that it can not bee farre from vs, and therefore that it is full time, and more then time, to turne vnto God by hearty repentance, and faithfull receiuing of his worde. For surelie the sentences of the Prophets, of some men partially and affectionately applied to the Clergy and ministers only, do in right and true meaning touch vs all, of al states and conditions. But I wil returne to my matter againe.

The testimonie of *Malachy* vsed of some to like effect, as

the other before, I haue purposely left to this place: because
it speaketh particularly of priestes, and therefore will they
haue it more nighly to touch our bishops &c. *And now O yee
Priestes* (sayth the Prophet) *this commandement is* Mala. 2.
for you, &c. And a litle after, making comparison betweene
Leui and the Priests of that time, *The Law of trueth was in
his mouth, and there was no iniquitie founde in his lippes, he
walked with me in peace and in equitie, and hee turned many
from their iniquitie: but yee haue gone out of the way, yee haue
caused many to fall by the Lawe, ye haue corrupted the couenant
of Leui, sayth the Lord of hosts: therefore haue I made you
despised, and vile before the people.* These wordes of the
Prophet doe so touch our bishops and clergie men, if they be
so euill as they are made, as all sentences wherein the
Prophets blame the Priests of their time, doe touch euill
Ministers of the Church: but howe they eyther specially
nippe our bishoppes, as it is thought, or any thing pertaine to
the proofe of the principall matter, or reproouing of Preachers
liuings by Landes, I see not. In deede this sentence of *Malachi*
might bee rightly vsed against the Pope and his Prelates,
which neglecting the whole dutie of Gods ministers, both in
preaching and liuing, stayed themselues vpon the authoritie of
Saint *Peter*, and of succession, as though the Spirite of God
had beene bounde to their succession, though they taught and
liued neuer so corruptly. For so in deede did these priestes
whom *Malachi* reprooueth: they neglected the true worshippe
of God, and yet woulde they bee accompted his good and true
Priestes, because they were of the tribe of *Leui*, with whom
God had made his couenant, that hee and his seede Num. 25.
shoulde haue the office of the high priesthood for euer. But
Malachi sayth they haue broken the couenant on their part.

That our Bishops and Ministers doe not challenge to holde
by succession, it is most euident: their whole doctrine and
preaching is contrary: they vnderstande and teach, that
neither they, nor any other can haue Gods fauour so annexed
and tyed to them, but that, if they leaue their dueties by Gods
worde prescribed, they must in his sight leese the
preheminence of his Ministers, and bee subiect to his wrath
and punishment. They knowe, and declare to all men, that
the couenant on the behalfe of *Leui*, that is, on the behalfe of
the Ministers of God to be perfourmed, consisteth in these

three branches: by preaching to teache the right way of saluation, and to sette foorth the true worshippe of God: to keepe peace and quietnesse in the Church of God: and thirdly, by honest life to bee example vnto others.

These branches of the couenant, if our Bishops and Preachers haue corrupted and broken, they haue to answere for it before God, and their punishment will be exceeding grieuous.

As for their doctrine, I am right sure, and (in the feare of GOD I speake it) will hazarde my life to trye it, that all their enemies shall neuer bee able so to prooue it, but that it shall bee founde sincere and true: so that I doubt not, but GOD him selfe will beare witnesse vvith them, as hee did vvith *Leui*, that *trueth is in their mouth,* and (as touching their doctrine) *no iniquitie founde in their lippes.* For they doe both teache the trueth according to the Scriptures, sincerely, and confound the errours of the Antichristian Church, learnedly and truely.

They therfore that speake so much against them, may seeme lesse to regarde this part of their obseruing the couenant of *Leui*, then the duetie of Christians requireth. But I trust, our mercifull God will fauourably consider it, and beare with some other their imperfections in them. I pray God wee be not lighted into that time, that men haue itching eares, and can like no Preachers, but such as clawe their affections, and feede their fantasies in vanities and newe deuises. The couenant of peace they keepe also, liuing in vnitie and peace among them selues, and studying (so much as they can) by teaching, and by good order, to keepe it among other. And that is no small cause of their misliking at this time, because they, being in some place of gouernment, according to their dueties striue to represse those, which by vntemperate zeale seeke to disturbe the Church, and to giue cause of faction and disorder, by altering things externall in a setled and refourmed state.

As touching their liues and conuersations according to the Lawe of God, (as before I haue said) if I must iudge according to that I knowe, I must thinke the best, because I know no ill. Though there be imperfections in some things: if men woulde charitablie consider, in vvhat time vve liue, and whose Messengers they are, and somevvhat vvithall descend into their owne bosomes, and lay their owne dueties before their eyes : I thinke surely they would iudge of them more christianly then many doe.

Obiection.

But they will say, that according to the wordes of Malachie, God sheweth his iudgement against them for their wickednesse, because hee hath made them so contemptible, so vile and despised before all the people: for (say they) wee may see howe all men loath and disdaine them.

Answere.

It must needes be true (I confesse) that *Malachi* spake of the Priests of his time : but I doe not take it to be alwayes an vnfallible token of euill Priests and Ministers, or a certaine signe of Gods displeasure towarde them, when the people doe hate, disdaine, and contemne them. I see more commonly in the Scriptures, that it is a token of vnthankefull, stubborne, and hard-hearted people, which smally regarde the worde of God, and therefore also mislike his Ministers. *Elias, Micheas, Amos*, and other Prophets were smally esteemed, you knowe, among the Israelites. *Esay, Ieremie, Ezechiel*, were euen of as small credite and estimation among the Iewes. It may appeare so to bee, seeing *Esay* signified, that they lilled out their tongues, in mocking of him, and other of his time. And I am sure, you knovve the fauour and entertainement that the Apostles had also among the same people. I trust then you will not say it was a token of naughtie and corrupt Ministers, or of Gods iust iudgement against them : for they were the right and true Prophets, Apostles, and Messengers of God, and yet were in great hatred and misliking of them that thought themselues to be the people of God.

It may be surely, and in deede I thinke it to be very true, that God hath touched our bishops and Preachers with this scourge of ignominie and reproch, for their slackenesse and negligence in their office : And I pray God they may take this mercifull warning, and shunne his greater plagues. But I must say withall, as Christ sayth of the *Galileans*, whose blood *Pilate* mixed with their sacrifice, and of them Luke 13.
vpon whome the Tower of *Siloe* fel : *Doe you thinke, that they onely are sinners? nay I say vnto you, if you do not repent, you shall all taste of the same sharpe iustice.* If God punish his Ministers, hee will not suffer the other vntouched. *Nowe the time is*

come that the iudgement beginneth at the house of God, and if God punish those that hee sent with his worde, what will hee doe to them that vnthankfully receiue his worde?

1. Pet. 4.

That this matter of Ecclesiasticall mens liuings may seeme to be of great importance, and such in deede as God hath had much care of in all times: as before it hath beene countenanced by the Lawe and Prophets, so must it nowe bee drawen also through the vvhole course of the nevve Testament. Yea, whatsoeuer is vsed, eyther of Christ himselfe or of his Apostles, against couetousnesse, or the loue and care of this worlde, and delight of this life: all that, either by fayre meanes or foule, is brought into this fort, to batter and shake the lands and possessions of Bishoppes, and other of the Cleargie.

Proofes out of the Newe Testament against the rich liuings of Bishops.

And first men are willed, to call to remembrance the example of Christ our Sauiour, his birth, the state of his life, the choice of his apostles, and his perpetuall doctrine, exhorting to pouerty and contempt of the worlde. His parents (say they) were poore, and liued by an handie craft, descended of a stocke and kinred growen altogether out of credite in the worlde: in steede of a princely chamber, borne in an Oxe stall, wrapped in poore clothes, in steede of white and fine linnen: layed in a cribbe for want of a rich cradle: and in place of vvorthie seruitours, hee had the presence of an Oxe and an Asse. And that hee might shewe himselfe to delight in pouertie and contempt of the worlde, his natiuitie was first reuealed vnto poore Shepheards watching their flockes. As hee was borne, so was hee bredde, in the poore and contemptible Towne of *Nazareth*, out of the vvhich *Nathaniel* thought nothing worthy credite coulde come: in which Towne, as it may bee thought, by the exercise of an handie craft, hee liued in obedience of *Ioseph*, and of his Mother. Such as his birth and breeding was, such was the state of his liuing, when the full time of his dispensation came: for hee was not borne to any Landes or possessions, neyther had hee any great wealth and riches to susteine him selfe, yea, not so much as an house to put his heade in, but was maynteined by the almes as it vvere, and by the charitable deuotion of certaine vvealthie vvomen of Galiley, and other godly persons. His Apostles that he chose to follovve him, and to bee the Ministers of his kingdome, he tooke not out of the state of Princes, noble men, or great and rich Lordes, with Landes and dominions: but out of the pore state, and condition of fishers, Tent-makers, and toule-gatherers. And thus may vvee see our Lorde and Christ altogether vvrapped in pouerty, and besette on euery side vvith the base and contemptible state of the vvorld.

But to what purpose is all this alleaged? Forsooth, that wee may vnderstande, that it is not lavvfull for such as bee guides of the Lordes flocke, to liue in any other state, then in that the Lorde gaue example of: For vvhosocuer secketh Christ (say they) in other state and sort, then hee gaue example of, secketh not Christ, but Antichrist and the pompe of the vvorld. So that the sense and effect of the reason is this: Christ was borne, bredde, and liued in pouertie, and chose vnto him Apostles of poore condition : therefore bishoppes and Ministers of the Church must haue no Landes or possessions, but stay them selues in like poore state, as Christ and his Apostles did. I doe not frame this argument (good Reader) of purpose to cauill, but to admonish thee of the principall state, and that considering the proofe to bee naked in it selfe, thou mayest the better iudge of the strength thereof.

Surely, I will hencefoorth cease to marueile at the wrested and violent interpretations that Hermites, Monkes and friers haue made vpon the scriptures, to iustifie and set foorth their superstitious life of voluntarie pouertie and forsaking the world : seeing professors of the gospel, to maintaine their new doctrines, take vpon themselues the like liberty and boldnesse, in abusing the holy Scriptures and worde of God : And yet surely it doth grieue mee, and make my heart bleede to see it. What shall the aduersarie thinke of our dealing vvith the Scriptures? Surely, that wee doe in so earnest manner pull them from the interpretation of the Fathers and of the Church, to the ende that by applying them according to our owne fantasies, we may set foorth and seeme to iustifie to the worlde, what doctrine soeuer we shall thinke good our selues : And so shall this bee an occasion to discredite all the particular doctrines of the Gospell, which hitherto, as well this Church of England, as other Churches reformed haue taught. But to vnderstand the weight of this reason before vsed against the wealthie liuings of our Clergie, wee must trie it by a right and iust balance ; that is, by the true meaning of the holy Ghost. First therefore, let vs consider the causes of Christes pouertie, and of the choyce of such Apostles, which in mine opinion are two: The one is the necessitie of our redemption: the other is an example and iust instruction set foorth vnto Christians.

The right causes of Christes pouertie and his Apostles.

As touching the first, when the certaine purpose of God had determined that his sonne shoulde come into the worlde, to worke the redemption of mankinde, and his deliuerance from sinne: necessarie it was for him to satisfie the iustice of God, in sustaining all those difficulties and punishmentes, that were due to man for sinne: that is to say, affliction, ignominie, reproch, contempt, pouertie, and all worldly troubles and miseries, and last of all, death. This is it that the Prophet *Esay* spake of long before. *Hee is despised and abhorred of men, hee is such a man as hath goode experience of sorowes and infirmities: we reckned him so vile that we hidde our faces from him. Howbeit hee onely hath taken our infirmities on him, and borne our paynes. Yet wee did iudge him as though he were plagued and cast downe of God.* This is that humiliation and debasing of himselfe that *Paul* speaketh of, when hee sayth, *Hee being in the forme of God, thought it no robberie to bee equall with God, but made him selfe of no reputation, taking on him the forme of a seruant, and made in the likenesse of men, and founde in figure as a man, hee humbled himselfe, made obedient vnto death, euen to the death of the Crosse.* These places (good Christians) declare vnto vs, both the pouerty and contemptible state of Christ here in earth, and also the very roote and principall cause thereof: that is, the saluation of mankinde. The sonne of God became the sonne of man, that he might make vs the children of God: he was borne a weake and tender babe, that hee might make vs strong men in him: hee was tied in swadling bands, that hee might loose and deliuer us from the bondes of the fraile and sinfull flesh: hee was wrapped in poore clowtes, that with the garment of his innocencie, he might hide our nakednes: he was borne and liued poorly, that he might make vs rich and plentiful in him: he was a stranger in the worlde, and had not an house to put his head in, that he might purchase for vs a citie and heritage in heauen: he was borne vnder bondage, and payed tribute to *Cæsar*, that hee might deliuer vs from the tyranny of Hel: he was debased euen to the company of bruite beasts, that hee might bring vs to the glorious company of Angels: he laye in hay in a Crib,

Esai. 53.

Phil. 2.

that hee might procure euerlasting food for our soules: finally, hee was accused of sin and put to most cruel death, that we being iustified by his merite, might appeare innocent in the sight of God. These be the sweete and comfortable cogitations that good Christians should conceiue vpon the consideration of Christs poore and base state in this life. For pouerty in Christ was not so much for example of life, as to satisfie a punishment due to sinne. Riches is the good blessing and gift of God : but pouerty came in at the same door that death did, that is, by the disobedience of our first father. We may not therefore thinke with Monks and Friers, that pouertie in it self is a more holy state of liuing, then wealth and riches is. But of that more hereafter. Now let vs consider what maner of pouerty this was in Christ. Christ was in himself exceeding rich, both as the son of God, and as the sonne of man. As God, he had al things common with Ioh. 16. his father. *All things that my father hath* (saith he) *are mine*. And againe, *All thine are mine, and mine are thine.* Iohn 17. As touching his humanitie, hee is likewise of great possessions. For his Father sayth vnto him, *Desire of me, and* Psal. 2. *I shal giue thee the heathen for thine inheritance, and the vttermost parts of the earth for thy possession.* How hapned it then, that Christ being in right Lord of so great possessions, became in the time of his dispensation, almost in the state of a beggar? certainly, *quia ipse voluit*, because he would himself. For he that filleth heauen and earth, was borne in an Oxe stale in *Bethleem* : he that had al power in the whole world, was a banished person for a certaine time in *Egypt* : he that feedeth with sustenance man and beast, foule and fish, partly by labor gate his liuing, partly was fed with the liberalitie of other. He that prouideth apparel for al things, hung naked vpon the Crosse : he that sitteth in heauen as his throne, and hath the earth for his footestoole, at an others mans charge was buried and layde in a strange Sepulchre. Christes pouertie therefore was willing, not of any necessitie of holynesse, as I haue said, but to beare that for which sinne was due to vs. Nowe, I pray you, marke the strength of the former reason. Christ, to sustaine the punishment due to our sinnes, liued in great pouertie and humilitie in this worlde : therefore Bishops and Ministers of the Church, of necessitie, must liue in pouerty, and not haue any wealthy liuings, by landes or otherwise. I trust they that haue care of their consciences, will not easily be led to any perswasion by such reasons. They will say, Christ did this also for our example. I graunt, in some respect he did so : By his example he teacheth vs humblenesse and modestie, that we may not bee loath to doe those things, that he did, for the benefit and commoditie of our christian brother. If we so swel with pride, that in respect of our Noblenesse, or birth, or great estate in the worlde, wee disdaine other, and thinke our poore neighbour doeth vs iniurie, if hee in respect of christian brotherhood require of vs a benefit for his better reliefe : then is it time for vs, to behold the Sonne of God lying poorly in a cribbe or manger, betweene beastes : who, although he were God eternall with his Father, and by his mother borne of the most noble family of manie Kinges and Prophets : yet for our sake hee did so humble and debase himselfe, that he came in so poore and vile condition before men. Furthermore, Christ by his example, hath as it were consecrated pouertie, trouble, miserie, and affliction, that they may not be accompted token of the wrath of God, or such things as doe hinder true piety and holines, or let the saluation of our soules, For as mans nature doeth abhorre al afflictions; so chiefly doe men thinke pouertie and neede, to be not onely one of the greatest miseries that can happen to man, but also hatefull to God himselfe. Thus we see men commonly to think of such, as are any way fallen into pouertie and misery. Let *Iob* hereof be an example. In this cause also it is expedient for vs to looke vpon our poore Christ, and to set him before our eyes, that wee may both more patiently beare these thinges, when for Gods cause they light vpon vs, and more charitably iudge of other, whom God therewith toucheth : yea, it is good to teach vs to pull downe our bristles, when we waxe proude of those giftes of plenty and riches, that God hath giuen vs. Thus you see what profit the example of Christes pouerty bringeth : but I pray you, to whom is Christ an example ? to bishops and Ministers only ? did he liue in poore and miserable state for Ministers only ? did he die for their sinnes onely ? God forbid. He was borne, he liued, he died for all mankind, and all faithful haue the fruit of this his birth, his life, and his death. Therefore the example of Christs life must stretch further then to Bishops and Ministers. It is a farre truer argument to say, Christ liued a simple and poore life, while he was here on earth : therefore all Christians ought to liue in the same manner that he did, then to apply the same onely to Ministers and Ecclesiasticall persons. Therefore I will all Christians to be beware of this hereticall and Anabaptisticall assertion :

Whosoeuer seeketh Christ in other state and sort then hee gaue example of, seeketh not Christ, but Antichrist, and the pompe of the world.

For if this sentence be applied to the example of the poore state of Christ, it is the very ground of Anabaptisticall communitie, and that none can be saued, but such as renounce all their goods and possessions. Albeit the example of Christ in this place be applied to Ministers onely: yet in trueth it apperteineth to all other faithfull, as wel as to them. And if the Argument shal be counted good now: hereafter with as good likelihood, and farre truer interpretation, it may be vsed against al that shal truely professe Christ. As touching that Christ chose so simple Apostles, and of so poore estate, *Saint Paul* sheweth the reason and cause thereof. 1. Cor. 4. *Brethren* (saith hee) *you see your calling, howe that not many wise men after the flesh, not many mightie, not many Noble are called : but God hath chosen the foolish things to confound the wise, and the weake things to confounde the mightie, and vnnoble things of the world, and things that are despised, God hath chosen, and things that are not, to bring to nought things that are, that no flesh should glorie in his presence.* If Christ in the entrance of his Kingdome, going about to subdue the world to his knowledge, shoulde haue vsed the seruice and ministerie of Princes, Noblemen, great, wealthie, and rich men : or of such as had bene wise, learned, and eloquent, and politique : the glorie of his mightie conquest would haue bene attributed to the power and might, to the wealth and riches, to the wisedome and learning, to the eloquence and policie of those, which had bene his ministers, and so the glorie of God in that worke of mans saluation, should haue bene diminished. Therefore God, to shewe his power in heauenly things, ouerthwarted the wisedome of the world, and chose his Apostles poore, vnnoble, simple, vnlearned, without eloquence, farre from the cunning, wisedome, and policie of the word, and by them and by their preaching in a few yeeres wanne the whole world to his knowledge, and defaced the kingdome of Sathan, consisting in superstition, idolatrie, and wickednesse. And in deede, this order of Gods woorking by these poore and vnlearned men, preuailed against all the Nobilitie, the honour, the might, the wisedome, the policie, learning, the eloquence of the worlde, so that it might be truely sayd, *Non est potentia, non est prudentia, non est consilium aduersus Dominum.* But what hereof is to bee concluded to this purpose? forsooth, that as Christ thought it fittest to chuse onely poore men to his Apostles, and sent them abroade without any stay of Liuing in the worlde: so hee thinketh it meetest, that his Ministers in his Church in all times and places should be in poore estate, and not to haue any wealth or riches.

It is good to consider this reason also, that you be not more ledde with it, then the weight and force of it requireth. The office of the Apostles was, to goe from Countrey to Countrey, from place to place, to plant Churches vnto God, so that they could not haue any certaine stay of Liuing: It is not therefore like reason, that in a setled Church where the Gospel is receiued, the Ministers and Preachers thereof may haue no certaine forme of Liuing appoynted them, eyther by land or otherwise. As Christ chose his Apostles poore, so hee chose them simple, and vnlearned, without eloquence, or any kinde of knowledge, that his glorie thereby might the more be set foorth: Shall we therefore inferre thereupon, that it is fittest alwayes for the Ministers of the Church, to bee simple, without learning, eloquence, and knowledge? It is well knowen that the Anabaptists, and some other phanaticall spirits troubling the reformed Churches beyond the seas, vpon the same example of the Apostles haue gathered, that learning and knowledge is not to bee respected in the choyce of Ministers: because God needeth no such helpes to set forth his Gospel, yea they say that learning and eloquence are perillous instruments, to corrupt the simplicitie of the Gospel, and to giue countenaunce to errour. Wherefore such persons doe vsually admit among them to the Ministerie handicrafts men, and such as challenge to themselues the spirite of God onely, without further knowledge. But the godly, I doubt not, vnderstand that all things neither can, nor ought to be like in the state of the Church beginning and vnder persecution, and in the Church setled and liuing in peace and quietnesse.

The Ministers and Preachers of our Church, beside the example of Christ and his Apostles liuing in pouertie, are willed diligently to looke into the perpetual doctrine, which Christ in all the Euangelists doeth teach them, touching the state of their liuing, namely against riches, couetousnesse, the glorie of the worlde, and care of this life. To this doctrine apperteyneth that which Christ teacheth. *Matth.* 6. That they *shoulde not hoarde vp treasure for themselues vpon earth, where thieues breake through and steale them, but that they should lay vp treasures in heauen &c.* That they can not serue two masters, God and Mammon: That they shoulde not *bee carefull for their life, what they shoulde eate, what they shoulde drinke, or what apparell they shoulde put on: but cast all their care vpon God, and seeke his kingdome, and the righteousnesse thereof,* for that it is heathenish carefully to seeke after those other things, which God of himselfe will plentifully cast vpon his: that riches, and the pleasures and cares of this life, are resembled to *thornes* which choake vp the good seede of Gods word, and make that it cannot prosper: *That it is as vnpossible for a rich man to enter into the kingdome of God, as far a Camell to goe through the eye of a needle:* That hee cryeth out, *woe to them that are full, for they shall bee hungrie: and to them that bee rich, because they haue alreadie their comfort and consolation:* yea, he willeth them to *sell all that they haue, and giue vnto the poore,* with a number of other places: wherein hee instructing his disciples and followers, vtterly willeth them to renounce this world and the treasures thereof. Whereupon it is thought it may be very well concluded, that the Ministers of the Church may not haue any wealthy liuings, and especially by landes and lordships: and therefore that our Bishops bee not the true followers of Christ, but walke in the steps of Antichrist. Surely our Sauiour Christ did see, that as the perpetuall enemie of mankinde did continually seeke by all wayes to drawe men from God: so he did not vse any meane more commonly, then by honour, glorie, riches and wealth. And therefore when he saw that Christ coulde not by other temptations bee ouercome, he assaulted him with ambition and desire of principalitie, honour, and lordship. This temptation is therefore the more dangerous, because mans corrupt nature is of it selfe greatly inclined to the loue of the worlde and earthly pleasures. Wherefore I cannot denie, but that our carefull and louing sauiour did often and in many places warne his disciples, and by them all vs, to beware of this working of Sathan, and so much as they could, to shunne his snares. But shall wee thinke therefore, that hee condemneth principalitie, lordship, dominion, wealth, riches, landes, in them that bee his true and faithfull followers? No surely; for that is the full grounde of the Anabaptists doctrine, to be shunned of al right christians. And yet before I begin to answere this, I must needes protest it is a queisie and dangerous matter, to speake of wealth and riches of the worlde, for feare of mistaking, either on the one part, or the other. For whatsoeuer a man shall say in that case, among the vngodly will bee drawen according to their priuate affections.

The rich, when they heare the possession of riches and the right vse of them defended, by and by if Gods special grace stay them not, waxe more confident and secure, and with contempt and disdaine of other, thinke themselues free maisters and Lordes of Gods giftes, to vse them euen at their owne pleasure, and to the fulfilling of their owne fleshly fantasies. On the contrary part, when they that bee poore and destitute of those giftes, shall heare the rich blamed for the abuse of their wealth, and signification giuen, that what soeuer is aboue the sufficient maintenance of their own state, is due vnto the poore: they also as rashly enter into iudgement, and condemne al rich men as couetous, as greedy gatherers, as theiues and extortioners, and cruel detainers of that which by Gods law is due to others. Some there be also, that think all vse and administration of riches to be dangerous, and to bring no smal hinderance to the saluation of mens soules. Vnto which perswasion, the phanaticall spirites of the Anabaptists adde more difficultie, not onely taking away al possession and property, and allowing a *Platonicall* community of al things: but also denying superioritie, and Lordship and dominion, and bringing in a general equalitie, most dangerous to the societie of man. Wherefore, it behooueth mee so to speake of riches and possessions, that (so neere as I can) none of these offences may be iustly taken.

First therefore to begin, we may not thinke that Christ in them that be his, condemneth either the possession or the right vse of Lordship, dominion, lands, riches, money and such like: for they are the good gifts of God, wherewith he blesseth his people, as the whole course of the Scriptures declare. *The blessing of the Lord* (saith *Solomon*) Pro. 10. *maketh rich, and bringeth no sorowe of heart with it. Blessed is the man* (sayth *Dauid*) *that feareth the Lord &c. his* Psal. 112. *seede shall be mightie upon earth, the generation of the faithfull shall be blessed, riches and plenteousnesse shall bee in his house &c.* And againe, *His horne shall bee exalted with honour : the vngodlie shal see it, and it shall grieue them.* Therefore wee see many of the good saints of God, that haue bene indued with great riches and possessions, as *Abraham* the Father of the faithful, *Iob, Ioseph, Dauid, Salomon, Daniel*. And in the New Testament, *Nicodemus, Ioseph of Arimathea, Lazarus of Bethania, Mary Magdalene, Sergius Paulus* Proconsul of *Cypres*, the *Centurion*, and manie other. Wee may not thinke therefore, that Christ condemneth the giftes and blessinges of God, or the vse of them, in his seruantes. And that the trueth taken out of the Scriptures may be of more authoritie with you, I wil let you vnderstand it by the wordes of the ancient and learned Fathers: so shal you perceiue, it is not my interpretation, but theirs. And first *Hieroms*, Ioseph, *which both in pouertie* Hierom ad *and riches, gaue triall of his vertues, and was both a* Saluinam. *seruant and a maister, teacheth vs the freedome of the minde. Was hee not next vnto* Pharao, *adorned in royal furniture ? and yet was he so beloued of God, that aboue al the* Patriarkes, *hee was a Father of two Tribes.* Daniel, *and the three young men, had such rule ouer the power and riches of Babylon, that in apparell they serued Nabuchodonosor, but in minde they serued God. Mardocheus and Hester, in the middest of their purple, silke, and precious iewels, ouercame pride with humilitie, and were of such worthinesse, that they being Captiues, bare rule ouer Conquerours.* My speech tendeth to this end, that I may declare that this young man that I speake of, had kinred of royall blood, aboundance of riches, and ornamentes of honour and power, as matter and instrumentes of vertue vnto him. S. *Augustine* disputeth this question, writing to *Hillarius*. *Thou writest vnto* Epist. 89. *me* (saieth hee) *that some say, that a rich man remaining in his wealth, cannot enter into the kingdome of God, vnlesse that hee sell all that he hath, and that it shal not profit, though in his wealth he keep the commandements of God. Our fathers, Abraham, Isaac and Iacob, vnderstoode not this reasoning : for they all had no smal riches, as the holy Scriptures witnesse, &c.*

And least that some might say, that those holie men were vnder the old Testament, and vnderstood not the perfect law ^{Matt. 19.} that Christ giueth, when he sayeth, *Goe and sel al that thou hast, and giue it vnto the poore, and thou shalt haue treasure in heauen,* the same *Augustine* addeth, *If they will say so, they may speake with some reason: but let them heare the whole: lette them marke the whole: they may not in one parte open their eares, and in an other part stoppe them. Hee spake that to one that asked him, What shall I doe to obtayne euerlasting life? and Christes answere is not, If thou wilt obtaine euerlasting life, sell all that thou hast: but, if thou wilt haue euerlasting life, keepe the Commaundementes, &c. And a little after, our good Maister doeth make a distinction betweene the keeping of the Commandements, and that other rule of perfectnesse.* For in the one part he saide, *If thou wilt enter into life, keepe the Commaundements:* And in the other hee saide, *If thou wilt bee perfect, sell all thou hast, and come and followe me. How therefore can we denie, that rich men, although they haue not the perfection, shall come into euerlasting life, if they keepe the Commaundementes, and giue, that it may be giuen vnto them?* And in the ende he concludeth his reason in this manner, after hee had spoken of the vncharitable minde of the riche glutton. *This pride* (sayeth hee) *wherewith this riche man did contemne the poore iust Lazarus lying before his gates, and that trust that hee did put in his riches, whereby he thought himselfe a blessed man, because of his purple, silke, and sumptuous feastes, did bring him to the tormentes of hell, and not his riches.* By which wordes of *Augustine,* it may appeare, it is not riches, Landes and possessions, that GOD condemneth in his seruauntes, but the euill vse [of] them. Wherefore the ^{Psal. 51.} same *Augustine* sayeth, *When the Lord had sayde, It is easier for a Camell to passe thorowe the eye of a needle, then for a riche man to enter into the kingdome of GOD: and the Apostles maruailing thereat, answered, Who then can bee saued? What respected they I pray you?* surely, non facultates, sed cupiditates: *not great substaunce, but greedie desire of them.*

Immediately hee sheweth, that riche Abraham had preheminence in heauen, before poore Lazarus. *Reade the Scriptures,* (saieth hee) *and thou shalt find riche Abraham, that thou maiest knowe, it is not riches that is punished. Abraham had great store of golde, siluer, cattell and householde. Hee was rich, and yet was poore Lazarus brought into his bosome: the poore* man in the bosome of the rich, or rather both rich before God, and both poore in spirite &c. Marke this, that you do not commonly blame rich men, or put trust in poore estate. For if a man should not put his trust in riches, much lesse in pouertie. To the like effect speaketh *Hierome, Is it euill to haue riches iustly gotten, so that a man giue thankes to God that gaue them ? No, but euil it is to put a mans trust in riches. For in another Psalme it is sayde, If riches come vnto thee, set not thine heart vpon them. A man may haue riches for his necessitie, but hee may not possesse them to delight in them.* Well therefore saith *Chrysystome,* _{Homil. 2. ad popul. Antioch.} *As I haue said, wine is not ill, but drunkennesse is ill : so say I, riches are not ill, but couetousnesse is ill. A rich man is one thing, and a couetous men is another. A couetous man cannot be a rich man.* And to the same meaning _{Homil. 13. ad popul. Antioch.} in another place: *Let vs not falsely accuse either riches or pouertie : for both riches and pouertie are such, as, if we will our selues, bring instruments of vertue. Let vs therefore so frame our selues, that we iudge not so, as we may seeme to blame Gods giftes, but the euill affections of men.* The same *Chrysostome, Riches* (saith hee) *killeth not : but to be a slaue to* _{Homil. ad popul. Antioch. 58.} *riches, killeth, and to loue couetousnesse. And againe, the rich glutton was punished, not because he was rich, but because he wanted mercie. For it may be, that one hauing riches, ioyned with mercie, may attaine to all goodnesse.* By these testimonies of the ancient learned Fathers, grounded vpon the examples and doctrine of the Scriptures, you may perceiue, that riches are the good gift and blessing of God: that the Saintes of God haue vsed and enioyed them: that wealth and possessions of them selues are not hinderous to pietie and godlinesse, but rather instruments of vertue and meanes to come to heauen : that God doeth not condemne them in his seruants : that it is not a man voyde of lands and possessions, but a heart voyd of couetousnesse that Christ desireth: that it is not riches, but the sinfull affections of man that he reproueth. How then can it bee prooued by Christes doctrine, that any state of his disciples or faithfull seruants and followers, ought not to haue landes, possessions, or ample and large liuings ? or that they be by his word so expressly prohibited, that neither Prince may suffer it without danger, nor faithfull Minister with good conscience inioy them ? Let vs somewhat better consider the particular places of this doctrine of Christ,

whereon this assertion is grounded. Where Christ saith,
Matth. 6. *Hoarde not vp treasures for your selues on earth*, he saith not, you shall haue no treasures. To haue treasures, and to hoarde treasures, be diuerse. Hee that hoardeth vp treasures, sheweth that hee hath a carefull minde to keepe them : but a man may possesse treasures, and yet with free heart bee willing to imploy them to godly purposes : like as *Iob* did, who had his riches alwayes readie to pleasure other. When Christ affirmeth, that *where a mans treasure is, there is his heart :* by treasure, he meaneth not the possession of riches simply, but hee meaneth that, wherein a man reposeth his chiefe treasure and felicitie to consist. And in deede it cannot be, but that hee that esteemeth his chiefe felicitie in any thing, doeth set his heart also vpon it. Hee that setteth his felicitie in honour and dignitie, hath his heart possessed with ambition. Hee that thinketh it to bee in worldly pleasure, hath his whole minde on playing, banqueting, feasting and riot. He that reposeth his felicitie in building, giueth ouer his cogitations vnto that. So hee that iudgeth his blessednes in this life to be in possession of riches and lands, vndoubtedly cannot but haue his heart fastened vpon them. And seeing that God chalengeth vnto himselfe all our whole heart, and our whole soule and minde, they that so do, must needs offend God most grieuously, and make of their riches their God, and so as *S. Paul* saith, become very idolaters. Therfore if either Ecclesiasticall persons, or lay men, do so set their minds on riches, this place nighly toucheth them. When Christ saith, *No man can serue two masters &c. and ye cannot serue God and Mammon*, Marke, I pray you, that he saith not : *No man can serue God and get riches.* For godly men both haue before time, and now may get lands and riches, procured either by heritage or by gift, or by any other
Gene. 30. lawfull meanes. Consider the Patriarch *Iacob* : who passed *Iordane* onely with a staffe in his hand, and in the time of his liuing in a strange Countrey, gate so great riches, as he returned with two great companies of seruants and cattel. And yet vndoubtedly this Patriarch was a good Christian, being saued by the same religion that his Grandfather *Abraham* was, the father of the faithfull, who with reioycing sawe the day of Christ. Neither doth Christ say, *No man can serue God and possesse riches.* For as it is said

before, *Abraham*, *Iob*, and *Ioseph*, possessed great wealth and riches, and yet vndoubtedly, truely, and sincerely serued God. Riches are the blessings of God, neither may any more rightly or with better title possesse them, then the good and faithfull seruants of God. What saith Christ then? forsooth, *No man can serue two masters:* or *No man can serue God and Mammon.* Getting or possessing is one thing, and *seruing* is another. *Seruing* presupposeth a mastership or dominion in him that is serued. Hee that *serueth riches*, acknowledgeth them to be his Lord and Master. *Seruitude* or bondage hath this condition, that hee wholly obey his master: that night and day he doe nothing but that pleaseth his master: that hee shall be contented to haue the displeasure of al other, so that he may haue the good will of his master: Finally, whatsoeuer a seruant doth, what labour soeuer he taketh, whatsoeuer by his paines he getteth, he doth it to the vse and behalfe of his master. Whosoeuer is such a bondslaue to riches, is a traitour reuolted from God, neither can it be possible for him to serue God. Such a seruing of *Mammon* it is that Christ in this place rebuketh, with which seruice, the seruice of God cannot be ioyned.

But it were great rashnesse to thinke all that possesse lands, lordships, and riches, of necessitie to be subiect to this slauish seruice of *Mammon*, as some men vncharitably iudge of the Bishops and Clergie of England. Ioseph of *Arimathea* was a rich man, and yet in time of great perill did more seruice to Christ, then all his poore Apostles which had so little to leese. It is written in the Euangelists *When euen was come, there came a rich man from Arimathea* Matt. 27. *named Ioseph, which also himselfe was Iesus his disciple. He went to Pilate and begged the body of Iesus. Then Pilate commanded the bodie to bee deliuered, and when Ioseph had taken the body, hee wrapped it in a cleane linen cloth, and layde him in a newe tombe &c.* Consider the circumstances of the historie: weigh the danger of the time: call to remembrance how many thinges might haue hindered, and staied *Ioseph* from this doing, and you shall perceiue that possession of landes and riches, may be ioyned with a free and faithful seruice, yea, often times more faithful, then pouerty and base estate in the worlde. Good Christians therefore may not condemne as slaues and seruants to Antichrist, al such as haue lands and possessions. Experience in England (God be thanked) hath taught, when a number of poore Priests and Ministers reuolted from Christ to the *Mammon* their Masse, that many which had the greatest liuings in this land, were most readie not onely to bee banished their countrey, but also to shead their blood, and giue their liues to serue faithfully their Lord and maister Christ: and I doubt not, wil doe againe, if euer God giue the occasion. Iudge therefore more charitably of your Ministers and Preachers, (O ye English professours) which haue seene these things with your eies, and knowe not how soon, to the sorow of your own hearts, ye may see the same againe. But they which at this day mislike the state of bishops, and doe write or speake against them, are those persons, which in the time of affliction, eyther were not borne, or els were very yong, and therfore haue no sense of that temptation, which that persecution did then bring. As God of his goodnes granteth vs now some *Halcion* dayes: so I beseech him against that day to giue vs the grace of his mighty spirit, so that we may haue the like constancie.

It is further alledged out of Christs doctrine, that when he answered the Pharisees, *Matt.* 22. he giueth a plaine commandement, that landes and possessions should be at the pleasure of the Prince, and that Ministers of the church ought to giue them vp vnto him. For this he saith, *Giue to Cæsar, that which is Cæsars, and to God, that is Gods,* Matth. 22.

But (say they) all temporall landes are *Cæsars,* therefore they ought to giue them vnto *Cæsar:* and our *Cæsar* is our gracious Prince and Soueraigne.

Truely it woulde make any Christian heart to lament in these dayes, to see Gods holy word so miserably drawen, racked, and pulled in sunder from the true meaning thereof. If the Bishops, and other of the Cleargy of England did grudge or murmure to haue their landes and Liuinges to bee tributarie to the Prince, and subiect to all taxes and seruices, that by the lawes of this realm may be, either to the maintenance of her person, or to the defence of our countrey: Or if they did challenge such an immunitie or exemption from the authoritie of the Prince, as the Pope and his Cleargy did: Or if they did finde themselues grieued to bee punished by the Prince for the breach of her Lawes, as the *Donatists* in old time did, and some now in our age doe: If they were such enemies to Princes and Gouernours, as they woulde exempt them out of the state of true christianitie, and of the Church of God, and make them onelie to serue their turne in euill affaires: then in deede did this place make strongly against them. But I trust the Clergie of Englande, are with all good men out of the suspition of these pointes. They are as willing and readie at all times to bee contributarie, as any other subiectes are: they claime no exemption from her authoritie: they willingly submitte themselues to her correction: they humbly acknowledge their obedience in all thinges, that anie Christian prince may require: and this doe they principally for conscience sake, because it is the ordinaunce and commaundement of God: but much moued thereto also, as men, in consideration of their owne state, which next vnder God dependeth of her Maiestie. Seing therfore the hand of God hath more straightly bounde them vnto her, then other common subiects: I doubt not, but she willingly hath, and shall haue all dueties of obedience at their handes, that any Christian subiects by the word of God are bound vnto. Neither are they in any feare that her Maiestie will presse them to any thing, which shall not stande with the glorie of God, and furtherance of the Gospel. But how these words of Christ before mentioned, doe commaund them presently to yeeld vp into her Maiesties hands such lands and possessions, as by the graunt of her goodnes, and by the law of this realm they nowe inioy, indeede I see not. If such a prince shall come (as I trust in my daies neuer to see) that shal put them to this choise, either to forgo their landes and liuings, or to loose the free course of the Gospell: it is before declared, what their duty is to do therin. And I doubt not, but in the late time of persecution, there were many of them that would haue bin glad with al the veines in their heartes, by that choice to haue enioyed in this Realme the freedom of their consciences, though they had bin put to as pore estate, as possibly men might haue liued in. But how that christian princes are warranted, either by this place of the gospel, or by any part of the worde of God, so hardly to deale with the state of the ministery, I haue not as yet learned, though it be in these daies by some boldely affirmed. *Amb.* had a worthy saying, wherin he plainly noteth both what a christian prince may do in these things that appertain unto the church, and how a godly bishop should in that case behaue himselfe. *VVhen it was proposed vnto me* Epist. lib. 5. in Orat. contra Auxentium. (saith he) *that I should deliuer the plate or vessel of the church, I made this answeare: If there were any thing required that was my owne, either land, house, gold or siluer beeing of my owne priuate right, that I would willingly deliuer it: but that I coulde not pull anie thing from the Church of God. And moreouer I said, that in so doing I had regard to the Emperours safetie, because it was not profitable either for me to deliuer it: or for him to receiue it. Let him receiue the wordes of a free Minister of God: If he wil do that is for his owne safetie, let him forbeare to doe Christ iniurie.* By these words yee may perceiue, both that *Ambrose* woulde not deliuer the Church-goods, nor that he thought it safe for the Emperour to require it. The me[a]ning of Christ is in those words, to teach his to put a difference between the duty that they owe to the Prince, and that they owe to God: and to declare, that within their due boundes, they may both stand together. Therfore they that will rightly follow Christ in this doctrine, must consider, in what consisteth the duety towards a Prince or Magistrate, and wherein resteth our duetie towards God. Wee owe to the Prince, honour, feare, and obedience: obedience (I say) in al those things that are not against the worde of God and his commandementes. Those things that God commaundeth, a Christian Prince cannot forbid: Those things that God forbiddeth, no Prince hath authority to command. But such things as be external, and by Gods word left indifferent, the Prince by his authoritie may so by lawe dispose, either in commanding, or forbidding, as in wisedome and discretion he shall thinke to make most to the glory of God, and to the good and safe state of his people. Among these things external, I think lands, goods, and possessions to bee, and therefore that the same ought to be subiect to taxe and tribute in such sort, as the lavves and state of the country requireth: yea, and if there shall happen in any country a magistrate, which by violence and extortion shall vvrest more vnto him of the lands and substance of the people, then lavv and right requireth: I see no cause vvarranted by Gods vvorde, that the inferiour subiects can rebell, or resist the prince therein, but that they shal euidently shew themselues to resist the ordinance of God. For they haue not the sworde of correction committed into their hande, and often times God by euil princes correcteth the sinnes of the people. Wherefore, if subiects resist the hard dealings euen of euill Magistrates, they doe in that respect striue against God himselfe, who will not suffer it vnpunished. Wherefore *Ieremy* willeth Ierem. 28. the Iewes to submit themselues to the obedience of *Nabuchodonosor*, a wicked and cruell king: and *Baruch* teacheth them to pray for the good estate of the Baruc. 1. saide *Nabuchodonosor* and his nephewe *Balthasar*. And Saint *Peter* and saint *Paul*, will Christian subiects not 1. Pet. 1. Rom. 13. onely to bee obedient to the heathen tyrants, which 1. Tim. 2. were in their time, as *Nero*, and such other: but also to make most humble and heartie praiers for them, that his people might liue vnder them a quiet and peaceable life, vvith all godlinesse and honestie. *Tertullian* also shevveth Tertulli. ad the same to haue beene the practise of the primitiue Scapulam. Church, euen toward the enemies and cruell persecutours of the faith of Christ.

A Christian (saith he) *is enemie to none, and least of all to the Emperour, whome hee knowing to be ordeined of God, must of necessitie loue, reuerence, and honour, and wish to be in safetie together with the whole Romaine Empire.* And againe, Tertul. Apolog. *We pray for all Emperours, that God woulde graunt vnto them long life, prosperous reigne, strong armies, faithfull Counsell, obedient Subiects. &c.*

We may learne then by this, that Christian duetie of a subiect consisteth in louing, in reuerencing, in obeying the Prince and Magistrate in all things, that lawfully he commandeth: and in those things that he commandeth vnlawfully, not by violence to resist him, though the same touch our goods, our lands, yea and our life also. As touching our duetie toward God, wee owe vnto him, our selues whollie, both bodie and soule, and all thinges and partes to the same appertaining, according to that his Lawe requireth, *Thou shalt loue God with all thy heart, with all thy soule, with all thy minde, and with thy whole power.* For wee are his creatures, and hee is our Lorde and maker. But forasmuch as Princes, Magistrates, Rulers, Parents, Masters, and all superiours, haue a portion of Gods authoritie ouer vs, as his officers and Lieutenants in their callings: therefore God doeth permit vnto them some part also of his honour, but so farre,

and in such things, and such maner as before is declared,
retaining vnto himselfe our faith and religion, with all the
partes of his diuine worship consisting in Spirite and in trueth,
the calling vpon his blessed name, the confession of his holy
trueth, and the obedience of his morall Lawe : which thinges
hee doeth not make subiect to anie Princes authoritie. And
if any Prince or Magistrate by violence and crueltie shall
breake into the boundes of our duetie towardes God, I say
not that priuate subiects may by violence resist it : but surely
they may not obey it, but rather yeelde into his hands, goods,
Lands, Countrey, and life too. For so did the Prophet *Daniel :*
so did the yong men his companions : so did the whole
number of the martyrs of GOD, by whome the Church of
<small>August. de Agon. Chri.</small> Christ increased as *Augustine* sayeth, *Non resistendo
sed perferendo*, not by resisting but by suffering.
<small>Hierom. ad Theophil.</small> And *Hierome : The Church of Christ was founded by
suffering reproch, by persecutions it increased, by
martyrdomes it was crowned.* To this end sayth *Tertullian*
also, *Semen Euangelij Sanguis Martyrum*. This is the true
doctrine of the wordes of Christ before mentioned, by which
wee are taught to put a difference betweene our duetie
towards God, and that we owe toward the Prince, yeelding
to each that which is his : A doctrine most profitable and
necessary to all Christian Churches and common weales.
But who can gather of this, that the Ministers of the Church
of Christ, liuing vnder a Christian Prince fauouring and
defending the Gospell, must of necessitie giue vp into the
Princes hands those landes and possessions, which by the
graunt of the same Prince and the Lawe of the Land is
assigned vnto them ? For if the land be *Cæsars*, and therefore
must be deliuered to *Cæsar :* then are all goods, *Cæsars*, and
must be also yeelded into his hands.

God saue vs from Princes that will vse like violence and
tyrannie toward our Landes, goods, and bodies, as these
men vse to the word of God. I haue not as yet noted vnto
you (good Christians) the very grounde of this corrupt
interpretation of the doctrine of Christ, and the mischiefe
that is hid vnder it. I pray you therefore consider, to whome
doth Christ speake in al those places of his doctrine before
mentioned ? Whome doth he teach ? whom doth he instruct,
that they shoulde not hoarde vp treasure vpon earth ? that they may not

serue God and Mammon? that they may not bee carefull what to eate and what to drinke? that they must sell all that they haue and followe him? that they must renounce all that they haue if they wil be his true Disciples? and lastly that they must yeelde to Cæsar that which is Cæsars?

Are these things spoken to Ministers onely? doeth Christs doctrine pertaine to Bishops and Ministers onely? Is it his will that they onely shoulde followe his godly instructions and commaundements? Then of likelihoode, as hee came onely to teach Ministers, and to be example of life to them alone: so hee came to saue Ministers onely. But what a wicked vanitie were it so to speake or thinke?

Now if Christes doctrine be generall to all the faithfull, as in deede it is: (that beeing the true interpretation that they woulde haue to bee) it must of necessitie followe, that no true Christian can keepe lands and professions, nor abide in any wealthie or rich estate: which is the very ground of the *Anabaptistes* doctrine, as all learned men doe knowe. In so much, that all the famous men, that in this our age haue expounded the Scriptures, or written against the *Anabaptistes*, doe note, that by this interpretation of the speeches of Christ before mentioned, they do ground their communitie, and taking away of propertie and possession of goods, with sundry like other doctrines. We may see therefore, and it is time to take heed of it, how Sathan, vnder pretences seeketh to thrust the Spirit of the *Anabaptistes* and the groundes of their learning into this Church of *England*. The inconuenience then of this kinde of reasoning is, either, that these sentences of the Gospel touch bishops and Ministers onely, and all other are left free, which is a very great absurdity: or else that the same doctrine gathered out of these places in the same sense that they vse, doth belong to all Christians, which with the *Anabaptists* taketh away all proprietie and possessions of lands and goods, and (as I haue before saide) bringeth in a Platonicall communitie. I say not, that they which vse these places doe meane it: but surely that inconuenience and daunger followeth vpon it. Therefore, they that haue any feare of God, ought to take heed, that their immoderate stomack and affections against bishops and other Ministers, doe not ouermuch blind them, and carrie them away, eyther to the affirming, or to the maintayning of corrupt and daungerous doctrines, both to the Church and common wealth.

If this their doctrine spread in libelles, shall once become familiar vnto the common people of this Realme: it may happily breed such a scab and daungerous sore, as al the cunning in this lande wil scant bee able to heale it. God send grace, that heede may be taken thereof in time.

They will say (I knowe) That this is but a shift of Logike that the false Sophisters the Bishops doe vse, to turne the matter from themselues, when they say, that this doctrine of Christ pertaineth to al Christians, asvvell as to them: and vvill aske me hovve they vvill auoyd those plain euident vvords that Christ speaketh to his Apostles and disciples onely, vvhen hee sendeth them abroad tvvo and tvvo, to preach the kingdome of God. This (say they) doth belong to Ministers and Preachers onelie.

As ye goe, preach, saying, that the kingdome of heauen is at Matth. 10. *hand: heale the sicke, clense the leapers, raise the* Mar. 3. *dead, cast out deuils, freely ye haue receiued, and freely* Luke 9. *giue you. Possesse not gold, nor siluer, nor money in your purses, nor scrip toward your journey, neither two coates, neither shoes, nor yet a staffe. For the workman is worthy of his meate.* These wordes, I must confesse, doe not appertaine generally to all Christians, no more doe they generally to al ministers and preachers of all times and places. Is it euill in it selfe to haue golde or siluer? or to haue a staffe on the way to walke with? or to weare shooes to saue his feete in iourneying? I thinke there is no Christian that will so iudge. Christ himselfe had a purse, wherein *Iudas* carried money for his prouision, and hee suffered certaine rich women to goe with him, and to minister to him and to his Disciples. *Peter* also bare a sworde, and ware sandalles on his feete, when the Angell bade him put on his sandalles. And *Paule* writing to *Timothie*, willeth him to bring his cloake with him, although vndoubtedly hee had another garment before. Wee must consider then what it is that Christ in this place meaneth, seeing neither himselfe nor his Apostles did obserue it according to the strictnesse of the letter.

There bee some that say these precepts bee personall, and for a time onelie, not generall or perpetuall: for that which goeth before may seeme to take away the continuance of these precepts, *Go not in the way of the Gentiles, but to the lost sheepe of the house of Israel.* Which precept the Apostles at this time obserued, but afterward they preached the Gospel vnto al the nations of the earth: so doe they thinke, that Christ, for the time of this message onelie, commaunded them to possesse no golde nor siluer, &c. and from thenceforth that this commaundement was abrogated. This interpretation I can not reiect as euill, or not pertinent to the meaning of Christ. There bee also some hypocrites, and Pope-holie persons, which will haue these preceptes perpetuall, and builde thereon friery and monkish superstition: They wil not touch any money: They wil weare no whole shooes: They wil not haue a staffe to walke with, thinking that they shew themselues the holy seruaunts of God therein. To this interpretation verie nighly commeth that, which these men vse to proue, that bishoppes and preachers may haue no landes nor possessions, nor riches, no nor money, further then will barely prouide them meat, and drinke, and cloth, and whatsoeuer is aboue, to be of superfluitie. Some other thinke, that Christ in those woordes onely compareth the Ambassadours of other princes with his: as if he had sayde, I sende you foorth to preach the kingdome of God: and the state of an ambassade or message doeth require, that I should deliuer vnto you money, and all other like thinges conuenient for this voyage, as princes vse to their Ambassadours: but deceiue not your selues: the maner of this message is diuers from such messages as ciuil princes vse. In ciuill ambassades, great furniture (I know) is thought conuenient: but this message of mine is such, as needeth no such matter to set it out. For the maiestie of the thing it selfe, and the myracles that you shall worke, shall sufficiently giue authoritie vnto it. This interpretation also I think not amisse: but in my opinion, and that by the iudgement of some other learned men also, the true and simple meaning of Christ was, to teach his Apostles to put their trust and whole confidence vpon the prouidence of God onelie, and for the better perswasion, would haue them at this time to make triall thereof, and by experience to learne, that though they haue nothing in the sight of the world to feede them, to helpe or to defend them: yet that hee wil so prouide for them, if they continue in their vocation and calling faithfully, that they shall want nothing: yea, that the fowles of the air shall rather feede them, then that they shoulde lacke sustenance. That this was Christes meaning, it may appeare in Saint *Luke*, where he sayeth to Luke. 22. his Apostles, *When I sent you forth without wallet or scrippe, or* shooes, lacked you any thing? and they saide, No. *Then saide he vnto them, But nowe hee that hath a wallet, let him take it vp, and hee that hath none, let him sell his coate and buy a sworde.* The Apostles vndoubtedly had great need of this instruction, and to be taught to put their whole trust in the prouidence of God, and to depende vppon that onelie. For he did see that in the execution of their office they shoulde bee cast into all the difficulties of this world, which either Sathan or his ministers were able to raise against them. This lesson is very necessary also for all other Christians, but principally for the Ministers and preachers of the Gospel, whensoeuer God for the profession and teaching of his trueth shall cast them into the like difficulties. For if they doe not rest vpon that onely, they shall finde lands, possessions, power, authoritie, kinred, friendshippe, and al other helpes of this world, to be but as a broken staffe to leane vnto.

But what maketh this against that, that Ministers of the Church in the calme times of quietnesse, may enioy the benefites and liberalitie of good and gratious Princes, whome he hath appoynted as fosterers and nourishers of his Church and people, wherein soeuer those benefites of their liberalitie shall be imployed, bee it landes, possessions, goods, money, or any other maner of prouision?

For further proofe of this matter against the wealthie state of the Cleargie, the example of S. *Peter* also is brought in, Actes 3. who sayeth in the *Actes* to the poore lame man, *Siluer and golde haue I none, &c.* Loe (say they) Sa[i]nt *Peter* was a right Apostle, and was in so poore case, that hee had neither siluer nor gold, no not so much as he could bestowe a meane reliefe vpon a poore begger. His example should our rich Bishops and Preachers follow. And Saint *Paul* to *Timothie, Hauing foode and rayment, we shoulde therewith be content.*

Here wee may learne (say they) what maner of liuing Ministers of the Church should haue, that is, so much onely, as will prouide them meate, drinke, and cloth : whatsoeuer is aboue, that is superfluity, and more then Gods word requireth.

Who seeth not (good Christians) whereat these men shoote, and what state of the Ministerie, this earnest zeale that nowe is pretended, woulde settle in this Church? that is, more miserable and worse prouided for, then any other state of the lande beside. Those heartes wherein is true deuotion, and the right loue of the Gospell, are rather ouer bountifull toward the Preachers thereof, then too sparing. For they are thus affected, that they thinke nothing too deare for them, yea, if it were possible, they would giue their eyes vnto them out of their heads, as *Paul* saith to the *Galathians*.

What spirite this is therefore that woulde so hardly pinch and wring the Ministers of the Church, it is euidently to be gathered. The principall purpose at the beginning was, to prooue that the Ministers might not by the word of God inioy any temporall landes: but nowe forsooth, through the goodnesse of their cause, in the vehemencie of their reasoning, and fulnesse of their proofe, it falleth out so, that Ministers may not haue so much as any peny in their purse to prouide them sustenance; but must liue vpon the charitable almes of the people, and content themselues with meate, drinke, and apparell onely, as the Apostles did. For they are no spirituall men (say they) that haue temporall liuing. Yea, of the very tithes they ought to claime no more, then may serue them to meate, drinke, and cloth. And if the same be denied them, they may not by lawe sue for it. *For if their coate be taken from* Matth. 5. *them, they should deliuer their cloake also.*

This doctrine doeth very well iustifie the couetous and vncharitable dealings of many Parishioners, which partly by violence, partly by craftie meanes detaine from the Ministers their portion of tithes appoynted by the lawe. This doctrine giueth good countenance to corrupt patrons, who will not bestow their benefices, but by composition of a good part of the fruites to their owne vse and commoditie. And when the liuing shall be worth 100. poundes by the yeere, they will aske, whether thirtie or fourtie pounds be not a sufficient portion for the Parson? This dealing before time hath bene accounted little better, then sacrilege or simonie: but now it may be thought (if this doctrine be good and allowable) that it is lawfully done, and according to the word of God: yea, and that the Minister is a couetous worldling, and worthy great blame, that will not content himselfe with such a rate, as they willingly shall allowe him. What care they which thus reason haue, I will not say of the preaching of the Gospel, but of the state of learning and knowledge in the Church of Christ, all men may euidently perceiue. Either they iudge, as I haue before written at large, that men bee Angels without corruption, and will followe the course of learning for conscience sake, though there bee no hope of rewarde to allure them; or els they thinke, that God will miraculously giue knowledge to such as he shall incline to the Ministerie, as he did in the primitiue Church to his Apostles and other.

As touching the example of Saint *Peter*, it is before declared, what cause Christ respected in the choosing of so poore Apostles, and leauing them in so base state and condition of life: that is, that the worke of winning the whole world to the doctrine of saluation by so simple and poore instruments, as in the iudgement of men they seemed, might be the greater glorie to God, as Saynt *Paul* sayeth: Especially seeing hee did set them foorth, and furnish them with the heauenly riches of his holie spirite, that is to say, extraordinary knowledge, rare giftes of vertue, and power to worke myracles.

But vpon this extraordinarie dealing of God in the founding of his Church, to grounde a generall and perpetuall rule, to binde the Ministers of al places and times, is such maner vsing the Scriptures, as must needes breede great inconueniences among the people of God.

As for the words of Saint *Paul*, there is no man I thinke, but that hee may perceiue they are spoken generally, and not to Ministers onely, as they are in this place applied. Remember the place: viewe the circumstances: consider what goeth before, and what commeth after, and you shall vnderstande it to bee true. For Saint *Paul* there, speaketh to the same purpose that Christ doth *Matth.* 6. when he willeth men not to be carefull what to eate, what to drinke, or what to put on, but that they shoulde seeke the kingdome of GOD and the righteousnesse thereof, and all other things shoulde by the prouidence of God bee cast vnto them. So, I say, Saint *Paul* exhorteth men not to be in loue with the riches of this world, which they shall neuer cary away with them: that they shoulde not practise wicked waies to gaine, but account godlines their chief gaine and commoditie, holding themselues contented with those things that the necessity of nature requireth, that is, foode and apparell: For whatsoeuer is aboue that, may seeme to bee superfluous. This wholesome doctrine, the spirit of God in the Scriptures doth often cast vpon the consciences of Christians, as a necessary bridle, to stay the wicked affection of couetousnesse and greedie desire of the world, wherto the corruption of our nature is giuen. And yet he doeth not condemne riches, or a more plentifull life, as euill in it selfe. It is the heart, the minde, and the affection, that God would haue staied and kept vnder in his obedience, and not the forbearing of the externall creatures as before is at large declared. *Iob* in the middes of his greatest wealth had as poore and as contented a heart, as he that had a small liuing, and did no more exceede in gluttonie, or other riotous excesse, then hee did, which had not a peny more then to prouide meate, drinke and cloth. This doctrine, as it doeth generally pertaine to all Christians: so I denie not, but it very nighly and chiefly ought to touch Preachers and Ministers of the Church. Wherefore I must and doe confesse, that so much as our Bishops and Clergie want of the perfourmance heereof, they want of that perfection that by the worde of God they shoulde haue. But howe can it bee prooued heereby, that they may not haue more ample or large allowance then shall suffice them for necessarie foode and apparel? In deede that contentation of mind they should haue, whensoeuer God calleth them to that necessitie, yea and when they be in their wealthiest state that any condition of a Christian common weale doth giue them, they ought not in those things to exceed, but to keepe that moderation that godlines requireth: and whatsoeuer is aboue that, they are bound in conscience to see godly and honestly bestowed, or else they grieuously offende God, and giue euill example to other. This rule (as I haue said) pertaineth in like maner to all christians: and therefore it can no more follow vpon this, that the lands and liuings of ministers must be taken from them, because it bringeth superfluitie vnto them and more then the necessitie of nature requireth, then you can conclude the same against all other Christians that haue more ample lands and liuings then will suffice them to the like purpose. As I haue said before, so say I now again, If our bishops and other clergy men, imploy the ouerplus of their large and plentifull liuings vnto euill and naughty vses, neither I nor any other can therein defend them.

For the better vnderstanding of my aunswere to these places, and of the imperfect manner of reasoning vsed by the aduersary: it behoueth to consider, that God in his worde layeth downe a perfect measure of his iustice, and an absolute rule of that life that Christians shoulde leade. As for example, when hee sayth in the Law, *Thou shalt loue the Lorde thy God with all thy heart, with all thy soule, with all thy minde, with all thy power, and thy neighbour as thy selfe:* This commaundement requireth, that all the parts and members of our soule inwardly, and our bodie and goods outwardly, should be bent and giuen ouer to the setting foorth of the glory of God. Our *heart* is the roote of our affections: therefore we are commaunded to loue or hate nothing, to feare or hope for nothing, to desire or shun nothing, not to be sory for any thing, nor reioyce in any thing, but onely in God and his glory. By our *soule*, is meant all the course of our life: our infancie, our young age, our middle age, and our old age. Wherefore in this it is required, that the whole time of our life, from the beginning of our birth to the houre of our death, shoulde bee imployed to the seruice of God. Our *minde* comprehendeth our reason and vnderstanding: so that by that branche, wee are taught that our understanding, our reason, and all the cogitations of our minde should bee occupied in nothing, but in the loue of God. Our *power* noteth all the strength and sences of our body, and the abilitie of worldly substance and outwarde giftes of God. So that there is nothing apperteining to vs, eyther invvardly, or outvvardly, (as I haue saide) but God wholly requireth the same to his seruice: and if wee doe fayle therein, wee offend his iustice, and want of that perfect rule of life that is prescribed vnto vs: Insomuch that if the mercie of God in Christ our Sauiour helpe not, wee deserue for the same euerlasting damnation. To the declaration of the latter part of this rule, *that wee should loue our neighbour as our selfe*, apperteineth the doctrine of Christ, *Matth.* 5. *that we should not so much as once bee moued with anger toward our neighbour, that wee should not looke vpon a woman to lust after her, that wee should not onely loue our neighbour as our selfe, but that we should loue our enemies, blesse them that curse vs, doe good to them that hate vs, pray for them that persecute vs. &c.*

As for our money, lands, goods and possessions, wee should haue our mindes so litle giuen to them, and our hearts so smally set vpon them, that we nothing at all should care for them further, then that they may bee vnto vs, either instruments of vertue, or necessary helps of our fraile life. Yea, there is nothing so nigh, nothing so deere vnto vs by Christes rule, eyther eye, or hande, or foote, or whatsoeuer it bee, but we should cut it off, and cast it from vs, if it be a let or hinderance vnto vs to enter into the kingdom of God. Finally, our bodies being here in this vale of miserie, our minds, and hearts and conuersations shoulde be in heauen: *they that haue wiues, as though they had none: they* 1. Cor. 7. *that weepe, as though they wept not: they that reioyce, as though they reioyced not: they that buy, as though they possessed not: they that vse this worlde, as though they vsed it not.*

To this rule of Christian perfection, apperteine all those sentences and exhortations of Christ and of his Apostles, which before you haue heard alledged, tending all to this ende, to pull away the hearts of men from the loue of riches and care of this worlde, that they may set the same wholly vpon God. This rule is layde downe not onely for Ministers of the Church, as though they onely were the seruants of God, but also for all other faithful Christians, whom it bindeth as streightly as it doeth the Ministers. For it is a marke, vnto which they both should direct their whole indeuours.

They therefore that will apply this rule to some one state of men, and not to other, fal into like error as Monkes and Friers did, dreaming a more straite order by God to be appoynted to one, then to another. The Minister so much as he lacketh of this perfection, so much is hee indebted and in daunger vnto God: And if he flye not to the mercie of God purchased by the merite of Christ to wash away that want and imperfection, vndoubtedly there resteth nothing, but eternall damnation.

Nowe, as I haue sayde of the Minister, so must I say of all Christians beside. Therefore out of this doctrine is no particular application to bee made more to one state then to another, but onely this, that ministers, because of their calling, should shew themselues to come neerer to this marke, then other. Where the errour in reasoning is, you may nowe by this perceiue, which consisteth in two points. First, that the branches of the rule of Christian perfection generally giuen to all, are applied onely to Ministers of the Church, as speciall precepts to binde them: And secondly, that the performing of this rule is more imputed (as the Monkes and Friers did) to the outwarde refusing of Gods creatures, then the brideling of the affections and humble contentation of the mind before God.

By this corrupt manner of reasoning in these dayes, are framed sundry daungerous arguments against the state of the Ministerie heere nowe with vs in England. As for example,

Our Bishops and Ministers are euill men: they aunswere not the perfect rule, that is prescribed vnto them by the worde of God: therefore they shoulde bee deposed, their state altered, and their Lands and liuings taken into the Princes hands, or be otherwise imploied as it shall be thought good.

The daunger of this argument will be easily perceiued, if you apply the same to other states, as thus:

Princes, Magistrates and noble men are euill, they do not fulfill that rule of right and perfect gouernment that the worde of God requireth: therefore pull them downe, set other in their places, or alter their state cleane.

This is a seditious and perillous argument, especially when common and inferior subiects, not hauing authoritie, shall take vpon them to bee iudges in such cases, as nowe they doe against bishops.

VVith this manner of reasoning (as I haue before noted) the Deuill filleth the heads and hearts of his troublesome instruments, when hee intendeth to worke mischiefe, eyther in the Church of God, or in the state of any common weale.

This manner of arguments they alwayes vse, which for priuate respects, pretend generall reformations or alterations in the state of a Church or Countrey, wherein they liue. Let the bishops and Cleargie of England haue such iudges and triall, as the word of God requireth, and euer hath beene vsed in the Church of Christ: yea, or such as other states woulde thinke reasonable and indifferent for them selues in their calling: and then, on Gods name, let them abide the hazard of the sentence eyther with them or against them, and the daunger of such penaltie as in iustice and equitie may be assigned. Another daungerous Argument is this:

Bishops and Preachers by Christ are commaunded not to bee carefull for the world, not to hoord vp treasures in earth, yea to renounce all they haue and follow Christ: therefore they ought not to haue any lands or Lordships, or great and wealthie Liuings, but to be contented with meate, drinke and cloth. &c.

The hardnesse of this reason will be the better vnderstanded, if the like bee applyed to some other person.

Noble men and gentlemen, if they wil bee right and true Christians, by Gods worde are commaunded not to be carefull for the worlde, not to hoord vp riches heere on the earth, yea to renounce all that they haue, and followe Christ: therefore they may not haue so great and ample liuings more then other, but shall content themselues vvith such a moderate portion, as may tollerably mainteine them, in seeing the adminstration of iustice in their countreyes, and the residue that nowe is spent in gaming and vnnecessarie pompe, and vanitie of the world, to be imployed to the maintenance of a great nomber of the Princes subiects, and people of God, that are not able in meane estate to liue.

For in such case were the noble men and Gentlemen of the Israelites called *Principes familiarum*, the Princes and chiefe of each tribe and familie among the people of God.

A many of such factious and seditious arguments may in like manner be framed, more meete for rebels, then for good subiects or faithfull Christians, which I do in this place for good considerations omitte. For if they shoulde bee so countenaunced with particular allegations of the Scriptures, and furnished with such learning and examples of histories, as factious heades are able to deuise: happily they woulde carrie as much credite, and drawe as great a number of followers and mainteiners, as nowe the like dealing doeth against the Clergie. I will not therefore tarrie any longer in this point. I haue set foorth vnto you an example or two nakedly and barely, to this ende onely, if it might bee possible, to open the eyes of some, which seeme in part to bee blinded eyther with affection against bishops, or with a desire to worke and bring to passe some speciall drift and purpose that they haue deuised: for what cause, it may be more easily by wise men coniectured, then safely by mee layde downe in writing.

For the further examining of this matter, and that it may be the better vnderstanded, whether ecclesiasticall men may with safe consciences enioy the state of their liuings by landes or no, Let vs briefely consider the condition of the Church, and hovve Ministers haue beene mainteined from the beginning, euen to this day. And heere I must protest, that the Histories and writers, especially such [How Ministers were mainteined from the beginning.]

as bee of credite, are so imperfect in this point, as the trueth must bee gathered by coniecture of certaine braunches, rather then by any discourse in their writing.

For the space of the first three hundred yeeres after Christ, it is well knowen to all such as haue looked into the Ecclesiasticall Histories, that it was almost in continuall persecution vnder heathen tyrantes, which with all indeuour sought meanes to oppresse Christian Religion, and the true professours thereof. Wherefore in all that time it was not possible for the church to haue any setled state, by Landes or certaine reuenewe to mainteine the Ministers thereof: but they were sustained onely by the liberall contribution of godlie persons, collected at certain times for that and other like Christian vses.

For Saint *Cyprian* signifieth, that to certaine persons _{Lib. 4. epi. 5.} appointed to the office of readers, hee distributed the measure of gifts and distributions, as were assigned to _{Canon. 5.} the Priestes. The Canons attributed to the Apostles, make mention of oblations and the first fruites to bee brought home to the house of the bishoppe, beside such thinges as were offered in the Church. *Origen* somewhat more straightly seemeth to require the tenthes and first fruites of such increase as Christians haue by the blessing of God: _{Hom. 11. in Numer.} his wordes bee these. *It is comely and profitable, that the first fruites should be offered to the Priests of the Gospell also, for so the Lord disposed, that he that preacheth the gospell, should liue by the Gospell. And as this is good and comely: so contrariwise, it is euill and vncomely, that one that worshippeth God, and commeth into the church, knowing that the Priestes attend on the Altar, and serue the worde of God, and ministerie of the Church, should not offer vnto the Priests the firstlings of those fruites that God giueth by bringing foorth his sunne and seasonable showres vpon them. For such a soule seemeth not to mee to haue any remembrance of God, or to thinke, that it is God that giueth those fruites.*

It may appear also, that euen in this time the Church had certaine houses allotted to their Bishops. For when *Paulus Samosatenus* after his deposition, would not depart out of the _{Euseb. ecclesiast. hist. lib. 7. cap. 30.} house that belonged to the Church, it was appoynted by the authoritie of the Emperour *Aurelius*, that he should bee remoued from it, and the house assigned vnto him, to whom the bishops of *Italie* did agree in doctrine. *Origen* also mentioneth certaine rentes and reuenues due to the Church. *Many of vs* (sayeth he) *haue neede of this warning, that wee bee both faithfull, and also wise,* ad dispensandos Ecclesiæ redditus, *to bestowe the rents of the Church.* ^{Orig. tract. in Matt. 31.}

And one *Petrus de Natalibus* writeth, that in the time of *Vrbane* bishop of *Rome,* about two hundred twentie and sixe yeeres after Christ, the Church first beganne to possesse landes towarde the finding of the Ministers. Certaine it is, that many godly disposed persons, notwithstanding they were letted by the crueltie of tyrantes, euen in that time gaue large and ample giftes vnto the Church, not onely in money and plate, but as it is to bee gathered, in reuenue also. For *Optatus Mileuitanus* writeth, that *Mensurius* Bishop of *Carthage* before *Cecilianus,* when hee was sent for to the Emperour, fearing that hee should returne no more agayne, left in the custodie of certaine persons *Ornamenta plurima et aurea et argentea, many ornaments of golde and siluer.* The restoring of which ornamentes and iewels afterwarde, was one great occasion of the schisme of the *Donatists,* as the same *Optatus* sheweth. Wherefore it may appeare, the Church was not in those dayes so poore and needie, as some men woulde haue vs thinke it was: though it were then vnder heathenish and cruel tyrants, with all extremitie forbidding, that any persons should giue eyther goodes or Landes to the releefe of it. *Sabellicus* writeth, that in the time of *Maxentius* the Emperour, one *Lucina* a noble and rich gentlewoman of *Rome,* appoynted the Church of *Rome* to bee heire vnto all her substance and possessions. Which, when that cruell tyrant vnderstoode, hee for the time banished her out of the Citie. But when *Constantine* that good and first Christian Emperour, vndertooke the defence and maintenance of Christian religion, he not only liberally bestowed vpon the Church himselfe, but by lawe made it free, to all that woulde giue any thing vnto the Church, were it in Landes or otherwise. Which lawe *Valentinianus, Theodosius,* and other afterwarde confirmed, nor euer was it abridged but by *Iulian* the Apostata. A copie of one decree of *Constantine* is in *Eusebius.* Those thinges that belong to the right of other, we ^{Opt. lib. 1.} ^{Ennead. 7. Lib. 8.} ^{Lib. 1. de sacrosancto eccles.} ^{Lib. 16. Cod. Theod.}

will not onely not to haue retayned, but plainly to be restored.
_{Lib. 10. cap. 5.} *Wherefore our will and pleasure is, that so soone as thou shalt receiue these our letters, if there be any goods belonging to the Catholike Church of Christians, eyther in cities, or other places, taken in possession by the citizens, or by any other, that the same presently be restored in like right, as before they had it. See therefore that all things, eyther houses, or gardens, or whatsoeuer, bee with speede restored to the Church againe.* By this meanes, not only the Emperors themselues gaue both lands and many other riche giftes, but also sundry other rich and godly persons. *Constantine* gaue lands in the countrey about *Sabine*, and an house and a garden at *Rome*.
_{Sabell. Ennead. 7. lib. 8.}

_{Sozom. lib. 1 cap. 8.} The same *Constantine* out of the tribute of euery citie, gaue a portion to the Churches for the maintenance of their Ministers, and established them to continue as a Law for euer.

Eusebius writeth, that beside many other benefites (as contribution of corne, building of Churches, &c.) he granted to all Ecclesiastical persons, free immunitie of all seruices and taxes, sauing only for their lands. For the lands of the Church were subiect to tribute, as other were, by an ordinance made by the sonnes of the forenamed *Constantine*. This may appeare also by *Ambrose*, writing of the second *Valentinian*. *If he require tribute, we denie it not: the lands of the Church do pay tribute.* The church then had lands, and that a good while before *Ambrose* his time, which was about the yeere of our Lord three hundred sixtie and eight. Yea, *Ambrose* himself liued by his owne lands being Bishop. Therefore it may appeare hee did not thinke it to be against the worde of God, for a Bishoppe or Minister of the Church to liue vpon the reuenewe of landes.
_{Euseb. eccles. hist. 13. ca. 7.}
_{Lege tertia. Cod. de episc. et clericis.}
_{Lib. epist. 5. in orat. cont. Auxentium.}

After the time of *Constantine*, the wealth of the Church increased, as well in landes as other substance and prouision, not only by the gifts of Emperours, Kings, and Queenes, but partly also (as I haue said) by the deuotion of other godly persons, who oftentimes left to the vse of the Church, eyther a great part, or their whole substance and possessions, partly by the gift of Bishops themselues, partly by other Ecclesiasticall persons, which, because they were not maried, nor had issue or heires, were
_{Basil. epist. 140.}

by order bound to leaue vnto the church, all their possessions, both lands and goods. Sometime also by the punishment of offendors. For it is read, that one *Bassus* a gentleman falsely accused *Sixtus* bishoppe of *Rome*, and when *Sixtus* had cleared himselfe in a synode of Bishops, *Bassus*, for his slaunderous accusation, was banished, and his landes giuen vnto the Church. The same *Sixtus* gaue landes vnto the Church himselfe also. *Crescentius* a noble man gaue vnto the Church of *Rome* all his substance, and a manour in *Sicilie* called *Argianum*. *Eudotia* the Empresse, wife to *Theodosius*, adorned the Bishops house at *Constantinople*, and gaue vnto it a yeerely reuenue. By the counsell at *Berythe* it may appeare, the Church of *Edessa* had rentes, manours, woods, and plate set with precious stones, &c. This state of wealth the church grewe vnto, not much more then in the space of one hundred yeeres after it pleased God to giue peace vnto it from outwarde and Heathenish enemies: and yet in the meane time had it other tempestes and bitter stormes of aduersitie, that did more hinder deuotion and godlinesse, then the bloody persecutions of the Emperors did: as namely the troubles raysed by the *Arian* heretikes, by the space of many yeres, and especially in *Asia*, *Greece*, and all the East parts of the world. And shortly thereupon folowed the horrible inuasion of the *Goths*, *Vandals*, *Herules*, and other barbarous people, which as swarmes came out of the north parts, and with maruellous cruelty ouerwhelmed all the west Countreyes of *Europe*, to the great hindrance, daunger, and vnquietnesse of the Church of God. After these stormes and tempests were somwhat ouerblowne, the riches of the Church did very much increase, both in lands and otherwise, by such meanes as before I haue rehearsed. And this generally I obserued in all histories, and in all times, that the wealth thereof vnder Christian Princes was neuer diminished, but rather increased: nor euer did they murmure at it, or thought it too much, vntill the Pope chalenged his vsurped dominion, and did seeke to bring the neckes of Princes vnder his girdle, and to alter Empires, Kingdomes, and Principalities at his will and pleasure, saying, that he had *Ius vtriusque gladij*, the power of both swords.

 Heere (I knowe) some will say, that by my ovvne confession, I am fallen to acknowledge that botch that first bredde Antichrist, and set him vp into his throne aboue Kings and Princes, that is to say, the immoderate vvealth of the Ecclesiasticall men, vvhich then did corrupt religion, and so, say they, doth it novve vvith vs.

No, no (good Christians) they that so say, eyther are blinded with ignoraunce, or looke into thinges with partiall eyes, and seeke rather a secrete furthering of priuate purposes, then the knowledge of the true causes of that, whereof they speake. For they that will indifferently consider the states of time, and with true iudgement weigh the circumstaunces of them, may easily discerne, that it vvas not the wealth of the Cleargie, but other causes of great weight and importaunce, that sette vp Antichrist aloft in his throane, and wrought him the dominion of the Church, which I pray God may bee more carefully looked vnto among vs, then yet I perceiue that they haue beene: especially if we meane so earnestlie to keepe away from vs the returne of his corruption, as many now would seeme to doe.

The first cause that aduaunced Antichrist, was *Schisme and heresie in the Church*, for the space of two hundred yeeres and more, together with the barbarous irruptions which before I spake of. The second cause was, *the generall decay of learning*, and especially of *the knowledge of the Scriptures, and of the tongues*. Thirdly, *the vsurpation of Ecclesiasticall Discipline*, practised against Emperours and Princes, by which hee conquered more then by all other meanes. The helping causes to these principall, were these two: first, the negligence, the vnskilfulnesse, the vnworthinesse of many emperours and gouernours, giuen ouer rather to wantonnesse and voluptuous pleasures, then to the care of their charge: and secondly, the superstitious deuotion of the people, maintained by corrupt doctrine. But the graund cause of all causes was, *the iust iudgement of God*, for the generall vnthankfulnesse of the world, in receiuing the knowledge of his gospell, which he sent among them.

The true causes that set vp Antichrist.

And this cause was vniuersall in all estates and kindes of persons, as well ecclesiasticall as other. The bishoppes and Ministers were giuen ouer to maintaine factions and hereticall doctrines: Princes looked more to their sensuall pleasure, then to the godly gouernment of their subiects: the people were bent wholly to superstition and wickednes of life, so that (a small number onely excepted) none did studie howe in life and godly conuersation, to frame themselues to the good and wholesome doctrine of the Gospell, which at the hande of many godly men, they at the beginning had receiued. Sundry of these or the like causes haue we now also growing and encreasing among vs: and therefore haue we great cause to feare the like iust iudgement of God, that eyther shall cast vs againe vnder the tyranny of Antichrist, or bring upon vs some plague no lesse grieuous then that is.

Our ministers and Preachers breake out to Schismaticall factions and curious Doctrines. The people, in steede of superstitious deuotion, haue conceiued an heathenish contempt of Religion, and a disdaynefull loathing of the ministers thereof. Vice and wickednesse ouerwhelmeth all states and conditions of men. None almost, vnlesse it bee some that God reserueth to his secrete knowledge, studie to shevve them-selues thankfull to God, and in life to expresse that, which in doctrine they will seem to approoue. I pray God, that by abusing this long suffering of the Lorde, wee heape not vp wrath for our selues against the day of wrath. God hath dealt as mercifullie with this land, as euer hee did with any. I beseech him, that in time we may repent with *Niniue*, and turne to him in sackcloth and ashes, while hee may bee founde, and while hee stretcheth vnto vs the hande of his gratious goodnesse, least when it is too late, and hee hath turned his face from vs, we crie vnto him with vaine gronings and mourne with vnprofitable sighings. Hee sent the light of his trueth into this realme, first in the time of K. *Henry* the eight, and brake the power of Antichrist among vs: but because hee sawe neyther thankfull receiuing of the Gospell, nor any thing studied for by men generally, but the benefite of Abbey lands, and possessions, to enrich them-selues: hee by and by cut off the comfortable sweetenesse of his word, with the bitter sauour of the sixe articles, and sharp persecution of them that professed true religion.

His iustice indeede coulde no longer abide the full ripenesse of the superstition, idolatrie, and wicked life of the Monkes and Friers, and such other swarms of Antichristian impietie: but our vnthankfulnesse deserued not to haue the same turned to our benefite, nor the freedome of his Gospell to be continued among vs to our further comfort.

In the time of that gratious Prince King *Edward* the sixt, hee gaue vs a larger taste of his word and a greater freedome of all points of sound and true christian doctrine, to our vnestimable benefite, if wee coulde haue receiued it accordingly. But euen then also, hee perceiued, that wee sought not so much the increase of his glory, or to frame our liues according to our profession, as wee did studie vnder countenance of religion, by al meanes we could, to work again our owne worldly benefite and commoditie. And therefore did hee the seconde time take from this realme his fatherly blessing, and cast vpon vs that heauie scourge of persecution, which immediately followed, keeping vs vnder the rodde of his correction by the space of certaine yeeres.

Neuerthelesse, as a mercifull Father, declaring that by his chastening he sought not our confusion but our amendment, euen for the glory of his names sake onely, beyonde al hope and expectation, hee shewed vs againe the light of his countenance, and that more fauourably and bountifully then euer hee did before, raysing for vs as it were out of the dust of death, a Noble Queene, a gratious Prince, as a nurse or protectresse of his church : Vnder the shadow of whose wings, although but a Virgine, he keepeth vs in great safetie and quietnesse, against al the ancient enemies, both of his Church and of our naturall countrey. Notwithstanding all this, our olde vnthankfulnesse and forgetfulnesse of our duetie still continueth, and we shew our selues the same men that euer we did before.

And therefore beside the earnest preaching of his worde, calling vs continually to repentance, vvho seeth not, that diuers times he hath shaken the rod of his displeasure ouer vs? as in the Northren rebellion, and in many signes and tokens from heauen, thereby, if it were possible, to waken vs out of our sinfull securitie, wherein wee sleepe so confidently ? Yea, and the more to keep vs in feare, hee hath made vs to nourish in our bosomes the apparant instrument of his wrath, by whome wee coulde not choose but see, that in a moment hee might haue taken from vs both the comfort of his Gospell, and the freedome and happinesse of our state. Heere must I put you in minde againe of his exceeding mercies shewed toward vs euen in these fewe Monethes, deliuering vs from the bloody crueltie of our enemies.

But to what effect, I pray you, commeth all this carefull working of our mercifull God, by fayre meanes and foule meanes thus labouring to drawe vs vnto him? Doth it quicken in vs the care of our saluation? doth it increase the feare of his displeasure? doth it stir vp any more zeale and loue of his Gospell? hath it any thing diminished our vncharitable strife and contention? doth it any thing abate the obstinacie of the aduersarie? hath it any way diminished the loosenes of our liuing? hath it taken from vs our pride in apparell? our daintines in feeding? our wastfull and pompous building? hath it made lesse any euill among vs, and not rather encreased euery thing, to an higher degree then euer it was before? Shall we thinke then, that this our vnsensible dulnesse and vnthankfulnesse, can be without imminent punishment? Surely, me thinketh the song of *Esay* the Prophet painteth out our state and condition with the euent that will follow of it, *The Lord hath chosen this lande, as his beloued vineyard, hee hath mounded it* with his gratious Esay. 5.
fauour and diuine protection, *hee hath stoned it* by casting out the rubble of the Synagogue of Antichrist, the broken stones I meane, of idolatrie, superstition, false doctrine, and corrupt worship of God: hee hath planted among vs the sweete grape of his most wholesome Gospel, and the true vine Christ Iesu: he hath *set vp a watch Tower* of Christian gouernment, *and a wine presse* of earnest preaching of repentance, to presse and wring mens hearts, if it were possible, to yeelde foorth the sweete iuice of the fruits of the gospel to the glorie of God. And he long hath looked, (for these his great benefites) that wee should haue brought foorth *sweete grapes*, and we haue yeelded nothing but sowre and stinking fruite, discord and dissension among our selues, couetousnesse, oppression, extortion, drunkennesse, banquetting, voluptuous pleasure, whoredome, adulterie, securitie in sinne, contempt of God, disdaine of his Ministers, despising of his worde, selfe-liking in our owne doings, confidence and trust in our owne wisedome and policie &c. I pray God therefore in time wee may take heede of that heauie iudgement that followeth, I meane, that hee will *take away the hedge, and breake downe the wall* of his mightie protection, whereby onely wee haue hitherto remayned safe, and that hee will lay vs waste that the beastes of the fielde may ouertrample vs: that hee

vvill take from vs the teaching and preaching of his Gospell, vvherevvith in vayne hee hath so long digged and delued in our barraine heartes: that hee vvill forbidde the cloudes of his heauenly prouidence to rayne dovvne vpon vs his great and manifolde blessings, vvhich beforetime hee hath giuen vs, so that wee shalbe left as a desolate ground, breeding nothing but bushes and brambles of ignorance, errour, idolatrie, superstition, heresie and vvicked life, and bee made subiects and slaues vnto our greatest enemies. The Lorde turne away that, which our vnthankfull hearts may iustly feare to be at hand. &c.

By this that I haue written, as I doubt not but the godly may perceiue it was not riches and vvealth of the Cleargie that first set vp Antichrist in the vsurped throne of his dominion ouer the Church, but that there vvere other more true and right causes that bredde that mischiefe: so likewise that conscience, that feareth God, and vvithout affection looketh into the state of this time among vs, and rightly weigheth and considereth things, may easily iudge, that it is not the Landes and great liuings of bishops and Ecclesiasticall persons, but other matters, more heynous and more grieuous, that will hasten the wrath and displeasure of God against this Realme, which in deede, it behooueth bishops principally, and all other in their states and conditions to haue care of, and in time, while wee may, by all godly meanes to preuent it.

The affection of them, which at this day speake so much against the Landes and liuings of bishops, and other Cleargie men, is much like the dealing of those persons, that murmured against *Marie* of *Bethania*, which in the house of *Simon* the leper, in testimonie of her thankfulnesse, for the great mercies that shee had receiued of Christ, powred vpon his head the precious oyntment of Spikenard. For euen in like manner our gracious Queene, when God had deliuered her out of the iawes of the greedie lyons, and cruell wolues that sought her blood, and by his mightie hand had set her in the throne of this her Fathers kingdome: to testifie her thankfull minde, and to shevve her liberall and bountifull heart towarde the Church of God, shee povvred vpon it this plentifull gift, towarde the maintenance of the Ministers and Preachers of his vvorde, that shee might declare to the worlde, that in imbracing the Gospell, and restoring the same to this Realme, shee had not that minde and affection, vvhich some other haue shewed, that is, vnder colour thereof, to make the increase of her owne benefite, and the commoditie of her Crowne. But as then *Iudas* and some other Disciples murmured at *Marie*, and vnder pretence of holinesse and charitie toward the poore, founde great fault with that superfluous excesse (as they thought it) euen so nowe, many Disciples among vs, with like colour of religion and holinesse, and of zeale towarde the perfection of the Church (forsooth) murmure at the liberal benefit of our prince, which she hath bestowed vpon the Church, and think the same a great superfluitie, that might bee better imployed sundry wayes, to the benefite of the common weale. VVhatsoeuer is pretented, I pray God the cause of the griefe bee not the same that *Iohn* mentioneth to haue beene that, which first Iohn. 11. began the murmuring at that time. But whatsoeuer is the cause of this reproouing of the liberalitie of our gracious Prince and soueraigne: if the time did now serue, I coulde with better reason and authoritie prooue the Contrary Proposition to that which they take vpon them to maintaine: that is, *That it is not lawfull to bestow such liuings vpon Lay men, as are appointed by godly lawes for Ministers and Preachers of the worde of God.* But the shortnesse of the time will not nov, serue to followe that course.

IMPRINTED AT LON-
don by the Deputies of Chri-
stopher Barker, Printer to the
Queenes most excellent
Maiestie,
1589.

UNWIN BROTHERS, THE GREHSAM PRESS, CHILWORTH AND LONDON.

www.ingramcontent.com/pod-product-compliance
Lightning Source LLC
Chambersburg PA
CBHW032139160426
43197CB00008B/706